TH[illegible] R
OF ABERDEEN

Edward Ranson

Centre for Scottish Studies
University of Aberdeen

First published 1996

ISBN 0 906265 21 5

Printed by BPC-AUP Aberdeen Ltd.

CONTENTS

Introduction

List of Illustrations

Chapter One	Early Business Career. 1838-1848.	1
Chapter Two	Monarchist and Patriot. 1848-1856.	13
Chapter Three	Foreign Diversions and Local Interests. 1856-1861.	43
Chapter Four	Martin and the American Civil War. 1861-1865.	87
Chapter Five	Royal Events and Royal Statues. 1861-1866.	111
Chapter Six	Politics and Reform. 1865-1868.	127
Chapter Seven	Military Pride and the Aberdeen Wapinschaw. 1868-1876.	145
Chapter Eight	Liberal Supporter and Royal Sympathizer. 1868-1874	157
Chapter Nine	The Final Years on Union Street. 1874-1885.	189
Chapter Ten	Epilogue and Retrospect.	217

LIST OF ILLUSTRATIONS

1. Frontispiece: Photograph of Samuel Martin from William Skene, *East Neuk Chronicles* (1906).

All the remaining illustrations are advertisements from Aberdeen newspapers as under:-

2. *The Aberdeen Herald*, February 19, 1842. opp. p 6
3. *The Aberdeen Herald*, September 2, 1848. opp. p 14
4. *The Aberdeen Herald*, May 12, 1855. opp. p 28
5 *The Aberdeen Herald*, September 15, 1855. opp. p 30
6. *The Aberdeen Herald*, January 10, 1857. opp. p 44
7. *The Aberdeen Herald*, September 11, 1858. opp. p 58
8. *The Aberdeen Herald*, August 10, 1861. opp. p 90
9. *The Aberdeen Herald*, January 3, 1863. opp. p 98
10. *The Aberdeen Herald*, February 27, 1864. opp. p 118
11. *The Aberdeen Herald*, November 4, 1865. opp. p 128
12. *The Aberdeen Herald*, February 23, 1867. opp. p 132
13. *The Aberdeen Herald*, September 28, 1867. opp. p 134
14. *The Aberdeen Herald*, May 21, 1870. opp. p 148
15. *The Aberdeen Herald*, June 29, 1872. opp. p 152
16. *The Aberdeen Herald*, April 10, 1869. opp. p 158
17. *The Aberdeen Herald*, April 20, 1872. opp. p 172
18. *The Aberdeen Herald*, May 10, 1873. opp. p 174
19. *The Herald And Weekly Free Press*, April 7, 1877. opp. p 198
20. The *Aberdeen Journal*, October 21, 1885. opp. p 208

INTRODUCTION

Samuel Martin entered my life by accident. In perusing Aberdeen newspapers in the years 1861-65, and especially *The Aberdeen Herald*, in order to gauge the amount of information regarding the American Civil War being laid before the local population, my attention was frequently caught by Samuel Martin's advertisements. Increasingly I found myself turning first to page four of *The Herald*, in exactly the same way as contemporary readers, in order to read Martin's comments before turning to the news items and editorials. Frequently his account and interpretation of events was livelier than that written by either the Aberdeen journalists and editorial writers, or by the American newspapers whose reports were often reprinted.

My curiosity regarding Samuel Martin's reasons for advertising in this individual style, for his announcements stood out from those of other Aberdeen businessmen and traders, was thoroughly aroused. As a result I began to trace his career as a successful manufacturer and retailer of hats, as a publicist and self-promoter, and as a local character. Here was a man who, as it turned out, both literally and figuratively blew his own trumpet. Having started in the 1860s, in the middle of Martin's career, my research went in two directions - backward to his early life and arrival in Aberdeen, and forward to his retirement and death in the 1880s.

The study which has evolved out of this research is not a conventional biography, a business history, a social history of a local community, an investigation of public opinion in Victorian Scotland, or even a history of the development of some aspects of advertising. It is a mixture and an amalgam of all these things. In good part this is because of the nature of the resource material available. This book is not based on diaries or journals, it is not derived from any autobiography or personal letters, and information has not been gathered from dusty business ledgers or account books. Whereas Martin was sufficiently well known in his day to be mentioned in a number of published reminiscences by nineteenth century Aberdonians, and once in a while his unconventional approach to life and commerce earned him a few lines in the local press, most of the information about the man who liked to call himself the "Hatter to the People" is drawn from his regular advertisements. But these were not conventional announcements confined to the merits of the goods offered for sale and the expert attention promised by the seller, though these matters were eventually drawn to the attention of potential customers. Instead, Martin offered his readers over several decades his advice, opinions, and interpretations of local, national and international affairs. In many ways he epitomized public opinion on such matters as civic and social reform, politics and parliamentary matters, war and peace. He was forthright in his comments, though anxious not to give personal offence, and he rewarded his faithful followers, who appear to have been numerous, with many details about his own business and personal life alongside comments on the issues of the day.

Where his personal flamboyance, showmanship and astute sales technique ended and outright eccentricity began is open to argument. Nor is it clear whether the title of "Mad Hatter" is fully or partially justified, or merely a convenient name for someone whose behaviour was unconventional. After reading the following pages each person may make his or her own judgment.

CHAPTER ONE

EARLY BUSINESS CAREER. 1838-1848.

On Saturday, February 10, 1838, *The Aberdeen Herald* and *The Aberdeen Constitutional* both carried the announcement that a "NEW HAT ESTABLISHMENT" was due to open that day at 34 Union Street. In the conventional and formal language of the day the advertisements informed the reader that "SAMUEL MARTIN respectfully intimates to the Public of Aberdeen and its vicinity, that he will Open the above Establishment THIS DAY (SATURDAY the 10th February), with a large Stock of HATS, Caps, &c., and his system of doing business being to sell a good article at the smallest possible profit, for CASH, he trusts by a strict personal attendance, with a wish to please, to merit a share of public favour." the notice also contained the information "A BOY WANTED."[1]

Thus was the unsuspecting public of Aberdeen advised of the launching of the business career of a man who was to prove one of the city's shrewdest traders, a manufacturer, and especially a retailer, of hats, who for nearly half a century not only made a comfortable living from his business, but proved to be a pioneer in the practices of advertising and self promotion. Over the years Samuel Martin gained at least a local reputation, though one that sometimes spread beyond North East Scotland, as an amiable eccentric whose ideas and behaviour were the cause of much amusement and comment.

Samuel Martin was not, however, an Aberdonian, nor even a Scot, by birth, although his father, William Martin, was a native of Hamilton in Lanarkshire. William Martin came from a family of weavers and was intended by his father to enter that trade, but, apparently, he was fired by martial enthusiasm as a result of constant contact with the soldiers whose headquarters were in his native town. As a result William ran off and joined the army, and though his friends bought him off and he returned to the weaver's loom for a while he still longed for a military life and he enlisted a second time. Little is known of William Martin's career in the army, except that it was relatively successful. He served abroad with his regiment, and rose from the ranks to be appointed a cornet in the 6th Dragoon Guards (Carabineers) on July 16th, 1812, and was by one account a riding master. Although continued in service after the end of the Napoleonic Wars he was placed on half pay on May 9th, 1822, and died in 1825.

At some point William had married an Irish girl, Rosina Wilson, who bore him seven children, including Samuel who was born in Preston, Lancashire, where his father's regiment was stationed at the time, in 1814. Samuel had three brothers and three sisters, one of the girls being his twin. According to one source his brothers all entered the army and held commissioned rank. One allegedly died of sunstroke in Calcutta, a second fell in a "forlorn hope" attack in Spain, while the third rose to the rank of colonel and later held the appointment of Governor of a large public institution in Preston. Of his sisters even less is known. Samuel Martin's twin died when three years old, another married and died in Russia.

Certainly there was a strong military flavour to the family and to Samuel Martin's childhood, much of which was spent, on account of his father's military vocation, in his mother's native Ireland. Samuel was later to claim that because of his English birth, Irish mother and childhood, and Scots father, he really belonged to three kingdoms and might therefore be pardoned for any unusual notions he might entertain regarding the doing of things in the ordinary routine style. Had not his father died in 1825 Samuel would, without doubt, have joined the army, but even though fate had other things in store for him he was always intensely interested in and knowledgeable about military affairs and extremely proud that his father had been an officer.[2]

Circumstances now demanded that Samuel follow a more peaceful calling, and he was apprenticed to the hat trade in Glasgow in about 1826 or 1827, when he would have been twelve or thirteen years old. It is known that he worked for some time as a journeyman in Stockport before returning to Glasgow where he and one of his brothers entered business as hatters, though how that ties in with the alleged military career of all his brothers in unclear. At all events Samuel suffered ill-health and received medical advice to live and work further north and he chose Aberdeen as his future home, and in his own words "he never regretted the selection." Sometime in 1837 he made the not inconsiderable journey north, for at that time the stage coach running time between Glasgow and Aberdeen was in the region of fifteen or sixteen hours. He arrived in Aberdeen as a smart young man looking for a business opportunity, and in February 1838 he began to trade in a comparatively humble manner at 34 Union Street, "himself and a laddie forming the entire establishment." Aberdeen at that time was a community of approaching 65,000 people, but such were the easy going business practices of the time that in those early days, although his premises were in the most frequented part of the town, he nevertheless closed the shop for an hour for lunch with the comment that any customer would have to wait till he returned.[3]

How much note Aberdonians made of the arrival of a new hatter in their midst it is impossible to say. No doubt many readers of *The Aberdeen Herald* that Saturday were more interested in the Theatre-Royal's reminder that this was the "Last night but one of Signior Witini and his celebrated Dog."[4] One authority has claimed that when Martin opened his doors there was only one other hat shop in the city, so that any newcomer might be expected to stimulate interest and competition. However, investigation reveals a number of rival establishments, not to mention such stores as gentlemen's outfitters and others who sold hats as a sideline. Indeed, the town appears to have been well provided with hatters and as a result competition was fierce, even though in the nineteenth century a hat, and one suitable for every occasion, was regarded as an essential item of attire. The promotion of one's own goods and services, and the denigration of rivals appears to have been the order of the day amongst those in the hat trade.[5]

Martin opened his establishment in the midst of a severe winter, which may have benefited trade or conversely driven potential customers from the streets. The newspapers of February 1838 spoke of storms, heavy snowfalls and of winter continuing with "unabated severity". On Wednesday night, February 14, the weather was reported as severe almost beyond precedent in that part of the country, with even the leading thoroughfares in the city blocked by snow.[6] Nearly ten years later, in December 1846, *The Herald* remembered:

> During the past ten or twelve days we have had a snow storm, such as has not been equalled since the memorable spring of 1838, when for three months the snow lay several feet deep over the whole country, and in damp sunless hollows had not disappeared, even when the joyous month of June was half way through.[7]

Martin obviously survived both the weather and the competition, including that of the established firm of Messrs Craig & Anderson, 85 Union Street, who had been in business for five years and claimed that:

> ...for goods of equal quality, our prices are lower than those of any vender

> of Hats in Aberdeen. We state again that, both as Manufacturers and Importers of Hats, we can afford to sell, are selling, and will continue to sell, goods of a superior quality, and at a cheaper rate than the common-place articles usually offered for sale by those Shops who depend for any little trade they can pick up on the Day & Martin system of puffing.[8]

The reference to "puffing" relates to Martin's early reputation as a man who saw and exploited the power of advertising. As one observer noted later, Martin "was the first shopkeeper who made advertising a fine art in the north of Scotland; he 'woke up' the inhabitants to a sense both of the merits of his goods and his own smartness....Mr Martin nonplussed his neighbours. They shook their heads and said it 'would never do in Aberdeen' - he was only 'wasting his money'. They changed their minds in a year or two."[9]

Martin replied to his critics with the unashamed claim that his shop placed all others in the shade as he offered decidedly the cheapest and best hats in the city. He continued:

> ...S.M. considers it a duty on his part to return his sincere thanks for the unparalleled support he has received since he commenced business in Aberdeen, thus proving that he, being a *Hatter by trade,* and *understanding* his business, is duly appreciated, which facts naturally give him material advantages over those *Jack-of-all-trade* individuals who, no doubt, would like to be *Hatters*, but evidently get *fat doing nothing*, and possibly know more of making *shirt-collars* and other *delicate* work, than of manufacturing Hats.[10]

Martin's rejoinder appeared in the same edition of *The Herald* as the announcement of the arrival on the scene of a fresh competitor, the "New, Splendid, and Extensive Hat Establishment" of David Smith & Co at 194 George Street, who disclaimed "any desire to *puff* themselves into favour, being perfectly satisfied that they have *real claims* to their patronage, which can be neither surpassed nor equalled in Aberdeen."[11]

Martin remained silent for three months until December 1838, when he returned to the attack. After drawing attention to his large stock of hats and caps for the winter trade, and announcing "The Small Profit And Ready Money System Triumphant at 34 Union Street," he went on to outline his claimed advantages over business rivals in detail that is worth recalling. He wrote:

> ...after reading the following *facts*, a discerning public will at once see the pre-eminence he has over all *would-be Hatters*, particularly over individuals who appear to have no regular system of their own, and consequently, make *vain and farcical* attempts to copy his.... The following are a few of S.M.'s many advantages:-
>
> 1st, Being A Hat Manufacturer, and well known as such in the principal towns of Scotland.
>
> 2d, A complete knowledge of the business in all its various branches, having had twelve years' practical experience.
>
> 3d, Great advantages in purchasing, having a thorough knowledge of the English markets (*part of his experience having been in England*), and well knowing *when* and *where* to purchase.
>
> 4th, Being a judge of the articles in their finished state, he has no fear (in purchasing) of having old fashions or stale goods pushed on his hands, which disaster frequently happens to those individuals who go to market without a proper knowledge of the *Trade*.
>
> Numerous other facts could be adduced, equally conclusive, that S. Martin continues to sell the cheapest and best Hats in Aberdeen.[12]

One of these other facts, was presumably, his ability to alter hats on the premises, an advantage that rendered his establishment "quite the *nonpareil; in Aberdeen*".[13] In May 1839 Martin advised his customers that he had returned from a personal visit to the principal manufacturing towns with new stock, thus giving him an advantage over the "*many minor Establishments.*"[14]

Occasional advertisements continued to stress the bargains to be had at 34 Union Street, and in November 1839, after repeating that competition from other hatters was out of the question, Martin broke into verse for the first time:

> If good hats you want to buy
> Martin's are cheapest, come and try;
> Their texture's fine, the shapes are neat,
> And his winter stock is now complete.[15]

That the manufacture and sale of hats was not a guaranteed road to business success at this time may be adjudged by the fate of Anderson & Co., at the sign of the Gilded Otter, 85 Union Street, successors to Craig & Anderson. *The Aberdeen Herald* carried advertisements for Anderson & Co. in December 1839 and January 1840, but in March 1840 appeared the announcement that Anderson & Co. was closing its Aberdeen shop to concentrate on the manufacture of hats in Edinburgh.[16]

By contrast Martin's success allowed him to refer to himself on December 19, 1840, as "S. Martin, the Practical Hatter...the most extensive *Retail Hatter* in the North of Scotland," and to boast of his "Plate-Glass Windows, in the most modern style."[17] Another evidence of his expanding business was his advertisement in April 1841 for "One or Two experienced Salesmen."[18]

In October 1841 began a new rivalry, one that was to be long lasting but essentially friendly, when Steele & Co., Hat and Cap Manufacturers, opened a shop at the near-by address of 20 Union Street, at the corner of Union Street and Broad Street. Steele & Co. also believed in the power of advertising, and on February 5, 1842, published an announcement, which ran for several weeks, praising the "NEW PATENT WASHABLE BEAVER HATS" they were offering for sale.[19] Martin responded on February 19 by placing an advertisement alongside Steele & Co.'s offering for sale "SUPERIOR BEAVER HATS...which...never require WASHING". This was also the first occasion Martin referred to himself as "HATTER to the PEOPLE."[20] By January 1846 he was calling himself the "HATTER KING OF THE NORTH," in October that year "THE INVINCIBLE HATTER," and by Christmas 1847 "Hatter to the People, AND ADVERTISING HATTER."[21]

March 1842 saw the appearance of a new competitor, William Thomson, who opened for business at the Sign of the Gilded Otter, 131 Union Street, and attempted to entice customers to purchase not only hats and caps, but also "Biggs patent HAT GUARD, a contrivance at once simple and efficacious for keeping the hat FIRM on the Head in the highest wind - combining at once SAFETY TO THE HAT, SIMPLICITY OF APPLICATION, AND COMFORT TO THE WEARER."[22] Martin continued to distain all competitors, claiming his stock of hats was unrivalled for variety, style, durability and price in the north of Scotland, and his establishment deserved to be called "THE HAT SHOP OF THE NORTH."[23] He reinforced his contentions with another sally into verse:

> Then come and buy from MARTIN, for 'tis plainly to be seen,
> That he has the most extensive Stock of Hats in Aberdeen.
> The shapes are really splendid, and they fit the head with ease,
> And, in quality, wear, and comfort, they're warranted to please.[24]

SATURDAY, FEBRUARY 19, 1842.

NO SLIDING SCALE!
BUT A FIXED MODERATE PROFIT.

TRIUMPHANT MAJORITY
FOR THE SMALL-PROFIT, READY-MONEY SYSTEM IN HATS,
AT
S. MARTIN'S,
34 UNION STREET, ABERDEEN. **34**

THAT S. M. has the most complete and best assorted Stock of Hats in town, will not for a moment be disputed; an idea of the extent of which cannot be conveyed through the columns of a newspaper; and, from the fact of his having (it may be said) the only extensive retail Hat trade in the north of Scotland, is the best proof that his Hats have given satisfaction, and that a discerning public have experienced the advantages of purchasing at this Establishment, where large profits have been done away with by the

SMALL-PROFIT, MUCH-BUSINESS

system. And S. M. being the first individual that has succeeded in bringing down the price of Hats in Aberdeen to the level of other manufacturing towns, and having all the advantages that can be derived from long experience in the Hat Trade, knowing the best markets, buying largely, &c. &c. he is thus enabled to surmount all

ATTEMPTS AT OPPOSITION

on the part of ordinary aspirants to public support in the Hat Trade; for, however anxious individuals may be to obtain the eminence which S. M. has attained, they may possibly find that they will have to be contented by seeing it in perspective; for, as

KNOWLEDGE IS POWER,

so S. M.'s *knowledge* of the Hat Trade gives him the *power* of continuing his scale of Low Prices, which it might be dangerous for establishments of less extent to attempt, and which S. M.'s ability to persist in, naturally gives still greater celebrity to his already

WIDE-SPREAD FAME FOR SELLING GOOD HATS CHEAP.

S. M. would respectfully attract public attention to a fresh supply of his ECONOMIC STUFF HATS, at 12s 6d. and SUPERIOR BEAVER HATS, at 15s; both of which qualities continue to be much admired, and being SHORT IN THE NAP, and having all other recent improvements, never require

WASHING.

An immense stock of CLOTH and GLAZED CAPS at wonderfully low prices, for samples of which, see Windows, at 34, UNION STREET.

☞ Strangers may at once find the Shop, by inquiring for the PRACTICAL HATTER, and HATTER to the PEOPLE.

Feb. 19, 1842.

NEW ARRIVALS
OF
SUPERIOR WATERPROOF HATS,
AT THE
WHOLESALE AND RETAIL HAT DEPOT,
20 UNION STREET, **20**
CORNER OF BROAD STREET.

A. STEELE & CO., grateful for the distinguished encouragement they have received since the opening of the above Premises, are ever anxious to introduce anything New in the HAT TRADE, and beg to inform their Friends and the Public of the arrival of a splendid Stock of HATS for the Season, amongst which is a large lot of the

NEW PATENT WASHABLE BEAVER HATS,

so much admired in the metropolis on account of their DURABILITY, CHEAPNESS, and COMFORT; these they have much pleasure in recommending to their Customers and the Public, being convinced that they will give satisfaction to the Wearer, and prove a saving of Twenty-five per cent.

The following qualities they would highly recommend, viz.:—
Finest WASHABLE BEAVER HAT, 16s., equal to any that can be got in town for 21s.;

SHORT-NAPPED WASHABLE STUFF HATS, 7s. 6d.,
superior to what can be bought in the North of Scotland for 10s.

Gentlemen will find it to their advantage to examine A. S. & Co.'s Stock previous to making a purchase at any other establishment.

A large lot of CAPS and COMP-DE-PARIS HATS, much cheaper, quality considered, than any other in Aberdeen.

WHOLESALE AND RETAIL WAREHOUSE,
20 UNION STREET, **20**
CORNER OF BROAD STREET.

☞ Country Orders punctually attended to.

In fact, a rash of new hat shops opened in Aberdeen in the years 1843-45, for example: Francis Bell, 38 Queen Street; Mrs Bennet, 10 Union Street; D. Burge, 38 & 40 Broad Street; the Central Hat Mart, 26 Union Street; and the London Hat Company (Millar Brothers), 31 Union Street.[25] Martin was undaunted by these developments, claiming his experience and business methods permitted him "to keep all attempts at competition by less extensive houses entirely in the background."[26] He reminded the readers of his advertising copy that:

> SAMUEL MARTIN was the first individual who adopted the Small-Profit Ready-Money System in the Hat Trade in Aberdeen - a system never before attempted in the North - a system which has given complete satisfaction, and a system which has enabled S.M. annually to extend his trade, and reduce his profits, and to such an extent, that the fame of his Establishment for selling good Hats cheap has spread over the length and breadth of the land; and which enables him triumphantly to remark that the grand equilibrium in business to insure public support is Mutual Advantage between Buyer & Seller.
> ...He has, within the last seven years, reduced the price of Hats in Aberdeen to the level of other large manufacturing towns, and he has reaped the benefits of doing so, by securing to himself an immense Trade, for which he returns his Friends and the Public generally his grateful thanks.[27]

Martin was certain his shop "stands alone in the Hat Trade in this quarter," and asserted, "it is no uncommon circumstance to hear an individual remark, on meeting a friend with a Neat and Becoming Hat, 'O, I see you encourage the Practical Hatter'."[28]

One of the intruders, the Central Hat Mart, which opened in June 1844, had the temerity to describe itself as "an establishment acknowledged by all to stand *unrivalled* and *unapproachable* for *elegance, fashion* and *real economy*."[29] Such claims only led Martin to refer to the "amusing attempts at Competition which he has met with occasionally within the last eight years." He added that the summit of the anxiety and ambition of his rivals had been "to attain to be Second Best to Him," which was the limit for "individuals of ordinary Capacity."[30]

By this time, 1845, Martin was no longer content merely to praise his own stock while disparaging his rivals' taste and abilities. He adopted the ploy of extolling the medical advantages, particularly in warm weather, of a light, durable, and easy-fitting hat in order to avoid headaches.[31] He was also referring to a range of new styles such as the "New Ventilated Hat, The New Cork Hat, The New Reflector Hat, and the Young England & Louis Phillippe."[32] It can only be surmised that Martin was the unnamed target of the claim by the Central Hat Mart that no fictitious names were given to hats sold by them, but their goods were "All *bona fide* Shapes as worn by the leading MEN OF FASHION OF THE DAY."[33] On April 25, 1846, the London Hat Company went so far as to head its advertisement "CAUTION TO THE PUBLIC", and then advised:

> From the number of (Hat) Shops at present in Aberdeen, who put forth huge pretensions to extraordinary cheapness, overwhelming stocks, &c. &c. - from the downright quackery used by some parties, in order to entrap the unwary, and induce them to purchase, individuals (*and persons from the country especially*) find it very difficult indeed to decide at which of the numerous Shops they can get a GOOD HAT at a Reasonable Price. In order to meet this dilemma and obviate the difficulty, the LONDON HAT COMPANY, Established 1843, invite the attention of all to whom economy in Hats is really an object, to their very extensive Stock of HATS and CAPS, which, from the extent of their premises, the nature of their connexions in the Hat Trade, and the facilities which they (as PRACTICAL HATTERS) enjoy above all others, they can say, without exaggeration, is the *largest in town*; and as to lowness in price, all they wish is one trial from those who have not already done so, which, they are quite certain, will convince the most fastidious of the superior quality of their goods, and the advantages to be met with by purchasing at their Establishment.[34]

If this thrust was directed wholly or in part at Martin he remained unabashed, continuing to extol the virtues of his stock in the advertising columns of *The Herald* and also via his window displays.[35] In response to his own question "WHY DOES MARTIN THE HATTER ADVERTISE SO MUCH?" he explained that he did so to remind the public where good hats could be obtained at moderate prices.[36] While one of the major hat emporia did cease to trade it was not Martin but the Central Hat Mart which announced in September 1846, "BARGAINS, such as have never before been offered to the Inhabitants of Aberdeen, will be given, in order to effect a complete clearance of the Entire Stock, by the 20th October next" as the business was being removed to Liverpool.[37]

Relief from competition from the Central Hat Mart proved to be short lived, however, as in July 1847 the premises at 26 Union Street reopened after refurbishment that rendered them "unequalled in extent and magnificence North of Edinburgh" retaining the name Central Hat Mart but now under the proprietorship of Messrs. Thom & Thomson. The new owners made clear their intentions to the world, or at least to the readers of *The Herald*, in rhyme:

> In this, our first appearance in the page
> Where puffing Quacks in numbers weekly rage,
> And ceaseless labour (so many may infer it),
> To gain by puffing what they want in merit -
> When Pillmen, Pigmen, Grocers, Drapers, rush
> To print - to advertise - and thus to push
> A new or sinking trade - gain or regain
> Their former customers - *the fools again.*
> We come not here to take a weekly place,
> Although we, too, may sometimes show our face:
> Then blame us not, if in our harmless rhymes,
> We strive to ape the spirit of the Times.
> For, lately, puffing's been so much in Fashion,
> The Public must, for puffing, have a passion;
> Against the Fashion 'tis in vain to strive -
> All puff a little who would wish to thrive.
> Constrained by Fashion's mandate, we must yield,
> And thus reluctantly we take the field.

Thom & Thomson went on to assure prospective customers that their stock had been selected by themselves from the leading houses in London, Manchester and Glasgow based on taste and judgement derived from long experience working in England. Their policies were small profits, ready money, one price, and personal attention to every customer. They concluded with the announcement that odd shaped and extra-sized hats could be made to order.[38]

By 1848, despite the problems of what appeared to be an overcrowded line of trade and cut-throat competition, Samuel Martin had survived a decade in business at 34 Union Street. His penchant for publicity undoubtedly helped to promote his image and to boost his profits. As he wrote on July 8, 1848, "I am sure it is no fault of

MARTIN'S if the Public don't hear enough about his Hats!", and he was satisfied from experience that the more his Hats were known the more their pleasing qualities would be appreciated.[39]

NOTES

1 *The Aberdeen Herald and General Advertiser For The Counties Of Aberdeen, Banff And Kincardine, (hereafter referred to as The Herald),* price 4½d, Saturday, February 10, 1838, p1, col 4. Also *The Aberdeen Constitutional; And General Advertiser For The Counties Of Aberdeen Banff, And Kincardine,* Vol I, 22, Saturday, February 10, 1838, p1, col 2.

2 Most of the details relating to Samuel Martin's family background are derived from his obituary notices published in *The Aberdeen Journal*, Monday, January 9, 1888, p4, col 6, and in *The Daily Free Press*, Monday, January 9, 1888, p4, col 6. Information regarding the life of Samuel's elder brother Lieutenant-Colonel William Martin, who was for twenty years, 1843-1863, Governor of the Preston House of Correction, may be gleaned from the *Preston Chronicle* for November 11, 1843, and December 12, 1863. The latter issue printed a lengthy obituary with details of William Martin's earlier career as an officer in the 16th Lancers, the 38th Foot and in a British contingent in the Spanish army 1835-1837. At the end of his military employment William Martin joined the Lancaster County Police force and rose to the rank of superintendent in the Leigh Division prior to his appointment as Governor of the Preston House of Correction. At his death in his 58th year William Martin left a widow and several children.

3 *The Daily Free Press*, Monday, January 9, 1888, p4, col 6. Figures regarding the population of Aberdeen, and many other fascinating details of early Victorian Aberdeen, may be found in *The Bon-Accord Directory 1845-1846* (Aberdeen, 1845).

4 *The Herald*, Saturday, February 10, 1838.

5 *The Aberdeen Journal,* Monday, January 9, 1888, p4, col 6, suggests the rival shop was that of Steele & Co., 20 Union Street, but, in fact, those premises were in early 1838 occupied by J. Telfer, who opened a "New Wholesale and Retail Hat Establishment" in April 1838, see *The Herald*, April 7, 1838, p53, col 3. Steele & Co. did not open their shop at this address until October 1841, see *The Herald*, October 9, 1841, p185, col 7. In August 1838 Messrs. Craig & Anderson claimed to have been in business selling hats for 5 years, see *The Herald,* August 25, 1838, p133, col 4. *The Herald* on September 15, 1838, carried an advertisement for David Smith & Co. a retail hat establishment, 194 George Street, and on

June 24, 1843, p97, col 3, *The Herald* contained the announcement, "James Cooper, Hatter, who for the last Thirty-one years, occupied that Shop, No. 59, Union Street, next door to the Royal Hotel, takes this opportunity of intimating to his Friends and the Public, that he has Removed to 15 Shiprow."

The New Statistical Account of Scotland, Vol XII, Aberdeen (Edinburgh, 1845), published figures for various professions and trades on pp38-39, though it is unclear which year in the period 1831-1845 they refer to. The number of hat-makers and hatters was given as 8, in a town that also found employment for 128 advocates, 25 apothecaries and druggists, 56 bakers, 43 blacksmiths, 26 booksellers and stationers, 17 brewers, 40 dress-makers and milliners, 208 grocers and spirit-dealers, 32 hairdressers, 36 linen and wool-drapers, 3 opticians, 27 physicians, 47 surgeons, 5 umbrella makers, 193 vintners and 8 musical instrument makers.

6 See reports on the weather conditions in *The Herald* for February 3, February 10 and February 17, 1838.

7 *The Herald*, December 19, 1846, p203, col 3.

8 *The Herald*, August 25, 1838, p133, col 4.

9 *The Aberdeen Journal*, Monday, January 9, 1888, p4, col 6.

10 *The Herald*, September 15, 1838, p145, col 3.

11 *The Herald*, September 15, 1838, p145, col 4.

12 *The Herald*, December 15, 1838, p198, col 3.

13 *The Herald*, May 25, 1839, p81, col 7.

14 *The Herald*, May 25, 1839, p81, col 7.

15 *The Herald*, September 28, 1839, p153, col 5, and November 9, 1839, p177, col 6.

16 *The Herald*, December 21, 1839, p202, col 2, January 25, 1840, p14, col 3, and March 28, 1840, p50, col 4.

17 *The Herald*, December 19, 1840, p226, col 4.

18 *The Herald*, April 10, 1841, p74, col 6.

19 *The Herald*, October 9, 1841, p185, col 7, and February 5, 1842, p22, col 2.

20 *The Herald*, February 19, 1842, p29, col 5.

21 *The Herald*, January 10, 1846, p6, col 1, October 24, 1846, p170, col 3, and December 25, 1847, p201, col 7.

22 *The Herald*, March 12, 1842, p41, col 8.

23 *The Herald*, June 11, 1842, p94, col 1.

24 *The Herald*, November 26, 1842, p189, col 8.

25 *The Herald*, June 24, 1843, p89, col 3, contained the first advertisment for Francis Bell; July 8, 1843, p105, col 5 the first advertisment for Mrs Bennet; and the October 12, 1844 issue, p162, col 2, the first advertisement

by the Central Hat Mart, which, however, stated the business had opened in June last. The London Hat Company was advertising by June 22, 1844, p98, col 1, and D. Burge by April 5, 1845, p53, col 5.

26 *The Herald*, February 11, 1843, p22, col 1. At the same time Martin commented that "The celebrity which this establishment has attained for selling *Good Hats Cheap* is without precedent in the annals of the Hat Trade in Aberdeen, and plainly shows that the advantages possessed by S.M. being a *Practical Hatter* has been experienced and duly appreciated by a discerning public."

27 *The Herald*, June 15, 1844, p94, col 1.

28 *The Herald*, October 5, 1844, p158, col 2.

29 *The Herald*, October 12, 1844, p162, col 2.

30 *The Herald*, November 15, 1845, p182, col 2.

31 *The Herald*, June 14, 1845, p94, col 1. In *The Herald* for August 9, 1845, p126, col 2, Martin was claiming that hats made from Ventilated Satin were "well worth the attention of all Hat-wearers, as they carry out the principles so CONDUCIVE TO HEALTH, viz., to keep the Head moderately cool, and are thus particularly adapted for individuals who perspire much, or who are subject to Headach (sic)."

32 *The Herald*, January 10, 1846, p6, col 1.

33 *The Herald*, December 6, 1845, p194, col 1.

34 *The Herald*, April 25, 1846, p66, col 4.

35 See, for example, *The Herald*, July 18, 1846, p114, col 1, where it was stated, "Martin's Windows are particularly attractive at present"; January 2, 1847, p2, col 1, February 1847, p22, col 5, when Martin modestly claimed "it may be considered *quite a treat* to look at MARTIN'S Windows"; May 22, 1847, p82, col 2, June 26, 1847, p102, col 3; and April 1, 1848, p54, col 2, where it was stated "Martin's Windows have just been decorated for the Season, and are much admired; and his CAP department is complete with all the new styles. In fact, the display of Caps in Martin's West Window may well be looked at with Wonder and Admiration; and his Hat Window, as usual, is a sight worth seeing."

36 *The Herald*, November 28, 1846, p190, col 3. Perhaps an additional but unpublicized reason why Martin had made himself known to the public in his early years in business is that when the doors of 34 Union Street first opened as a hat shop there was already another Samuel Martin trading in Aberdeen as a grocer, tea and spirit dealer and mealseller at 1 Causewayend, and it was necessary to avoid confusion.

37 *The Herald*, September 19, 1846, p149, col 4. See also *The Herald*, December 12, 1846, p198, col 2.

38 *The Herald*, July 24, 1847, p113, col 6.

39 *The Herald*, July 8, 1848, p110, col 1.

CHAPTER TWO

MONARCHIST AND PATRIOT. 1848-1856.

While Martin's use of advertising prior to 1848 had certainly been innovative, it was the early visits of Queen Victoria to Aberdeen and Deeside, closely followed by the Crimean War, that really marked the beginning of a more exhuberant period of self-promotion by the Hatter to the People.

In anticipation of Queen Victoria's arrival in Aberdeen on September 7, 1848, *en route* for a vacation at Balmoral, Martin published an announcement a few days earlier that astutely combined fervent loyalty with a new sales technique. His advertisement referred to the city's opportunity "on this momentous occasion, of showing the national feeling by receiving our illustrious queen, and amiable mother of Britain's future Sovereigns, with that loyal, enthusiastic, and genuine good feeling, which she so justly deserves," and called for a demonstrative reception that would become a matter of history, passed down to future generations. He then went on to suggest, however, in view of the fact that a hat was the most conspicuous part of a man's attire, the propriety of appearing on this day wearing a good one. He continued:

> Martin's idea is, that *all* should have Good Hats on this occasion; and, notwithstanding that Hats will, as a matter of course, be taken off as the Queen passes, Martin wishes the Public to avoid what *might* be an *unseemly* sight to Royalty - viz., to be received by the *Waving of Thousands of Old Hats*, which individuals can easily avoid by purchasing one of MARTIN'S beautiful SATIN HATS, with nice showy Linings, pleasing to the eye, and which MARTIN is Selling at very Moderate Prices.

As the Queen was understood to be an early riser, and might pass through the streets of Aberdeen at an early hour, Martin recommended to potential purchasers his Wide Awake Hats.[1]

Martin's wish that Aberdeen should make the most of the occasion of Victoria's visit was fully gratified as the newspaper accounts of the occasion reveal. *The Herald* reported:

> The progress along Union Street was grand almost beyond description, and the scene which it exhibited was one which certainly could not be excelled

> in any city in the kingdom. Flags and banners of the richest material and the gaudiest hues were suspended in large numbers, and so uniformly, that it is almost impossible to individualise the displays which were made.... The aspect of the street, when viewed from one end, was magnificent.[2]

The Queen's departure three weeks later was just as impressive, and as *The Herald* noted no expense or labour was spared to make the illuminated display that evening a worthy one:

> ...Every house in Union Street, Union Place, Castle Street, Marischal Street, and Regent Quay, was a complete blaze of light from top to bottom. One or two houses, where sickness exists, were the only exceptions....The flare of the light from Union Street was seen reflected on the sky many miles around.... Mr Martin, hatter, displayed a fiery hat, in the shape of the latest fashion.[3]

For the rest of 1848 and during early 1849 Martin contented himself with modest announcements concerning the value of advertising and the advantages of a respectable appearance. In May 1849 he referred to himself as "a most Scientific Hatter", and in July commented on the magnificent style of his immense stock of tweed caps, wide-awake hats and "the new SLEEPY HATS, which although in want of a *nap*, are not heavy."[4]

In January 1850 Martin enjoined his readers to study good taste, enjoy comfort and practice economy by purchasing one of his hats, and in March he claimed to have still further reduced his prices. That his business style, including advertising, really did pay may be judged from the fact that in August he announced that he had "found it requisite, from the magnitude of his trade, to enlarge his Premises, which he has done, by adding to his well-known Splendid Shop, a LARGE WAREROOM, directly above."[5]

Martin opened 1851 with a paean on the virtues of the hat, including its medical advantages, thus returning to a theme he had tried before. After offering the advice "YOUR HEAD! YOUR HEAD! TAKE CARE OF YOUR HEAD!!!" Martin discoursed on the vulnerability of the human head, but had "no hesitation in stating that a thorough Waterproof, proper fitting HAT is the best article extant for protecting the head from the effects of the weather."[6]

The passing years saw a number of comings and goings in the hat

SATURDAY, SEPTEMBER 2, 1848.

THE QUEEN'S VISIT TO BALMORAL.

THREE CHEERS FOR OUR NOBLE QUEEN.

HURRA! HURRA!! HURRA!!!

IT being understood that the Queen will land at Aberdeen, on her way to Balmoral, thus will Aberdeen have an opportunity, on this momentous occasion, of showing the national feeling by receiving our illustrious Queen, and amiable mother of Britain's future Sovereigns, with that loyal, enthusiastic, and genuine good feeling, which she so justly deserves; and, as Scotland has ever stood famously prominent in history for fidelity to, and loyalty in the reception of, her Sovereigns, so let it be a matter of history, handed down to after ages, the loyal reception which the City of Aberdeen gave to her Most Gracious Majesty Queen Victoria in 1848; and thus show to the World that Scotland has *not* degenerated from the loyal and patriotic feeling which has ever characterised her as a Nation.

MARTIN,

HATTER TO THE PEOPLE,

AND A LOYAL SUBJECT,

Being of opinion that a proper attention to Dress should be studied by all her Majesty's subjects, particularly on an occasion of this kind, and as the HAT is the most conspicuous part of man's dress, MARTIN would respectfully suggest to the Public, the propriety of appearing before her Majesty with a *Good Hat*. But it may be said, people don't wear Hats before the Queen; this is admitted, but, as the streets through which her Majesty passes will possibly be crowded with individuals, *many* of whom will, no doubt, have good Hats, Martin's idea is, that *all* should have Good Hats on this occasion; and, notwithstanding that Hats will, as a matter of course, be taken off as the Queen passes, Martin wishes the Public to avoid what *might* be an *unseemly* sight to Royalty—viz., to be received by the *Waving of Thousands of Old Hats*, which individuals can easily avoid by purchasing one of MARTIN's beautiful SATIN HATS, with nice showy Linings, pleasing to the eye, and which MARTIN is Selling at very Moderate Prices.

It being understood that our beloved Queen is an early riser, and may thus possibly land early in the morning, to those individuals who are *not* habitually early risers, but would, nevertheless, like to see her Majesty, MARTIN would recommend his

WIDE AWAKE HATS.

OBSERVE!

MARTIN, Hatter to the People,

AND A LOYAL SUBJECT,

34,

UNION STREET,

ABERDEEN

ONE CHEER MORE FOR

Her Most Gracious Majesty Queen Victoria.

HURRA!

trade, and in August 1851 one of the newcomers, A & D Burge's, 38 Broad Street, attempted to gain public attention with the following rhyme:

> After making one trial, encouraged you'll be,
> To Purchase your Hats ever after from me;
> The objects that's aimed at is simple and plain,
> 'Tis to study your interest, your custom to gain.[7]

Martin did not respond directly to this challenge, possibly because he was once more attesting his loyalty to Queen Victoria during her stay at Balmoral while simultaneously expressing the opinion that "*No article of Dress detracts so much from the appearance of the wearer as a Clumsey-shaped Hat. No article of Dress adds so much to the appearance of the wearer as a Becoming-shaped Hat.*"[8]

Just as Martin had greeted 1851 with a flourish, so he felt compelled to bid it an affectionate adieu:

> FAREWELL 1851!
>
> This is the last *Saturday* that I can have the pleasure of meeting with you, as it seems you cannot remain after *Wednesday first*. But in wishing you goodbye, I must say that, although you have only been a *twelve-months'* acquaintance, yet these twelve months have passed very satisfactorily to me, seeing my Business going on most prosperously; and, although you are leaving in a *cold* and *chilly* manner, *and which cannot but be felt*, yet it is to be hoped that your friend, 1852, will arrive in a more genial way, and, throwing warmth around, make himself agreeable, and I am satisfied that, when it does arrive, it will find me well able to continue to sell my HATS, CAPS, &c. &c. at such moderate prices as cannot but be pleasing to purchasers at my Establishment.[9]

Martin did, indeed, welcome 1852 in the columns of *The Herald*, especially as the weather had moderated,[10] but his attention was quickly caught by recent happenings in France, and he was soon reassuring his customers that the recent *coup d'etat* of Louis Napoleon "has had *no effect* in raising prices of MARTIN'S Hats."[11]

While the vagaries of French politics might not affect Martin's business, events in Aberdeen were not so certain. *The Herald* on March 27, 1852, carried two independent announcements. The first by W.M. Miller & Company advised Aberdonians of the appearance of a "NEW

HAT ESTABLISHMENT" at 69 Union Street, at the corner with Market Street. The second proclaimed a "GREAT CLOSING SALE" as one of Martin's old adversaries, the London Hat Company, was replaced at 27 Union Street, due to circumstances over which they had no control, by a draper.[12]

Within two weeks W.H. Miller & Company were claiming great success in selling first-class hats at moderate prices, and predicting that, "If the Public will only extensively encourage *this, the first attempt on a large scale, to* reduce the enormous Profits hitherto charged by HAT SHOPS IN THIS CITY," then Miller & Company would pledge themselves to work on a low profit margin looking to a large and rapid turn-over for success.[13]

Two further rivals appeared in April 1852 - Brown the hatter, 58 St Nicholas Street, and William Milne, Hatter and Shoe Merchant, at 10 Union Street where he was replacing Mrs Bennet in some branches of trade.[14] Presumably W.M. Miller & Company experienced continuing commercial good fortune as in early 1853 they announced alterations and extensions to their premises.[15] Martin did not appear to be unduly perturbed by the increased competition. In July 1852 he took the opportunity to write:

CHARMING WEATHER!
WARMTH EXTRAORDINARY!
NOTHING LIKE IT FOR MANY YEARS!
GRATIFYING APPEARANCE OF THE COUNTRY!

These headlines, however, were really preparation for the comment that those who bought hats from his shop had a fair chance of avoiding headaches and other unpleasant sensations caused by unnecessary weight or undue pressure upon the head during the heat of the day. He concluded:

Wide Awakes for Men and Boys,
Shade the face, protect the eyes;
Buy from MARTIN, his Stock's complete,
And view his Shop - 'tis quite a treat![16]

In November Martin waxed lyrical over the advantages of living in Britain, "TRULY A GREAT COUNTRY", where education, victualling and luxuries were all cheap due to the wisdom of enlightened statesmen and a sensible people "governed by reason, knowing what's right, avoiding what's wrong" leading to peace and satisfaction for all. Talk of Britain being invaded was as likely as Louis Napoleon being proclaimed King of England or Martin, the Hatter to the People, selling hats dear.[17]

The Budget of 1853 brought good news for Martin with the proposed reduction of the Advertisement Duty from 1s.6d. to 6d., which, as he pointed out, "will enable MARTIN at a cheaper rate to remind the Public of the advantages of Purchasing at his Establishment."[18] Even better tidings followed when the government bowed to pressure and repealed the Duty completely, and *The Herald* confirmed that it was "anxious to give the full benefit of the new arrangement to the Advertising Public."[19]

Martin may also have been gratified by the thinning of the ranks of his competitors in September that year by the winding up of the hat and cap shop of Robert Brown, at 58 St Nicholas Street, after only eighteen months.[20] More likely Martin was concerned with Queen Victoria's annual visit to Deeside which he celebrated with such comments as: "THE QUEEN! EVERY HAPPINESS ATTEND HER!!", "Happy Country to have such a Queen!" and "Ever keeping up the true dignity of a QUEEN, but never forgetting the kindly feelings of a WOMAN. Long Life to Victoria, our Beloved Queen!" He could not resist adding:

> But really there is something very pleasing to see her Majesty leaving the *Pageantry* of a *Court* to enjoy her *Rural Home*. But all have their enjoyments; and if Her Majesty should again visit Aberdeen, and ever condescend to visit Martin's Establishment [which, perhaps, is not very likely] - but suppose she did, and asked Martin what were *his* greatest enjoyments, Martin's answer would be - Please your Most Gracious Majesty, my greatest enjoyments are knowing that my efforts to please Customers are duly appreciated, and have enabled me to obtain an immense trade; that your Majesty's subjects who purchase at my Establishment *continue to be pleased with their purchases*, and show the fact by recommending others; and should your Majesty ever deign to order a purchase at my Establishment, I will ever consider it the GREATEST HONOUR I HAVE EVER HAD CONFERRED UPON ME. BUT - with all the true feelings of a Loyal Subject to *his Queen* for her many virtues so nobly shown forth - I would pray *ever to be allowed to retain my proud title of*
>
> HATTER TO THE PEOPLE![21]

The following week *The Herald* published "A HINT TO 'THE PRACTICAL HATTER' " recounting the story of a traveller in the United States who made a purchase at a celebrated hatter. On paying for it he was requested to go upstairs where he was shown into a daguerrotype saloon and his portrait was taken, neatly framed and fastened inside the crown of his hat, *gratis*. A rival hatter provided not only a picture of the purchaser, but also a portrait of his wife, sweetheart or friend. *The Herald* wondered if Samuel Martin would emulate this example of American salesmanship.[22]

Martin did not reply directly, but in January 1854 he made the point that he had prospered for fifteen years by close personal attention to his business and by his efforts in selling his headgear at moderate prices:

> And although his *advertising* propensities may possibly not have pleased *all*, yet MARTIN would, in the most polite manner remind that portion of the public who do not approve of advertising, that, from the march of intellect, the old prejudiced opinion that advertising is not respectable, is fast wearing out; and that the *legislators* of this *Great Country* having taken off the Advertisement Duty, have thus countenanced advertising as both *respectable* and *legitimate* - these prejudices should therefore no longer exist.[23]

The following month, February 1854, Robert Westley, then manager of W.M. Miller & Company at 69 Union Street, "in consequence of the Termination of his present Engagement with that Firm", announced his intention of entering business for himself as a hatter at the "Spacious and Commanding Premises" of 37 Union Street, a location virtually opposite Martin, in June that year with a "most Extensive and Magnificent New Stock of the leading and latest Novelties, in every description of HATS and CAPS...."[24] Clearly some change of plans intervened since Westley's shop did not open until August 3, and then not on Union Street but at 8 Broad Street.[25]

By this time Martin, as will soon be seen, was devoting much of his attention to the outbreak of the Crimean War, but Alexander Steele at 20 Union Street had meantime made an unexpected move by abandoning his normally extremely conservative advertisements in favour of a series of essays into verse. Perhaps Steele was aiming a pre-emptive blow at Westley, more likely he was seeking to counter the increased attention that his friendly rival at 34 Union Street was attracting with his discursions on the developing military and naval situations. Certainly the reference in the third stanza of the advertisement published by Steele in June 1854 is obvious:

When dandy Fashions first began,
'T was said that Tailors made the man;
But now-a-days, through a' the lan',
Folks judges better;
They ken that claes can never stan'
Without the HATTER.

What signifies fu ye are drest,
Wi' gowden chains athort your vest
If SANDY STEELE does not assist
To *crown* the matter?
What's a' your superfines at best
Without the HATTER?

Some Hatters o' the modern school
Tell warlike tales, the folks to fool -
Wi' naval actions try to gull
An' catch the flats; -
What sorrow has Sebastopol
To dee wi' HATS!

In UNION STREET, at Number 20,
HATS, CAPS, and BONNETS ye'll get plenty,
At prices, too, that must content ye,
And please you weel;
Then what on earth sud now prevent ye
To Buy frae STEELE?[26]

Three weeks later Sandy Steele made his second foray into poetry with Samuel Martin clearly his principal target on account of the latter's growing obsession with the Crimean War:

I'm a Dealer in HATS, an' I carena a sneeshin'
For seiges an' battles - I'm nae politician -
My business I mind, an' the public I tell
At the Corner of Broadgate I've gweed Hats to sell.

For Napier or Raglan be nae ways afraid,
On lan' or on sea they will stick to their trade;
They'll manage a' matters quite weel, I'll be sworn,
Tho' never a Hatter on earth soun's their horn.

I have Hats o' a' sizes an' shapes ye maun ken,
To please a' sorts of people, baith laddies an' men,
Frae the gent in his coach to the tar at his wheel -
Then come a' to UNION STREET, 20, to STEELE.[27]

On August 19 Alexander Steele published a new advertisement in rhyme, again with an indirect but clear reference to Martin who had recently advised his Aberdeen public what his policy toward Russia would be if he was Prime Minister.[28] Steele wrote:

If Bonnets, Hats, or Caps you're wantin',
As lang's the weather's sae enchantin,
For picnics or autumnal jauntin',
I'll serve you weel,
Or you wha want to use your *Manton*,
Apply to STEELE.

If ye will call at my Depot,
Goods cheap and good I'll shortly show,
And if you want a good Chapeau,
I'll lat you see
That nae *Prime Minister* mair low
Can strike than me.

I hate to make a lang palaver
To cultivate the public favour,
But still 't will aye be my endeavour
To welcome a'
At 20, UNION STREET, whenever
They please to ca'.[29]

Possibly, however, it was Steele's literary endeavours which spurred Robert Westley into imitation. The very next week the new arrival in Broad Street announced:

If Money you'd save, and the present times mend,
Purchase where best you'll secure this desirable end,
In all things pertaining to Bonnets and Caps,
Or the latest New Styles now worn in Hats.

At the Foot of BROAD STREET, the No. is 8,
ROBERT WESTLEY has opened a Modern Estate;
His stock is well sorted, his Shapes are all New;
His Expenses are small, and his Profit so too.

If Hats, Caps, or Bonnets you're wanting, to him you will go,
The way to Save Money in these things he'll show,
His rent and expenses being both very small,
The Price of his Goods must satisfy all.[30]

Only a week later Westley was again stressing his bargain prices and his intention to be satisfied with a small profit:

If to secure a Good HAT be really your aim,
While a very low price you would pay for the same,
Try what WESTLEY in Broad Street can do in this matter,
And he here begs to say he's a Practical Hatter.

The apparent reduction some "Great Sales" would imply,
Amounting to thirty per cent or somewhere hard by,
Gives proof to a statement once before made,
That extravagant profits have been had in the trade;
For, if after thus coming down, a profit they draw,
What on earth must have been the profit before!

To avoid a return to this system, then, WESTLEY support,
By selling remarkably cheap public favour he'll court,
And to produce the very best value in BONNETS and CAPS,
He'll not be found wanting while Selling Cheap HATS![31]

For the third time in as many weeks Westley published once more in verse on September 9, 1854, setting forth his business practices and philosophy:

At No.8, BROAD STREET, a HAT you can buy,
Which for finish and price will competition defy;
The Proprietor being at very small rent
Is enabled to sell on mere nominal per cent.

WESTLEY keeps all the New Styles, both in Bonnets and Caps,
And a Splendid Assortment of Fashionable Hats,
Which he sells at such prices all must admire
Whose means don't admit an expensive attire.

But a word now to those who are disposed this to doubt,
And very properly may ask what is all this about;
What can WESTLEY do above those in his line,
That he should make so much noise about doing it fine?

There is nothing more clear - nothing more plain,
Than very high rents require very large gain;
From this source of evil WESTLEY is perfectly free -
Small expenses enable him to sell very cheap, do ye see.[32]

Robert Westley's experience was quickly to reveal that advertising alone, even in verse, was no guarantee of commercial success. Perhaps his location in Broad Street was unsuitable, possibly he was aiming at the wrong sector of the market, maybe his merchantise was unattractive, perchance his business acumen was as limited as his poetic talent, but, at all events, less than two months after Westley opened his doors *The Herald* published a notice to his debtors and creditors requesting those with claims against him, or who were indebted to him, to register those claims or make payment within fourteen days.[33] Sadly, the only additional references to Westley's ill-starred enterprise were the announcements in October of a bankruptcy sale of what was claimed to be "decidedly the Best, Newest, and most Fashionable Stock of HATS, CAPS, &c. &c., by Auction, in Aberdeen. The whole having been selected and bought personally by Mr Westley, about two months ago, with the view of establishing a Customer Trade; and must now be sold immediately for behoof of the parties concerned." The sale was to take place each evening at half-past six beginning on October 31 until the entire stock was disposed of.[34]

As noted earlier, from mid-1853 Samuel Martin's attention was increasingly focused upon foreign and military matters, especially the likelihood of war between Britain and France on the one hand and Russia on the other. Should hostilities commence, Martin, whose attitude reflected the prevailing Russophobia of the day, was confident that British broadsides and French bayonets would ensure victory, "for what can withstand The British Lion and French Eagle side by side?" He continued with the optimistic and patriotic statement, which in the light of the subsequent history of the Crimean War was shown to be extremely dubious, that "Never, in Britain's history, was she better able than at present to meet her Enemies," and expressed pleasure that at such a moment the British government was headed by Lord Aberdeen.[35]

Martin's favourite British statesman was Lord Palmerston, whose perceived chauvinism at this time Martin could identify with. In the government of Lord Aberdeen (1852-55) Palmerston held the office of Home Secretary though he exercised considerable influence over the direction of foreign affairs. On Christmas Eve 1853 Martin's announcement in *Tbe Herald* lamented the news of the resignation of his hero while wondering whether it was due to differences in the cabinet over a pending parliamentary reform bill, "or is it that the *Eastern Question* is not handled in accordance with this able politician's ideas of *British* dignity?"[36]

Despite the fact that Martin's reflections on Palmerston's resignation occurred only eight days after the news was released they were already outdated by the fact that the erstwhile Home Secretary's popularity demanded that he be brought back into the government just a week after his resignation became public.[37]

However, Martin had already offered both comment and advice in response to his own question *"what's to be done?"*

> Is the Russian *Bear* to *beard* the British *Lion* with impunity? Certainly *not*. There are few people in this country who want WAR if it can reasonably be avoided. But is Britain's amicable intentions to be to all appearance *scorned* or held of little consequence by *any despotic* power? Never. Then *what's to be done?* Why, let Parliament meet sooner than they apparently intend to do, and at once deal with the questions, Is Russia to be allowed to destroy Turkey? or has Britain a right to interfere? That she *has* a right to interfere is certain - else she would not have interfered, as she has already done. *Then, interfere as becomes her,* for certainly a greater insult to Britain's amicable efforts could not be given than that, despite her peaceful intentions, the Russians are openly at war with the *Turks*. Now is the time,

> then, to interfere in earnest. *No half measures!* Send the Russians back to their own territories - ay, at the point of
>
> BRITISH BAYONETS
>
> if required. But if Britain is to be the friend of Turkey let her be so, and *act*, or possibly the Turks may have cause to think that it is better to deal with open Enemies than
>
> LUKEWARM FRIENDS!
>
> But what's to be done by the People of Aberdeen in the meantime? Why, buy their Hats from MARTIN, Hatter to the People! - he's sure to please all who purchase at his Establishment.[38]

Early in the new year Martin was advocating aid to Turkey and the humbling of Russian, claiming that Britain and France were ready for action. He added:

> Never must Britain be trifled with!
> Never must despotism gain the ascendancy!!
> Never must Russia have her own way with Turkey!!!
> Never must Scotchmen forget the *deeds* of *their forefathers*,
> but ever be ready and *willing* to defend their country!!!!

He concluded with the remark that never must the people of Aberdeen forget that Martin sold good hats at moderate prices.[39]

The British and French declarations of war against Russia and in support of Turkey came at the end of March 1854, on March 28 in Britain's case. This news was, of course, carried prominently in the next number of *The Herald* on April 1, as was Martin's enthusiastic response.[40] By the end of the month Martin was using a technique he favoured frequently in the future, namely a visually deceptive headline:

MARTIN, THE HATTER

Does not expect

TO BE MADE A FIELD-MARSHAL

Nor, he added did he expect to receive a naval command or even to be consulted on "matters of moment." He considered it his duty to attend to his own business and to continue to sell first-rate hats at modest prices.[41]

As the war progressed Martin's increasingly lengthy advertisements appeared at regular intervals proffering comment and advice which revealed a surprisingly detailed knowledge of diplomatic initiatives and military developments.[42] By the end of May 1854 Martin was in ebullient mood, looking forward to "A GREAT & GLORIOUS VICTORY," and a "Sharp but Short War."[43] In July Martin was still full of martial enthusiasm, but explained the relative lack of bellicose activity by writing:

> The Czar will find that Britain's power does not lie in Bravado. Never had Britain such a magnificent Fleet upon the waters; and with France as her ally, she will soon bring Nicholas to reasonable terms. 'T is pleasing to think that, in this enlightened age, there are few who advocate War, unless under necessity. But this is a War of necessity, consequently requires to be carried on *Prudently, Systematically,* and *Thoroughly.* No half measures will answer this end in view. Thus it is that no unnecessary waste of Life has taken place, nor uncalled for Skirmishing gone into.[44]

Approximately once every three or four weeks Martin changed the text of his advertisements, but they still concentrated heavily on the war, though he found time to welcome Queen Victoria on her annual visit to Balmoral in September.[45] On November 4 Martin was able at last to proclaim a "GLORIOUS VICTORY ON THE HEIGHTS OF THE ALMA" and to lavish praise on the British army, and especially the Highlanders, at the battle of Balaclava fought on October 25. Naturally, he added:

> **MARTIN THE HATTER**
>
> is delighted with the bravery of the Allies, and is determined to show the People of Aberdeen that his low charge for *good* Hats may well be compared to the Fixed Bayonet Charge of the Highlanders at the Alma -
>
> **NOT TO BE BEAT**
>
> So EYES RIGHT, and buy your Hats from MARTIN.[46]

The Battle of Inkerman on November 5, 1854, produced no direct comment, but Martin waxed lyrical on the bravery and the virtues of the troops:

> BRITISH SOLDIERS, as usual doing their duty - every man from the Private to the General, showing acts of bravery never before surpassed, if ever equalled in history. Proud should every true-born Briton be to see their

> countrymen doing such deeds of arms. 'T is enough to put a martial spirit into the most peaceful-minded individual in the land....
> Britain is proud of you - the eyes of Europe are upon you. Oh, thanks to you for your bravery; your countrymen feel that their homes and their welfare depend upon you, and well are you acting up to their expectations. Be assured that your *fatigue*, your *losses*, and your *courage*, are often thought of and truly appreciated at home.[47]

That Martin's regard for the valour and sacrifice of British troops in the Crimea was widely shared was demonstrated in this same week by a meeting held in the city Town-House on Thursday, November 16, 1854, at which the Patriotic Fund for the Relief of Widows and Orphans of Soldiers, Sailors, and Marines, Who Fell in the present War was set up in Aberdeen. An editorial in *The Herald* expressed the opinion that to subscribe liberally to this fund was for most people "as nearly an imperative duty as anything can well be." The meeting in the Town-House, called for the purpose of carrying into effect the recommendation of a Royal Commission to establish such a Patriotic Fund, was crowded, although the day was described as very unfavourable. The topic was introduced by Lord Provost Blaikie and Mr Thomas Todd of Maryculter House moved the resolution to create the Patriotic Fund in a "just and eloquent" speech. The subscription list was then opened with several exemplary donations. In words that would have done justice to one of Martin's own announcements *The Herald* concluded, "Let all classes contribute according to their ability, for not only is much due to the heroic conduct of our brave soldiers and sailors, but a large amount and an immense number of names will be useful as showing the Czar how earnestly and universally the people of this country are engaged in the struggle against his insatiable ambition."[48]

Not surprisingly Samuel Martin's name appeared on the original subscription list published in *The Herald*, and he was, no doubt, one of those referred to as making exemplary donations as he gave the not inconsiderable sum of five guineas.[49]

Martin's combination of patriotism and humour was appreciated not only in Aberdeen, but also wherever copies of *The Herald* were to be found. William Carnie, a reporter and editor with *The Herald*, later recalled that Martin's devoted attachment to the British Army was reciprocated, and that, "During the weary anxious winter of the Crimean

War - 1854 - letter after letter from soldiers in the Highland Brigade to friends in Aberdeenshire was brought to the *Herald* Office, dwelling fondly on general things happening at 'home', but all declaring that the first portion of the paper read around the snow-encompassed camp fires was that containing the poetical patriotic advertisement of the 'Practical Hatter'."[50]

Martin bade farewell to 1854 in his usual exuberant mood,[51] but his first advertisement of 1855 showed his awareness of the growing volume of adverse comment on the way the war was being directed and managed, although at the same time it demonstrated his lack of sympathy with the critics. He wrote:

> There is perhaps no feeling that causes so many pleasant emotions to the mind as the performance of a pleasant duty; thus it is that, at this the beginning of 1855, MARTIN THE HATTER feels extremely happy in thanking THE PEOPLE, and which he does *most heartily*, for their kind support for the past year - support which he felt anxious to deserve by continuing to sell *good Hats cheap*, and which he has had *ocular demonstration* has been truly appreciated by the true power of Britain - THE PEOPLE - the power which has enabled MARTIN to carry on a prosperous trade in Aberdeen for nearly *Seventeen Years.*
>
> 1854 will appear a great year, not only for MARTIN, but from the fact of Britain having a War thrust upon her after a Peace of nearly *Forty Years.* MARTIN, in advertising, has frequently commented upon passing events in the War, and feels inclined to continue doing so. And however vehemently opinions may be expressed upon the so-called *mis*management of the War, MARTIN feels his right, as a British subject, to give *his* opinion, and from resources which he believes to be authentic, that there ARE AS ABLE COMMANDERS IN THE CRIMEA AS EVER WERE IN THE PENINSULA. But in this *his* opinion, MARTIN has no wish to detract from the laurels of those Brave Men who died for their country in the last War - men who *so* often and *so* justly received the thanks of *Parliament* and THE PEOPLE for their brave deeds. But in respecting the memory of the dead, 'T IS NOT REQUISITE TO FORGET THE MERITS OF THE LIVING COMMANDERS. The Government, in sending out an Army to the Crimea, selcted Commanders no doubt, who, from their experience, they knew were capable of upholding the *honour* of Britain, and fighting her Battles. And the Battles already fought (all victories) show that their selection was good.[52]

On January 27, 1855, Martin was again defending the reputation and actions of the British commanders and expressing the hope that despite the resignation of Lord John Russell from the cabinet the Prime Minister, Lord Aberdeen, might "triumphantly pass through the ordeal of inquiry as to the state of the Army in the Crimea." While he regretted the death of so many brave men from disease, Martin offered the opinion that "these are casualties which all Armies are liable to in landing in a strange Country at the most inclement season of the year, and over which no Government (*that cannot manage the weather*) can have control, but which experienced Commanders cannot but calculate upon." The grumblers were, in his opinion, few in number and their strictures likely to cause more amusement than annoyance to the commanders in the field.[53] In fact, Lord Aberdeen and his government resigned a few days later, and a new ministry was formed under the leadership of Palmerston.[54] This event afforded Martin the opportunity to include in his next advertisement the news:

MARTIN THE HATTER

has not had an opportunity of refusing office, for the simple reason that he has not been

OFFERED A SEAT IN THE CABINET[55]

The unexpected death of the Czar of Russia, Nicholas I, on March 2, 1855, drew forth little sympathy from Martin who wrote: "DEAD! Yes, Nicholas is dead. That his death will be a matter of regret to his subjects is doubtful; but that it will prove beneficial to the peace of Europe is certain." Martin held Nicholas responsible on account of his "*ambitious, grasping, dogmatic, unfeeling,* and *unhappy* disposition" for the outbreak of war and death of so many men on both sides, and, therefore, laid aside false delicacy by positively welcoming the tyrant's demise.[56]

Throughout the early months of 1855 Martin looked forward to military success in the Crimea and the fall of Sebastopol and to an honourable peace. He welcomed the visit of the Emperor and Empress of France, (Napoleon III and Eugenie), to Britain in April as likely to advance the allies' cause.[57]

For many Aberdonians the major news on May 5 was no doubt the absence from the columns of *The Herald* of any announcement by Martin.

CONSTERNATION!
WONDER!! AND AMAZEMENT!!!

MARTIN the HATTER's Advertisement not in the *Herald* last Saturday. No doubt many people surprised—some may have thought that MARTIN had at last got an appointment in the Ministry, or a Command in the Crimea, there being so much talk at present about

RIGHT MEN IN RIGHT PLACES.

Others may have thought that MARTIN was unwell or from home, and that it was him that the Shoemaker in Paris

SHOT AT LATELY!

But all such conjectures would have been erroneous. The Ministry being full at present—*at least Martin has not been offered an appointment*—and the Commanders in the Crimea are doing so well, that MARTIN's abilities have very likely not been thought of nor canvassed

AT THE HORSE GUARDS.

MARTIN is happy to say that his health and energies are good as ever, and that he was not from home, consequently it was not *him* but a *great* man in *another sphere* that was Shot at in Paris. 'Twas

THE EMPEROR OF FRANCE!

Not the Emperor af Hats! But the fact was, strange as it may appear, the Advertisement was *overlooked*, and yet was *not* overlooked; *overlooked*, not being inserted; but *not* overlooked, because not seen by readers.

DESPATCHES FROM THE CRIMEA DAILY.

THE ALLIES GOING AHEAD!

Sebastopol Shaken the Second Time in Style!!

Disastrous Effects of the Bombardment upon the Enemy.

RIFLE PITS AND OUTWORKS TAKEN.

THE RUSSIANS CHASED INTO THEIR DEN.

The Allies steadily advancing—evident preparation for a Great Battle, preparatory to cutting off Russian resources from the North side. No doubt of the result—the Allies must be victorious!

Sebastopol will be Attacked for the Third and Last Time!

Then, Highlanders and Zouaves, prepare for the assault! Fix Bayonets, and with a thorough British shout of

DEATH OR SURRENDER!!

make the Russians fly before you—they will never stand the bayonet used in the true Highlander's style.

NEWS OF GREAT MOMENT EXPECTED SOON.

But at present all who want a Good Stylish HAT or CAP at a Moderate Price, should purchase from

SAMUEL MARTIN,

HATTER TO THE PEOPLE,

34, Union Street, Aberdeen.

Established SEVENTEEN *Years.*

Their curiosity or concern was abated on the following Saturday when his regular advertisement reappeared under the headline:

CONSTERNATION!
WONDER!! AND AMAZEMENT!!!

Martin explained that his advertisement had somehow been overlooked, and reassured his readers that he had not been offered a political or military post, had not been unwell or away from home, and had not been the object of an assassination attempt. The intended victim of a shooting in Paris had been the Emperor of France and not the Emperor of Hats.[58]

Martin welcomed the arrival of Sardinian troops in the Crimea to aid the allied cause,[59] and praised the preparations for sending more British troops to the seat of operations. He had joined many other local citizens in visiting the Links to witness Lord Melville inspecting the depot of the 79th Regiment and the Militia. The 79th were a regiment who ever "LOOK WELL, DRILL WELL, and FIGHT WELL," and in Martin's opinion the Militia went through their evolutions in a very satisfactory manner.[60]

During June, July and August 1855 Martin ran a series of advertisements full of patriotic sentiments, describing events in both the Crimean and Baltic theatres of war and in particular looking forward to the fall of Sebastopol.[61] By the beginning of September he was confidently expecting momentous news and predicting the complete humbling of the Czar.[62]

Finally, Martin's optimism and repeated predictions regarding the fall of Sebastopol were rewarded, when, on September 9, after a seige of 339 days, the Russian garrison evacuated the city following the loss of the key Malakoff fort to a French assault. Martin's response was a positively delirious outburst of joy and patriotic pride tempered only with regret for the heavy casualty lists involved and a plea for generous help for the widows and orphans of the fallen and care for the wounded and maimed. Even by his own standards Martin's advertisement was brazenly chauvinistic, and was spread across two columns with many headlines.[63] Half a century later A.S. Cook in his *Old-Time Traders and Their Ways* remembered this particular advertisement. Cook recalled that Martin was very particular about the exact lay-out of his notices in *The Herald*, and that any departure from the copy was a serious matter for the compositor.[64]

Martin ran this same exuberant advertisement for three weeks, but in early October he returned to the theme of defending the reputations of the country's military and naval commanders against the comments of their critics. His main headline on this occasion was "DO AS YOU WOULD BE DONE BY!", and he regretted the fashion of the day which seemed to be to find fault with men while they were living but to praise them when they were dead.[65] Martin was not only an inveterate champion of Lord Raglan, both before and after his death in June 1855, but also a defender of Raglan's chief-of-staff and successor in the Crimea Sir James Simpson. After Simpson resigned at the end of September as a result of differences of opinion with the Secretary of War, Lord Panmure, Martin used the moment to announce:

> 'Tis reported that General Simpson is to be relieved from the Command of the Army in the Crimea, and that his Successor will not likely be known until Government receives his acknowledgement of the appointment. But the People of Aberdeen and the North, will no doubt, be delighted to hear
>
> that
>
> **MARTIN THE HATTER**
>
> has not received any Despatches from Government,
> consequently he has no reason to suppose that he
> **Will be General Simpson's Successor.**
>
> And although MARTIN is just about the age to make what is called a SPIRITED COMMANDER, yet he never expects that the great responsibility will be thrust upon him; thus his mind is quite at ease, the more so as, from the fault-finding propensities of the age, he feels convinced that even HIS abilities as a Military Commander would be found fault with; so that, as it is perfectly evident that he is not to have the Command of a Large Army, he is determined to have the Command of a LARGE TRADE, by continuing to Sell first-rate Hats at moderate prices, and thus avoid all chance of being found fault with by the People.[66]

Almost at once Martin found a fresh topic to write about that raised his patriotic spirit. For much of 1855 British representatives in the United States had been engaged in an ill-fated scheme to raise recruits for service in the Crimea. A new Foreign Enlistment Act had become law on December 23, 1854, designed primarily to raise men in Germany and

SHAKEN, AND TAKEN TOO!

FALLEN AT LAST!!

Three times Three Cheers, and One Cheer more!—Hip, hip, hurrah!!
Let every true-born Briton hurrah! Let the Nation be glad!!
Let every true-born Briton rejoice, with heartfelt enthusiasm!!!

GLORIOUS NEWS, INDEED!

SEBASTOPOL IS TAKEN!!

☞ NO MISTAKE THIS TIME!!!

THE Lion of Britain and Eagle of France are floating over its ruins! The Bombardment reopened on the 5th, and the Assault was made on the forenoon of Saturday the 8th instant. The Allies attacking four points simultaneously, and after a struggle fearful to contemplate, the French obtained possession of the Malakoff—the British fighting bravely, *as they ever do,* were nevertheless twice driven back from the Redan, being mowed down in hundreds by the Russian Artillery, ramparts being, it may be said, formed by the bodies of their comrades; but the THIRD and FOURTH time they came FEARLESSLY on,

DETERMINED TO CONQUER OR DIE!

on which the Russians, as if thunderstruck at such indomitable courage (far beyond their powers to comprehend), though themselves fighting well, were gloriously driven from their Stronghold with fearful carnage, blowing up their Magazines, Ships, &c. and leaving hundreds of Prisoners—suffering a

Total and Ignominious Defeat.

Thus fell Sebastopol, that has been nearly HALF A CENTURY in preparing to defy the World, but which the

VALOUR, COURAGE, & PERSEVERANCE

of the Allies has completely destroyed, after an investment of little more than THREE HUNDRED DAYS. 'T will now be merely a matter of Time, and that comparatively short, on the part of the Allies, to reduce the North side of Sebastopol, and thus thoroughly humble the Power of Russia, hitherto the scourge and disturber of the Earth, henceforward to be classed as a Third or even Fourth Rate Power.

Great Anxiety--List of Casualties expected daily.

Meantime, 't is reported that the Allies have lost Ten Thousand Men in Killed and Wounded. But, however, this IS and OUGHT TO BE a matter of regret, yet the Country could not but expect serious casualties in obtaining so glorious a result.

Happy Britain! Surely there breathes not a British Subject whose heart does not expand with Delight, Enthusiasm, and Endearment to his Country, on hearing this Glorious News!! Oh, how Proud, how Happy, how Delighted should all be, who can place their Hand on their Bosom, and exclaim—Britain, the Pride of the World! Britain, the Enlightened Power of the Earth!! Britain, the Terror of Despotism!!! And Britain,

MY NATIVE LAND!!!!

Oh, what a thrilling feeling of satisfaction to all British Subjects, on hearing of this Great and Glorious Victory. But what words can convey thanks sufficient to their Brave Brothers in Arms who have thrust this great

HONOUR UPON THE BRITISH NATION!

No, no. Words fall short to convey the enthusiasm and good feeling of the Nation to her Brave Soldiers. 'T is deeds that must stand forth in bold relief, showing to the European Nations of the earth that, as British Soldiers ever fight well, and where they fight they ever conquer, so Britain, shows her just appreciation of her Brave Sons, by REVERING the Memory of the Dead,

HONOURING THE LIVING,

And providing for the Widows and Orphans of those who have died for her on

THE BATTLE FIELD!

Thus there need be no false delicacy—the Widows and Orphans of those Brave Men who have died in the Crimea HAVE A RIGHT to be provided for, the WOUNDED and MAIMED MUST be cared for and made comfortable in their latter days. 'T is common sense, 't is justice; as the Country that forgets properly to recompence the Power that PROTECTS and DEFENDS her, deserves to be ruled by the iron hand of Despotism, and her subjects to be treated like Slaves. But,

BRITAIN'S BELOVED QUEEN,

Ever, even at her lovely Highland Home at Balmoral, has apparently her mind's eye upon the Deeds of her Soldiers; and her NATURALLY GOOD and AMIABLE Disposition will remind her ever truly to appreciate and recompence the

Brave Defenders of her Crown.

SO THINKS

MARTIN THE HATTER,

Who is able and determined to continue selling his far-famed Hats at very Moderate Prices, and thus try to please all who purchase at his Establishment.

Observe!—SAMUEL MARTIN,

HATTER TO THE PEOPLE,

34, UNION STREET, ABERDEEN.

☞ ESTABLISHED SEVENTEEN YEARS.

LONG LIFE TO BRITAIN'S BELOVED QUEEN,

And One Jolly Good Cheer for her Brave Defenders---Hurrah!!!

Switzerland, but British attempts to secure volunteers in America threatened to breach the United States Neutrality Act of 1818. Resentment against British behaviour in this matter, long-running rivalry in the Caribbean and Central America, and the generally hostile comment of the American press plus a series of court cases arising from the recruiting campaign led to a dangerous deterioration in Anglo-American diplomatic relations and the strengthening of the British naval squadron in the West Indies. By October the position looked serious, and it was at this moment that Samuel Martin offered the citizens of Aberdeen his appreciation of the situation. In his opinion the crisis was due to a misunderstanding, largely America's fault, and there was no likelihood of war. America should stick to "commerce and counting dollars, which she thoroughly understands, and not interfere with matters beyond her comprehension." While Britain had no wish for a quarrel, and was already at war with Russia, America should beware as Britain still had the power to chastise anyone who insulted her, and any conflict would lead to a succession of American defeats "which might be beneficial to them in carrying off a little of their superfluous *bombast*, which certainly frightens nobody, but may injure themselves."[67] Martin's aggressive and condescending attitude toward America, Britain's largest trading partner and chief commercial rival, was not unrepresentative of British public opinion. However, since a war would have been unpopular in both countries the temperature was gradually lowered and the matter allowed to fade from the diplomatic agenda and from Martin's advertisements since he referred to it only once more, in June 1856, after the British minister in Washington was forced to leave his post on account of his diplomatic indiscretion. Martin hoped that this would resolve the contretemps with America and permit an amicable settlement.[68] In Martin's eyes a much larger question needed to be addressed, namely the terms of peace with Russia.

As was becoming his habit Samuel Martin seized the occasion of his last advertisement in 1855, at the end of December, to review the past year and to thank the people of Aberdeen for their continued support, which had contributed to his prosperous position and wide-spread fame. His remarks at this time were of more than normal interest since they threw considerable light upon his individualistic business practices and general outlook:

> MARTIN'S style of Business may possibly be considered *peculiar*, and perhaps it is, but his idea is to please as many as possible, and to offend NONE. His Advertising propensities are now pretty generally known. (By the way, he has lately got in what he calls a Slashing Account from *The Herald*, for the last Six Months, but which he paid freely, as Sebastopol was taken, and MARTIN had some extra lengthy comments on the War.) But, blessed with an ordinary Education, MARTIN likes to touch upon passing events in these
>
> MOMENTOUS TIMES
>
> and to comment upon them without that verbiage which makes News difficult to understand. And he feels highly pleased in believing (plainly seen by the magnitude of his Trade) that his Advertisements are read and appreciated by the People, and which is certainly encouragement to him to persist in carrying on his Business in his own peculiar style; and, although some of his ideas may be thought full-drawn, ludicrous, and laughable to an extreme, it will be admitted that they are generally amusing, and not far from the mark aimed at - viz. giving his opinion upon Political matters, and keeping the Public in mind that *he continues to Sell Good Hats at Moderate Prices.*[69]

Martin welcomed 1856, which he believed would be a year of terror for Britain's enemies, as twelve months that would astonish the world. He pressed for a vigorous continuation of the war against Russia and her complete humiliation, expressing his feelings in extravagant language. Only peace terms that left Russia prostrate and crippled for the future would satisfy Martin.[70]

News that a peace conference would meet in Paris drew from him deep suspicion regarding the motives of Austria and an insistence that no patched-up peace was acceptable. He called upon the Prime Minister, Lord Palmerston, whom he saw as the right man in the right place, to do his duty fearlessly. He urged:

> Then agree to no terms of Peace with Russia that do not distinctly settle ALL matters for which the War was commenced, and thus prove to the World, and *particularly* to Jonathan, that Britain is ever reluctant to draw the Sword; but when drawn, 't is never returned to the Scabbard until Enemies are humbled, and she obtains an
>
> **Honourable, Lasting, and Glorious Peace.**[71]

The peace conference actually opened in Paris on February 25, and lasted until March 30.[72] Naturally Martin discoursed upon the negotiations and assured his readers that Russian attempts to divide Britain and France would meet with disappointment. Had the Queen appointed Martin to be a British plenipotentiary then he felt convinced that he would quickly have brought the Russian diplomatists to their senses, dispensed with formalities and simply have handed the Russians a document containing British peace terms with a ten day deadline for acceptance under threat of continuing the war if they were not agreed to.[73] On March 29, 1856, the day before the conference closed, Martin wrote:

> If the Conference ends in making a Peace strictly in accordance with the objects for which the Allies went to War with Russia, then their honour is safe, but if they give way to the manoeuvring diplomatic efforts of Russia to make a *patched-up* Peace without the proper balance of power being thoroughly agreed to by Russia, then the objects of the War will not be obtained, and timid Nations may triumph in remarking that the Allies have Sacrificed their Brave Sons and spent their money to no purpose.[74]

The Herald announced news of the signing of the peace treaty in its April 5 number, noting the reservations felt by Martin:

> The coming Peace having cast its shadow pretty intelligibly before, the news of the actual event, when it arrived on Monday, did not create that burst of enthusiasm which it otherwise might have done. During part of the day, however, the bells rang out merrily - flags and bunting of various hues were displayed - and the laddies made a terrible noise at night in Union Street, threatening destruction to porters' hurlies and merchants' barrows of every description, in their endeavour to raise a beacon fire of rejoicing. On Tuesday most of the schools obtained a half-holiday; and every person apparently was glad except Martin, the practical hatter, who, doubtful in his wisdom of the "honourable" terms on which Peace had been arranged, and jealous for the credit of his country, filled his principal window with white beavers clothed in sackcloth.[75]

Still suspicious of the terms on which peace had been signed, but in the absence of details, Martin's advertisement of the same date, April 5, was spread across two columns and filled with foreboding and a deepening suspicion regarding France's role.[76] A week later he explained that his idea of a satisfactory peace was "Russia humbled, and her wings so distinctly clipped, that henceforward she will not be able to make any flighty attempts at aggression." He went on to criticise the buying and selling of commissions in the British Army, and recommended the promotion of deserving non-commissioned officers. If he were Minister of War he would seek not to reduce the army but to make it more efficient.[77]

Although the official text of the peace treaty was not released until April 28 when ratifications had been exchanged, the British press had already made clear its feelings. To the surprise of many the terms were better received than expected in view of the considerable criticism, led by the London *Times*, levelled at the management of the war.[78] In Aberdeen *The Herald* of May 3 joined in the general mood of approval and the following week concluded an editorial on the subject with the opinion that its readers would have little difficulty in agreeing with parliament that the final terms were "honourable to her Majesty's Crown, and fully accomplished the great objects for which the war was undertaken."[79]

Needless to say, Martin did not swell the chorus of approbation. His first advertisement following the publication of the official text of the peace treaty was headed:

THE PEACE, SUCH AS IT IS, RATIFIED,

Containing Thirty-four Articles, well worth perusal, being very ingenious and very amusing.

\- - - - - - -

Is it proper, is it right?
Is it pleasing to the Nation?
Is it Peace like Britain's might?
Is it viewed with admiration?

Martin went on to complain that the idea of the peace terms being in strict accordance with the generally understood objects of the war was distinctly beyond his comprehension. He concluded this particular advertisement with the statement:

> Thus does MARTIN differ in opinion from many people, even from the enlightened views of the Editor of *The Herald*, upon the nature and advantages of the present Treaty of Peace. And at this, the end of the War (the Fighting being over for the present), and in a manner taking leave of the subject, MARTIN has no wish to damp the feelings of the Nation. But let those rejoice that think fit to do so. MARTIN, as a true British Subject,

> anxious for the honour of his Country, conscientiously thinks that he has fully as much reason to Mourn as to Rejoice at the present Treaty of Peace, feeling, as he does, regret that so many Brave British Soldiers have died on the Battle Fields of the Crimea to gain so little for their Country.[80]

Three weeks later he was complaining about the dishonourable and niggardly treatment of returning soldiers whose extra war pay had been stopped precipitously, and the reduction in rank of some officers and men. The thanks of parliament for the efforts of the army was gratifying, "but fine words butter no parsnips."[81] Even though the war was now over, Martin continued over the following months to voice his suspicions and dissatisfaction regarding the peace and the treatment accorded the armed forces,[82] and he lamented that the war had not been carried on for twelve months longer.[83]

The exact degree and nature of the influence of the press during the Crimean War may be in dispute, although, undoubtedly, the newspapers, and the London *Times* in particular, did influence the course of the war and contribute to political changes in Britain. It is interesting to note that while the majority of the press attacked the military conduct and political management of the war, yet applauded the peace settlement, Samuel Martin was unimpressed by their opinions. He resolutely defended the governments of both Lord Aberdeen and Lord Palmerston, regretted the hardship and suffering of the troops but considered such things as the inevitable consequence of war, and condemned the peace treaty. His opinions were always consistent and there is no reason to believe they were not sincerely held.

By 1856 Martin's advertisments were attracting widespread attention, and he had achieved more than local notoriety.[84] It was, perhaps, no empty boast when, soon after the Crimean War ended, he referred to himself as:

> MARTIN, whose fame, it may be said, has spread over Europe! MARTIN, whose fame has been spoken of in the bloody and well-fought battlefields of the Crimea, where British soldiers so gloriously thrashed their Enemies! MARTIN, whose fame even reached and was spoken of in the Trenches before Sebastopol, midst the roar of Russian Cannon, which were ultimately taken from the enemy....MARTIN, whose fame was well known and spoken of on board Britain's magnificent Navy in the Baltic and Black Seas!....And MARTIN, whose fame, he has reason to believe, has been

> heard within the walls of the Scotch Castle of Royalty, where the admirable, adored, and amiable Lady who so ably fills the British Throne, sojourns for a few weeks during the Summer season.
> Long Life To her Majesty & her Beloved Family.[85]

Since, in fact, Martin was indeed a close and long time friend of John Brown, Queen Victoria's noted personal servant, the patriotic and loyal hatter's hymns of praise to the royal family may very well have been heard at Balmoral.[86]

Whatever his vanity Martin's business acumen was not to be doubted, and despite the comings and goings of competitors his establishment at 34 Union Street flourished in the years 1848-1856. He did, however, suffer one loss in these years. Neil N. Maclean attended King's College, Aberdeen, between 1853 and 1859, and has left an account of his experiences entitled *Life at a Northern University*.[87] Early in his academic career, probably 1853 or 1854, Maclean recalled calling upon another student, a Mr Lockhart, a friend of Maclean's cousin. Browsing in Mr Lockhart's room Maclean recalled:

> ....Passing to the sideboard, I was very much surprised to see it decorated with ornaments of a very curious nature - knockers of all shapes and material - while in the centre there was a beautiful brass plate engraved with the name of Samuel Martin, Hatter to the People. I inspected these very closely, and found them to be in every way excellently executed, some in the antique style of art, while all, or almost all, bore some inscription. These inscriptions I found to be the names of leading men in the town, such as Dr Dyce, Rev. Henry Angus, Rev. John Murray, Sir Thomas Wyllie, Peter Henderson, Dr Keith, Sir Thomas Blaikie, and a host of others.

Lockhart confessed, with pride, that it was a craze of his to collect these items, and that he had devoted himself "to this branch of antiquarian research" since coming to college, and those on display he had acquired that session. He had long desired to possess Samuel Martin's name-plate, and, he explained:

> "...was patiently awaiting for an opportunity, when a deputation of my fellow-students called upon me a short time ago, and after stating that they were aware of my proclivity for the acquisition of articles of this nature, begged my acceptance of this little mark of their esteem. I was so touched

with their kindness that I could scarcely find words to express my thanks. After treating them to a liberal supply of Bass, and bowing them out at the door, I returned to seat myself before my magnificent present, and to study its exquisite proportions. While thus occupied, would you believe that I had a visit from a man, accompanied by two policemen, declaring that I was the receiver of stolen goods? Of course I shut the door in their faces and returned to my post."

"And were you never troubled by them again?"

"Of course not: more especially as the two bobbies were old friends whom I am in the practice of occasionally treating."

Thus, Samuel Martin had discovered the cost and paid the price of his fame.[88]

NOTES

1 *The Herald*, September 2, 1848, p141, col 5.
2 *The Herald*, September 9, 1848, p147, col 3.
3 *The Herald*, September 30, 1848, p158, col 3.
4 *The Herald*, March 3, 1849, p34, col 5; *The Herald*, May 26, 1849, p82, col 3; and *The Herald*, July 7, 1849, p106, col 4.
5 *The Herald*, January 5, 1850, p1, col 2; *The Herald*, March 2, 1850, p34, col 6; and *The Herald*, August 31, p139, col 1.
6 *The Herald*, January 4, 1851, p2, col 1. Martin also seized this occasion to ussue a rejoinder to "a remark sometimes made, that a HAT is a very inconvenient article of dress, from its bulk, &c, the reasons given being, that you cannot take a HAT into a crowded hall, or even into a parlour conveniently; but individuals who make such remarks should keep in view the purpose for which a HAT was originally intended, and, by so doing, they will find that it is not the *use* but the *abuse* of the HAT that causes the inconvenience. As to the bulk of a HAT. The circumference of a man's head being about half the circumference of his shoulders, the height of crown, &c, of the HAT is required to correspond to a reasonable extent with the size of the body under it, and HATS, like many other articles, being intended for a particular purpose - viz., an article of dress for outdoor wear, to protect the head from the weather, &c. - they never were intended to be taken into crowded halls or parlours. Else it may be asked, What were anterooms or pegs in lobby walls intended for? But to expect a HAT to be a convenient article under all circumstances and in all places, would be equally absurd as to expect a *Plough to be useful in a Drawing room*, or to

attempt to *wind up your Watch* with a Coal Scuttle.... But the fact is, that the HAT of the present day, if put to its *legitimate* use, is really and truly a very useful article...."

7 *The Herald*, August 16, 1851, p130, col 3.

8 *The Herald*, September 13, 1851, p146, col 3.

9 *The Herald*, December 27, 1851, p206, col 3. Martin added that his expectations had been realised as he was selling lots of umbrellas. His establishment had three great requisites as it was "Large! Commodious!! and Attractive!!!"

10 *The Herald*, January 3, 1852, p2, col 2.

11 *The Herald*, January 31, 1852, p18, col 3.

12 *The Herald*, March 27, 1852, p1, col 4, and p4, col 6.

13 *The Herald*, April 10, 1852, p4, col 2.

14 *The Herald*, April 17, 1852, p4, col 2, and April 24, 1852, p4, col 4.

15 *The Herald*, February 19, 1853, p4, col 1.

16 *The Herald*, July 25, 1852, p4 col 2. Martin reemphasizes the point in *The Herald*, October 8, 1852, p4, col 4, when he wrote, "*...for, as all undue pressure upon the head has a direct influence upon the mind, it naturally follows that a* tight *Hat has a tendency to have an impairing effect upon the intellectual faculties.*"

17 *The Herald*, November 13, 1852, p4, col 3.

18 *The Herald*, May 7, 1853, p4, col 3.

19 *The Herald*, July 30, 1853, p4, col 3. In this same editorial *The Herald* remarked that "The duty of 1s.6., being uniform, pressed with peculiar severity on short advertisements that will experience the greatest relief from the repeal; but even on the average size of advertisements the amount of reduction will form a considerable percentage. Before our next publication, we expect that the repeal of this duty will come into operation, when, and in future, our lowest charge for an Advertisement will be ONE SHILLING, and on the whole graduation of our Advertisement Scale of Charges the reduction will be proportionate."

20 *The Herald*, September 3, 1853, p4, col 1.

21 *The Herald*, September 24, 1853, p4, col 1. For those interested Martin added a footnote to his advertisement in *The Herald*, October 29, 1853, p4, col 3, informing readers, "Please to observe that the QUEEN DID *Not* call upon Martin as she lately passed through Aberdeen."

22 *The Herald,* October 1, 1853, p5, col 6.

23 *The Herald,* January 7, 1854, p4, col 2.

24 *The Herald*, February 18, 1854, p4, col 4.

25 *The Herald*, August 12, 1854, p4, col 3.

26 *The Herald*, June 10, 1854, p4, col 3.

27 *The Herald*, July 1, 1854, p4, col 3.

28 Martin's advertisement with the deliberately misleading statement, "If MARTIN THE HATTER was PRIME MINISTER OF ENGLAND," with "If" and "was" in much smaller type, appeared in *The Herald* on June 24, 1854, p4, col 4. Had he been elevated to that high office Martin assured his readers "his policy would be to reduce Russia to the position of a *third* rate power, and thus keep her henceforth from disturbing the peace of Europe with her ambitious projects, which she evidently appears *unwilling* to *fight for.*"

29 *The Herald*, August 19, 1854, p4, col 5.

30 *The Herald*, August 26, 1854, p4, col 2.

31 *The Herald*, September 2, 1854, p4, col 3.

32 *The Herald*, September 9, 1854, p8, col 3. According to the Aberdeen *Rent Roll And Assessments For 1854-1855*, in the City Archives, Westley was correct in stating that his rent was low in comparison to other hatters. Robert Westley's figure for "Occupants Assessable Rent" at 8 Broad Street was £26 p.a., while Samuel Martin at 34 Union Street was listed as £56.10s p.a., Steele & Co., at 20 Union Street was given as £57 p.a., and W.M. Millar at 69 Union Street as £70 p.a.

33 *The Herald*, September 30, 1854, p4, col 4.

34 *The Herald*, October 21, 1854, p8, col 2, and October 28, 1854, p8, col2.

35 *The Herald*, July 16, 1853, p4, col 2.

36 *The Herald*, December 24, 1853, p4, col 3.

37 For details of Palmerston's resignation and reinstatement see J.B. Conacher *The Aberdeen Coalition 1852-1855* (1968) pp215-32.

38 *The Herald*, December 24, 1853, p4, col 3.

39 *The Herald*, February 11, 1854, p4, col 1.

40 *The Herald*, April 1, 1854, p4, col 6, and p4, col 3.

41 *The Herald,* April 29, 1854, p4, col 3. Four weeks later Martin remarked that it was no doubt a great satisfaction to the people of Aberdeen to know that he had not been offered either a naval or a military appointment but would continue to serve them. He ended that particular advertisement with the information that he was satisfied that "purchasers will see that the *tout ensemble* of his Establishment is amazingly attractive." *The Herald*, May 27, 1854, p4, col 1.

42 See for example *The Herald*, June 24, 1854, p4, col 4, where Martin discoursed on the Austrian intervention that persuaded Russia to evacuate the Danubian Principalities of Moldavia and Wallachia.

43 *The Herald*, May 27, 1854, p4, col 1.

44 *The Herald*, July 22, 1854, p4, col 3. On this date Martin ran a second, more modest advertisement in the same newspaper on p8, col 3, aimed at the farming community. He commented on the weather, the beautiful appearance of the countryside, the likelihood of good crops, and went on:

"FARMERS and Others visiting Aberdeen, next week, should avail themselves of the opportunity, and purchase a *Stylish, Becoming,* and *Durable* Hat From MARTIN, THE HATTER TO THE PEOPLE. The FIT of his Hats have a consolatory effect upon the mind. Their *appearance* delights the Organ of Vision, and their *low prices* cause delight; and MARTIN, having an anxious wish to please purchasers, has a happy style of dong so." He called attention to his large assortment of portmanteaus, coat cases, leather hat cases, carpet and leather bags, umbrellas, etc.

45 *The Herald*, August 19,. 1854, p4, col 1, and September 23, 1854, p4, col 1.

46 *The Herald*, November 4, 1854, p4, col 3. Martin's expectations regarding the fall of Sebastopol were premature, as the fortress was not captured until September 1855, and British losses at Balaclava were high so that it was a costly victory. Oddly, perhaps, Martin made no mention of the famous cavalry charges by the heavy and light brigades, the latter event giving rise to Tennyson's poem.

47 *The Herald*, November 18, 1854, p4, col 4.

48 *The Herald*, November 18, 1854, p5, cols 3-4, and p6, col 1.

49 *The Herald*, November 18, 1854, p4, col 6.

50 William Carnie, *Additional Aberdeen Reminiscences. Social, Civic and Personal Pencillings of the Granite City*, Vol III, (1906), p273.

51 *The Herald*, December 16, 1854, p4, col 3.

52 *The Herald*, January 6, 1855, p4, col 2.

53 *The Herald*, January 27, 1855, p4, col 4.

54 On the collapse of the Aberdeen Government see J.B. Conacher, *op.cit.*, pp492-548.

55 *The Herald,* February 3, 1855, p4, col 4.

56 *The Herald*, March 10, 1855, p4, col 2.

57 *The Herald*, March 24, 1855, p4, col 3, April 14, 1855, p4, col 2, and April 21, 1855, p4, col 3.

58 *The Herald*, May 12, 1855, p4, col 2.

59 *The Herald*, May 19, 1855, p4, col 3.

60 *The Herald*, June 2, 1855, p4, col 2. On p5, col 4 of the same edition *The Herald* carried a news item relating to the same event: "THE MILITIA:- Our local militia corps was inspected by Major General Viscount Melville, in the grounds at Gordon's Hospital, on Wednesday forenoon, and reviewed on the Links in the afternoon, under the command of Lord Saltoun. Lord Melville highly commended the appearance of the Regiment and their expertness at Manoeuvring."

61 *The Herald*, June 16, 1855, p4, col 2, June 30, 1855, p4 col 1, July 21, 1855, p4 col 4, July 28, 1855, p4, col 3, and August 18, 1855, p4, col 1.

62 *The Herald*, September 1, 1855, p4, col 1.

63 *The Herald*, September 15, 1855, p4, cols 2-3.

64 A.S. Cook, *Old-Time Traders and Their Ways*, (1902), p76.

65 *The Herald*, October 6, 1855, p4, col 2.

66 *The Herald*, October 27, 1855, p4 col 1. For the circumstances of Simpson's resignation see J.B. Conacher, *Britain and the Crimea, 1855-56. Problems of War and Peace* (1987), pp117-26.

67 *The Herald*, December 1, 1855, p4, col 2. For the background to the crisis, see William F. Liebler, "John Bull's American Legion: Britain's Ill-Starred Recruiting Attempt in the United States During the Crimean War," *The Pennsylvania Magazine of History And Biography*, Vol XCIX, No.3, July 1975, pp309-35.

68 *The Herald*, June 21, 1856, p4, col 2. Martin remarked: "The People of Britain have no wish to quarrel with America, then let Jonathan hold out the hand of friendship, and let there be Peace, Blessed Peace, between the two Countries. 'T will be more beneficial to both than going to War."

69 *The Herald*, December 29, 1855, p4, col 2.

70 *The Herald*, January 5, 1856, p4, col 3.

71 *The Herald*, February 16, 1856, p4, col 3.

72 For details of the negotiations see J.B. Conacher, *Britain and the Crimea, 1855-56*, pp184-202.

73 *The Herald*, March 15, 1856, p4, col 1.

74 *The Herald*, March 29, 1856, p4, col 1.

75 *The Herald*, April 5, 1856, p5, col 4. *The Aberdeen Journal*, April 2, 1854, p4, col 6, referred to the flags of Britain, France, Turkey and Sardinia being waved from the Town-House windows.

The Herald, April 12, 1856, p6, col 2, carried an account of the reaction when news of the signing of the peace reached the village of New Deer some thirty miles north of Aberdeen on Tuesday, April 1. The inhabitants "instantly determined on giving public demonstration of their own feelings and satisfaction, believing that the conditions of peace will be found satisfactory, and in accordance with the enlightened views of 'Martin the Hatter.' Consequently, at eight o'clock, P.M., a simultaneous blaze of light streamed out from every window in the village, and at the south end and entrance the scene was exceedingly brilliant....The greatest order and regularity were observed during the time of illumination, which continued till ten o'clock."

76 *The Herald*, April 5, 1856, p4, cols 3-4.

77 *The Herald*, April 12, 1856, p4, col 3.

78 J.B. Conacher, *Britain and the Crimea, 1855-56*, pp202-06 outlines the terms of peace and press reaction.

79 *The Herald*, May 3, 1856, p5, cols 2-3, remarked, "From this rough outline of the origin of the War, the objects aimed at by the Allies, and the actual

conditions on which Peace has been proclaimed, it is, we think, literally obvious that the settlement neither deserves those opprobrious epithets that have been heaped on it by a few journalists, who seem actuated by no principle beyond the desire to create a sensation, nor yet the more modified condemnation which it is receiving in quarters where some degree of moderation and right feeling might be expected." See also May 10, 1856, p4, cols 5-6, and p5, col 1.

80 *The Herald*, May 3, 1856, p4, col 2. Perversely it was the *Aberdeen Journal*, in which Martin did not normally advertise, that shared his views, see the *Aberdeen Journal*, April 30, 1856, p8, cols 2-3, and May 7, 1856, p8, cols 2-3.

81 *The Herald*, May 24, 1856, p4, col 4.

82 *The Herald*, August 2, 1856, p4, col 2, August 23, 1856, p4, col 2, and September 27, 1856, p4, col 4.

83 *The Herald*, December 13, 1856, p4, col 2.

84 On June 16, 1856, Samuel Chalmers, an Aberdonian employee of the East India Company in Agra, wrote home to his brother William Chalmers, "Martin's advertisements are well read.... and well laughed at." Letters of Samuel Chalmers, MS 2884/1/3/1-2 Letter No.58, in Letters and Papers of the Family of Alexander Wallace Chalmers, deposited in the Special Collections of Aberdeen University Library. I am indebted to Dr Marjory Harper of the Department of History & Economic History at Aberdeen University for bringing this reference to my attention.

85 *The Herald*, November 20, 1858, p4, col 2.

86 That Samuel Martin and John Brown were "fast friends" is attested to by *The Daily Free Press*, January 9, 1888, p4, col 6, in its obituary of Martin.

87 Neil A. Maclean, *Life at a Northern University*, Third Edition, (1914).

88 *Ibid*, pp55-60. According to the *Roll of Alumni in Arts of the University and King's College of Aberdeen, 1596-1860,* (1900), p180, a David Lockhart from Thornton is listed as a student from 1853-1857.

CHAPTER THREE

FOREIGN DIVERSIONS AND LOCAL INTERESTS. 1856-1861.

Although the excitement of the Crimean War had subsided by mid-1856, Martin was never at a loss to find a topic on which he could lecture his attentive public. For example, as an adopted son of Aberdeen and North East Scotland he was an ardent advocate of the beauties of the area. He missed no opportunity to laud its "Magnificent Scenery - Mountain, Wood, and Water," to sing the praises of "such lovely spots" as Banchory and Ballater and to compare the delights of the Deeside views with those of Switzerland.[1] It was also at this time that he began his tongue in cheek advocacy of a knighthood for himself.[2]

As a fierce defender of democracy and freedom he naturally complained against the activities of King Ferdinand II of Naples, and assured his readers that had he been in charge of the British naval squadron in the vicinity, "he would, by a Volley from Britain's Wooden Walls, soon bring the infatuated KING OF NAPLES to his senses."[3] Martin wondered why Britain hesitated to strike with decision, as she was well able, "and remedy the evils of a once happy Country, by (if needs be) relieving it from the sway of a Tyrant who appears only to rule it to its destruction."[4]

Martin rejoiced in his own ability, as a British subject, to exercise the right to comment on public men and events,[5] a point he reiterated when he took a retrospective look at 1856:

> MARTIN thanks the People most heartily for their kind support during the past year - a year of events great in British history, and which had a tendency to brighten MARTIN'S ideas, improve his wit, and sharpen his pen; and, at this the beginning of 1857, it may be gratifying to the People to know that MARTIN'S mental facilities are bright as ever. He intends to persist in his advertising propensities, ever, as usual, avoiding harsh or unbecoming language, but ever determined to form his own opinions of public men and public events, and will never be backward in giving publicity to his opinions - the more so, when he thinks they may be beneficial to the honour, welfare, and best interests of his Country.[6]

Martin exercised just that right to comment, when, in February 1857, he advocated a decrease in the war time level of income tax. He also revealed his appreciation of social conditions with the remark that he supposed the government to be well aware of the large number of working class people unemployed in London, and he expressed the opinion that remedial legislation should be brought forward to help them. It was his view "that the well-being and comfort of the working classes ever adds stability to a Government, and to the general welfare of the country."[7]

1857 was to prove an exciting year in many ways. Abroad there was the beginning of the so-called *Arrow* War with China which lasted until 1860, and the outbreak of the Indian Mutiny. At home there was the defeat of the government on the question of its policy in China followed by a general election, and the major event of the year in Aberdeen was the ceremonial visit of Queen Victoria to the city in October. Needless to say all these occurrences attracted Martin's attention and drew forth comment.

The Anglo-Chinese imbroglio arose out of an incident at Canton in October 1856, when Chinese officials arrested the crew of the junk, or lorcha, *Arrow*, and allegedly hauled down the British ensign. This was the culmination of a series of disagreements between Chinese and British officials, particularly the Chinese Viceroy and Commissioner for relations with foreign powers, Yeh Ming-chen, arising out of different interpretations of the terms of the 1842 Treaty of Nanking at the end of the Opium War. The British officials in Canton and Hong Kong decided on punitive naval action in retaliation, and news of the affair arrived in Britain at the beginning of December. Martin's first reaction was published on January 10, 1857, under the headline, "DESTRUCTION OF A HANDSOME PIECE OF CHINA," and he was enthusiastic about the rapid response to such an insult to the national flag.[8] He continued to endorse the actions of the men on the spot, especially when the matter took on a partisan political complexion in parliament, and lamented "a strong tendency in Britain of late years to find fault with her Diplomatists and Naval and Military Commanders," who, "Have the honour, dignity, and welfare of their country at heart" more than any other groups.[9]

Lord Palmerston's ministry felt compelled to back the actions of its diplomatic and naval representatives despite the fact that there were technical defects in the British case relating to the ownership and registration of the *Arrow*. The opposition adopted a high moral tone, criticized the use of force against the Chinese, whose case they showed sympathy for, and forced a debate and a vote on the ministry's policy. The

DESTRUCTION

OF A HANDSOME PIECE OF CHINA.

WORK FOR CHINA MENDERS.

AUTHENTIC NEWS ARRIVED.

INSULT

TO THE

BRITISH FLAG AT CANTON,

But Immediate Chastisement of Britain's Enemies!

HURRAH FOR ADMIRAL SEYMOUR,

AND BRITAIN'S BLUE JACKETS!!

TRUE Descendants of NELSON, nobly doing their duty by *thrashing* their Enemies *at once*, when the Union Jack of England was insulted. Oh, that the same decision had been allowed and practised in the late War with Russia. 'Twould have saved the Country thousands of Brave Men's Lives and thousands of Pounds of Money, and have proved to the World that Britain's Glorious Navy,

FAIRLY RANGED, BROADSIDES ON,

would have crushed the Battlements of Sebastopol and Cronstadt comparatively as easy as the twenty-five-feet-thick wall of Canton. Oh, Britain, Britain! your philanthropy may be your destruction. Certainly avoid War by all honourable means; but when at War, strike hard and spare not—'tis the best way to save life and money, and bring your Enemies to their senses. Think on your power—the greatest nation of the earth in wealth, and ever the governing Power of the world in a just War, by the support of a naturally Brave People, who have ever preferred

DEATH TO DISHONOUR,

willingly paying Extra Taxes to support their Government in a righteous War. But when the results of War are not in accordance with Extra Taxation, it can hardly be a matter of surprise to hear expressions of dissatisfaction at the Governing Powers of the Country.

SO THINKS

MARTIN THE HATTER.

MARTIN thanks the People most heartily for their kind support during the past year—a year of events great in British history, and which had a tendency to brighten MARTIN's ideas, improve his wit, and sharpen his pen; and, at this the beginning of 1857, it may be gratifying to the People to know that MARTIN's mental faculties are bright as ever. He intends to persist in his advertising propensities, ever, as usual, avoiding harsh or unbecoming language, but ever determined to form his own opinion of public men and public events, and will never be backward in giving publicity to his opinions—the more so, when he thinks they may be beneficial to the honour, welfare, and best interests of his Country.

MARTIN'S STOCK is very large at present.

LONG LIFE TO THE QUEEN!

HURRAH!!

OBSERVE!

SAMUEL MARTIN,

HATTER TO THE PEOPLE,

34, UNION STREET, ABERDEEN.

Established EIGHTEEN Years.

government defeated a critical resolution in the Lords on February 26 by 146-110, but was defeated in the Commons on March 4, 263-247.[10]

Martin's sympathies were clear. He was a Liberal whose political preferences could be traced back as far as 1841 when he was listed as a member of a committee to secure the election, as a member for Aberdeen in the Liberal cause, of Mr Alexander Bannerman.[11] He was also an ardent imperialist and an admirer of Lord Palmerston, so he had no hesitation in supporting the ministry for "countenancing the acts and nobly taking the responsibilities of their representatives at Canton, in gallantly chastising the Chinese for insulting the British flag; for, although there is evidently a diversity of opinion if high quarters, as to the intent and extent of the insult, yet that the flag was insulted there can hardly be a doubt, and MARTIN THE HATTER'S idea is, that whenever and wherever the British flag is insulted, the only answer should be **Prepare for Action and Fire away!**" In anticipation of a dissolution of Parliament and a general election Martin exhorted his readers with the blatantly partisan advice:

> **Hurrah for LORD PALMERSTON!**
>
> Well does he deserve the gratitude of his country for his transcendently efficient services, particularly for the masterly abilities he so often displayed during the War, nobly maintaining the honour and true dignity of his country against all her enemies, surmounting difficulties that to ordinary minds would have appeared overwhelming, but which disappeared before his master mind like dissolving views. Thus, if Parliament is dissolved, as evidently appears certain, then let
>
> **THE VOICE OF THE PEOPLE**
>
> be heard through the length and breadth of the land, proclaiming that as Lord Palmerston's policy has shown itself sound and beneficial to the stability of the country, he has the confidence of the nation. Thus will he be reinstated firmer than ever as Prime Minister of Britain, a position he so manifestly has the abilities to adorn. Thus showing Foreign Powers that Britain knows well how to appreciate the abilities of one of the greatest men of the age, whose intellectual attainments and governing talent will ever shed lustre on, and have a conspicuous place in, the brightest page of British History. Therefore, let the voice of the People be heard, so that his Lordship may have a large majority in the House of Commons, and let the People remember that in a Parliamentary crisis like the present, Britain has a right to expect
>
> **"That every man will do his duty."**
>
> Then a jolly good cheer for Lord PALMERSTON. Hurrah![12]

Only two days before the appearance of Martin's advertisement Palmerston, on March 5, 1857, announced the dissolution of parliament. During the ensuing election campaign Palmerston concentrated on the Chinese issue and especially on the wickedness of Yeh Ming-chen. In his election address at Tiverton Palmerston referred to Yeh as, "An insolent barbarian wielding authority at Canton" who had "violated the British flag, broken the engagements of treaties, offered rewards for the heads of British subjects in that part of China, and planned their destruction by murder, assassination and poisons."[13] Polling was spread over several days at the end of March and the early part of April, and though the election was not fought solely on the Chinese situation Palmerston's handling of foreign affairs in general was important. The result was a notable victory for Palmerston,[14] and, of course, considerable pleasure on the part of the practical hatter. Martin described it as a glorious majority, and picking up Palmerston's phrase referred to **"The Barbarian Yeh"** who might well "tremble in his Chinese slippers, covered as they are with the life's blood and gore of his countrymen, when he hears of Lord Palmerston's triumph, for so sure as the ground that Yeh walks upon is polluted by his fiend-like step, so sure is his day of reckoning at hand, as his diabolical sway must give way and end before the humanizing developments of enlightened Britain."[15] In fact, although the controversy in Anglo-Chinese relations dragged on for some time, China very quickly dropped out of the public view and Martin made few further references, though in May 1857, he approved of reinforcements being sent to China and of a hard line.[16] Not unnaturally, however, the disastrous British attack against the Taku Forts on June 25, 1859, by the Royal Navy and marines when 89 officers and men were killed and 345 wounded provoked an agonized outburst from Martin when news finally arrived in September that year.[17]

When the new parliament met in 1857 after Palmerston's electoral success Martin wrote:

> Lord Palmerston's triumphant, he's weathered the storm,
> But the cry of the Nation is now for Reform.

He went on to announce that he personally had not yet been elected Speaker of the House of Commons, which might be a decided loss to the Liberals, but on the other hand he was well aware "that he has long been considered a Great Speaker in Aberdeen." With his usual modesty, and yet with a serious appreciation of some of the pressing problems of the day, Martin was prepared to advise Lord Palmerston on any subjects that required reform, especially:

> - 1*st*, An efficient system of Education - one of the great elements of which ought to be an insight into, and a thorough knowledge of, the nature and responsibilities of Political positions, as a preliminary to lowering the Franchise. 2*d*, A definite and very plainly-understood system of promotion in the Army and Navy, so that merit and brave deeds, with the requisite educational abilities, will be the sure stepping stone to the highest grades in both services. 3*d*, Less expense in being elected and maintaining the position of a Member of Parliament. 4*th*,
>
> **A Revisal of the System of Taxation,**
>
> so that the hard-working Mechanic may obtain the necessaries of life at a cheaper rate; in short, a proper equalization of taxation in accordance with reason, so that they who make their *money easiest* pay proportionally more than those who earn their living by *bodily labour* and the *sweat of their brow*, &c. Matters such as these might be well worth
>
> **LORD PALMERSTON'S ATTENTION;**
>
> as MARTIN has often thought that, if Legislators were inclined to try but *twelve hours* at a Workman's Bench, their ideas of taxation might be very materially altered.[18]

Although Martin was rarely able to exhibit his patriotism after mid-1857 by reference to China, another situation arose that permitted him to demonstrate his rampant imperialist attitudes and sense of outrage at any challenge to Britain's honour, prestige and power. The event in question was the Indian Mutiny of 1857-58, which began in the early months of 1857, and for a time reached alarming proportions and threatened to challenge the rule of the East India Company and of Britain. The origins of the Mutiny were complex, but due in part to the fact that many influential groups in Indian society were concerned that their cultural, religious, political and economic traditions were under threat due to British policies carried out in the name of reform. The sepoys, or native troops, who far outnumbered European units, were deeply concerned by perceived attempts to attack their caste and their religion and forcibly to Christianize them. Their fears were brought to a head by the distribution of the new Enfield rifle whose cartridges allegedly were greased with cow or pig fat - the former an animal sacred to Hindus and the latter an animal considered unclean by Muslims. Beginning in February and March 1857 native regiments refused to accept the new cartridges and finally broke into open mutiny thereby attracting other disaffected groups to them.[19]

The popular picture of the Indian Mutiny received in Britain was one of repeated atrocities by mutineers against innocent British men, women and children. The British victims were seen as dedicated servants of empire carrying the burden of administering and defending India for the benefit of the local inhabitants. It is clear in retrospect that many, though not all, the atrocity stories were invented or exaggerated, but the British public reacted to the news without the benefit of hindsight and without proper appreciation of the way in which Indian sensibilities had been injured.[20]

Samuel Martin did not mention the Indian Mutiny until late June 1857, but his response was, perhaps, predictable. He headlined his advertisement with the words "**ALARMING NEWS FROM INDIA**" and referred to a murderous attack by a sepoy on a non-commissioned officer and a commissioned officer, presumably a reference to the incident at Barrackpur on March 29. Since few details were available at that moment Martin confined himself to general comments on the need to send additional troops to India and to punish the mutineers.[21] A month later, with firmer intelligence at hand regarding the mutineers seizure of Delhi and the British response, Martin's opinions were positively bloodthirsty. He recommended that there be:

> no imbecile philanthropy in this war; murderers of defenceless women and helpless children deserve to be
>
> **Blown to Atoms from the Cannon's Mouth.**
>
> Nothing but ocular demonstration of British power, and *no quarter to Mutineers*, will have the effect of securing British rule in India. Thus let
>
> **GRAPE AND CANISTER SHOT**
>
> be poured upon the last man of the Mutineers that holds out, and thus lay the foundations of hundreds of years of peace in India, and show to the world that Britain is ever prepared for fearful retaliation upon all treacherous or open enemies.

He struck a much lighter note when he continued:

THE RIGHT MAN IN THE RIGHT PLACE.

Let the People of the North be delighted, which possibly they will be, to hear that

MARTIN THE HATTER

has *not* been appointed to a Government situation, or

GOT A COMMAND IN INDIA,

but is still in Aberdeen, selling his far-famed Hats, and prosperous as ever....Should her Majesty solicit MARTIN'S advice upon Indian or Home affairs, her Majesty will ever find MARTIN a firm supporter of her Majesty's Throne, British honour, and matters that are conducive to the best interests and welfare of the true source of Britain's power,

THE PEOPLE.[22]

Martin's righteous indignation was further inflamed by early September as a result of the receipt of news in late August of the surrender of the British garrison at Cawnpore in June and the subsequent massacre of Major-General Sir Hugh Wheeler and his men by mutineers led by the Nana Sahib in violation of a promise of safe conduct.[23] Martin's advertisement on September 5 was headed:

MORE AND MORE

HORRIBLE NEWS FROM INDIA!

Martin was aghast at "DIABOLICAL AND DEMONIACAL ACTS OF THE MUTINEERS!!" whom he referred to as beasts in human form who had committed disgusting crimes. He was in favour of "exacting a fearful retribution upon the Mutineers of India" for their crimes and cruelties against European women and children, and supported sending out "such an army as will strike terror to the heart of India by cutting down and exterminating the mutinous monsters, in human form, as they would destroy obnoxious vermin," leaving their vile bodies unburied. Martin rounded off this particular advertisement with the advice he would give to Queen Victoria should she summon him to Balmoral.[24]

Whether at this time Martin was ever in Victoria's thoughts it is impossible to know, but she was certainly very much in his, due to the impending ceremonial visit to Aberdeen of the Queen and the Prince Consort. Victoria and her entourage had paid their annual visit to Deeside in September, and were due to pass through Aberdeen in procession *en route* south on October 15 after visiting Lord Aberdeen at Haddo House.

In his announcement of October 10 Martin reminded his readers of his:

> **LOYALTY AND PATRIOTISM**
>
> so often displayed in his remarks and strictures upon passing events, and suggestions made from time to time to Government upon political matters and general policy, plainly indicating his anxiety at heart for the honour, dignity and general welfare of Great Britain, it is quite within the bounds of possibility that many may suppose that
>
> **HER MAJESTY**
>
> IN PASSING THROUGH ABERDEEN
>
> WILL CALL UPON
>
> MARTIN THE HATTER.
>
> But MARTIN has no expectancy of such an honour, at least at present. But the good time may be coming for honour to MARTIN; and if her Majesty has any substantial honour, dignity, or title which her Majesty is anxious to confer upon MARTIN, he would humbly suggest that it be presented to him upon an early opportunity, as MARTIN would like to enjoy his honours in the prime of life.[25]

The official programme for the Queen's visit was published in *The Aberdeen Journal* on October 14. At noon that day the Lord Provost, Magistrates and Council would greet Queen Victoria and Prince Albert at the city boundary, on King Street near Nelson Street, where a triumphal arch would be erected. The royal party's approach would be heralded by the ringing of the city bells and the hoisting of the royal standard on the bartizan of the Town House. When the Queen reached the city boundary the ancient keys of the city would be presented to her, and the royal party and civic dignitaries would then proceed in their carriages along King Street, Castle Street, Union Street, Market Street and Guild Street to the station of the Scottish North-Eastern Railway Company.[26] A separate announcement by the Town Clerk, on behalf of the Lord Provost and Magistrates, took leave "to suggest to their Fellow-Citizens that all the Houses in the different Streets in the Line of Procession should be, as far as possible, Decorated with Flags of Ensigns, or in some similar way, so as to present a gay and cheerful appearance on the joyous occasion of Her Majesty passing through the City."[27]

The processional route would, of course, pass immediately in front of 34 Union Street, and Martin could be relied upon to make the occasion a memorable one. The Aberdeen newspapers covered the royal visit in detail, including long descriptions of the decorations. *The Herald* gave particular attention to Martin's contribution:

> ...But hark! what's that? by our veracity, if it is not our trusty friend, Mr Samuel Martin, energetically sending forth from a French horn or cornopeon, the well-known notes of - No; yes it is, he's got it again - "God Save the Queen." Nor was this all, for we were told - though, unfortunately for ourselves, not till some time after - that, Mr Martin observed the good old custom of "open table," and made all and sundry who liked to call, welcome to cake and wine. While we have our own notion of the music, and have no doubt but the wine was capital, we can have no hesitation in asserting that, for pure chasteness and simple beauty, the decorations of Mr M's establishment were unmatched in the city.[28]

Martin's advertisement two days after the event brimmed over with loyalty and civic pride. He congratulated the city for the splendid, magnificent and gorgeous reception given to the Queen, and expressed his opinion that the day might well be remembered with pride and satisfaction not only in the history of the city but of Britain. He proudly proclaimed:

> *ABERDONIANS,*
> **The Eyes of the Country**
> **were upon you**
> and well have you acquitted yourselves - oh! nobly, gloriously have you acquitted yourselves. There never was a QUEEN more deserving of such a reception and never! never!! was a QUEEN received by a body of subjects with more pure and respectful enthusiasm, and in so strict accordance with the Style that her Majesty so much values and appreciates, and which cannot but have added another to the many indelible impressions made upon her Majesty's virtuous heart by the loyalty, patriotism, and faithfulness of Scotland's Sons. Oh! it was a pleasing sight! Oh! it was a gratifying display. Oh! it was grand and thrilling! Oh! it was transcendently perfect! Aberdonians, generations to come will read with glowing admiration your doings on the 15th October, 1857,
> MARTIN THE HATTER
> was so enthusiastically delighted as to make himself if possible more than usually conspicuous, feeling a glowing sensation of pride, pleasure, satisfaction, and admiration, at the orderly and admirable conduct of the People, so conducive to their own comfort and the honour of the city. In short, MARTIN will ever look back with pleasurable emotions upon the display in Aberdeen last Thursday....[29]

Once the excitement of the royal visit had subsided Martin was able to redirect his attention back to the unfolding story of events in India. By late October the intelligence from India was much better, with news of Brigadier-General Sir Henry Havelock's recapture of Cawnpore and victory over the Nana Sahib in mid-July. Martin was jubilant that British power was again in the ascendant, that the Nana Sahib, a cowardly fiend in human form, and his followers were in retreat, and that the 78th Highlanders had played a conspicuous role in the successful action. Martin's desire for revenge remained unabated, however, as his remarks reveal:

> Let the British soldiers' war-cry be Extermination! No quarter to a single man that has committed or countenanced the late diabolical murders of European women and children; thus let the Mutineers be swept from the earth as loathsome vermin, unfit to live. This may be called vengeance and cruelty; pshaw! away with such imbecile philanthropy - its proper name is justice. The blood of treacherously-slaughtered British subjects cry aloud from the grave for justice upon their murderers, and the British soldier that withholds his arm from the work forgets his duty to his comrades and his country; and if Britain refuses to countenance such acts by her soldiers, she neither does justice to herself nor to the memory of those who have miserably perished by the heathen natives of India. So thinks MARTIN....[30]

The relief of Lucknow in late September was the occasion of renewed praise by Martin for the troops involved and for General Havelock when the news reached Aberdeen. The time lag between events in India and the arrival of reliable reports in Britain seems to have been in the region of six to eight weeks, and as the position of the British force in Lucknow, even after their success, was known to be precarious, Martin anxiously awaited the arrival of the next mail from the seat of operations.[31] This transpired to be:

GRATIFYING
NEWS FROM INDIA!
GLORIOUS
RESULTS OF BRITISH SOLDIERS' BRAVERY!

With obvious pleasure Martin continued:

> Mutineers thrashed in all quarters. Ringleaders taken daily and blown from the cannon's mouth. Serve them right; 'tis a pity that they have not a hundred lives each, so that they could be blown as many times from the cannon's mouth. 'Twould scarcely be penalty enough for their beastly and diabolical crimes - murderers of defenceless women and children. Go-a-head, British Soldiers, in your
>
> JUST RETRIBUTION!
>
> Strike, and strike firm! Hundreds of lives now may save thousands in time to come. Think of your countrymen and countrywomen beastily and horribly murdered at Cawnpore, when in the power of these fiends in human form.[32]

That not everyone in Aberdeen shared Martin's enthusiasm for military glory may be deduced from his following remark that "the martial spirit of Aberdeen does not appear conspicuously enthusiastic at present. But 'tis to be hoped that it is not on the wane." He was referring not so much to popular support for British troops in India, but to a dispute that had already lasted several weeks over the care and positioning in Aberdeen of two Russian guns, trophies of the Crimean War. The guns, according to Martin, were languishing in a "melancholy and uncared-for position," and were "apparently daily watched by a Policeman, whose weekly wages for doing so, since the Guns were placed as they are, would go far to pay the cost of a handsome railing round them, and placing them permanently....The Guns should either be placed properly or kept out of sight, *no matter if in a coal shed....*" As he understood the guns had been requested from the government Martin believed it was incumbent on the city council to place them "*permanently, handsomely,* and *properly* in the most conspicuous place in town," and certainly Castle Street was preferable to a kail-yard or a turnip field. This last remark being a reference to the proposal that the guns might find a home in the grounds of Gordon's Hospital.[33]

The final relief of Lucknow on November 17, 1857, by a British force, in which the 93rd Highlanders were conspicuous, commanded by Sir Colin Campbell, was not commented upon by Martin until January 2, 1858, on account of the delay in the arrival of news from India. Martin headlined, his advertisement **"GLORIOUS NEWS INDEED! INDIA AGAIN SAFE UNDER BRITISH POWER!"** He went on to refer to the "Gallant, brave, noble Army," and to describe Generals Campbell, Havelock and Outram as three of the bravest men of the age. Martin was delighted that Aberdeen's martial spirit and civic pride had been revived since his previous announcement, and with a fine sense of how to achieve an anticlimax he wrote:

> Therefore, let the news resound from Pole to Pole - let the Government be informed - let the bemedalled and maimed British soldiers, who have dyed the barren sands of Russia with their blood, be delighted - let the army of heroes in India keep up their hearts - and let all mankind be pleased: the Council have nobly, handsomely, and completely
>
> **Plugged the Two Russian Guns**
>
> *In Castle Street (Trophies of British Valour at Sebastopol), and caused the*
>
> **Conspicuous Policeman to Evaporate,**
>
> thus showing the world that Aberdeen is acting like herself, and that the much-talked of City Improvements are not likely to consist merely in getting up
>
> **MUSIC BELLS AND MUSIC HALLS;**[34]

This last comment was a reference to the contemporaneous campaigns to raise money from the citizens of the Granite City to purchase bells for St Nicholas Church and for the erection of a music hall. Indeed, on the same page as Martin's advertisement there appeared the latest list of subscriptions to the music hall fund. Only two months later Martin was recorded as giving half a guinea (10s.6d) to the Town's Bells appeal, and at the same time he made a donation of two guineas to the fund for the wives and families of soldiers and sailors in India.[35]

That Martin did not have the same charitable feelings toward the mutineers in India was reiterated on January 30, 1858, when he wrote of his detestation for them and his hope that their bodies would be left for the beasts of prey. He proclaimed his opinion that no prisoners should be taken, as they were an encumbrance, and that the bayonet and the rifle should do their deadly work. In this announcement he returned also to the situation in China from whence he hoped to hear shortly of the bombardment of Canton. With no sense of inappropriateness or incongruity Martin concluded by wishing long life to Queen Victoria and her family and by expressing the hope that the Princess Royal, who had married Prince Frederick William of Prussia on January 25, would enjoy marital happiness.[36]

As regards the bombardment of Canton at least his wishes were soon fulfilled and he was able to write one of his visually misleading headlines that had become a trademark:

GOVERNOR YEH A PRISONER!
BUT NOT LIKELY
TO BE SENT TO ABERDEEN,
NOR TO BE MADE
CHAIRMAN OF THE PAROCHIAL BOARD!![37]

Martin was also at this same time able to parade his often barely suppressed dislike of Napoleon III of France. On January 14, 1858, an unsuccessful attempt was made on the lives of Napoleon III and the Empress Eugenie by an Italian patriot Felice Orsini. When it was discovered that the Orsini plot had been hatched in London by Italian political refugees the French Ambassador protested in the strongest terms. Somewhat unexpectedly Lord Palmerston failed to respond, publicly at least, to the French complaint in the kind of terms the British public expected of him, but instead he introduced a Conspiracy Bill which would have strengthened the law in this field. On the evening of February 19 the bill was defeated on its second reading 234-219, and Palmerston and his cabinet resigned.[38] Samuel Martin was obviously not one of those disappointed by the moderate and conciliatory actions of his hero, Lord Palmerston, in response to the French protest. Rather, he leapt to the defence of the out-going ministry and mocked the attempts of the opposition to form a new government:

> Farcical affair, were it not that it may lead to serious results. There appears a feeling of satisfaction in the country at the defeat of the Ministry; but look the matter in the face - what has the country to be thankful for? Is it because a Coalition Opposition has ousted the Ministry, and by so doing exposed their own weakness and inability to govern? Is it for stopping the Parliamentary business of the country at a most momentous time? Is it for retarding, if not annihilating those useful and much called for measures of Reform, &c., which the late Ministry was in a fair way, and soon likely to bring forward? Is it for ousting a Prime Minister who was called into office, it may be said, by the almost unanimous vote of the British nation at a most critical period, and who, by taking the reins of Government, carried his country gloriously and honourably through what might have been a

disastrous war with a wily and powerful enemy? Is it for ousting a Prime Minister who, by his thorough financial knowledge, enabled the country to surmount the late monetary crisis? Is it for ousting a Prime Minister who has ever been brought forward and conspicuous in taking his country out of difficulties that other men shrank from? In short, is it for ousting from office the *master mind of the age - Lord Palmerston,* whose whole career proves him to be one of the greatest and most useful Prime Ministers that ever adorned the British House of Commons, whose vigorous mind, admirable intellectual abilities, literary attainments, and masterly Legislative and Governing Powers have shown themselves to be of the highest order, and which, from their very nobleness and magnanimity, are misconstrued, because so transcendently beyond the ordinary intellectuality of the present age. Talk of Palmerston giving way to foreign influence and jeopardising the honour of his country. Pshaw! mere nonsense; he has been found fault with for his high tone with foreign powers, but never for countenancing the dishonour of his country.

MARTIN THE HATTER

Will be delighted to hear that this highly-talented Statesman has again been returned to office (which at present appears very likely), believing that the true interests and honour of Britain are safe in his hands, whose antecedents plainly show that he has served his country well.

Then Hurrah for Lord Palmerston![39]

Whatever Martin's political opinions and loyalty to Lord Palmerston, who had now been replaced by the second ministry headed by Lord Derby, which lasted from February 1858 until June 1859, Martin was not to be dissuaded from the business of selling hats. In March 1858 he managed to combine two natural events and to use them as excuses to encourage purchasers. The first was a period of unusually cold weather and a snow storm which in his opinion would take the shine out of a good many hats. The second was the eclipse of the sun on March 15.[40] The coming of spring provided the chance to remind Aberdonians that a hat was the most conspicuous article of attire, and that this useful and indispensable item of dress would either add to or detract from a respectable appearance. As appearances had a great deal to do with welfare and prosperity it followed "that those who wear a GOOD HAT are performing a duty devolving upon them by the forms of Society." This was the time to buy at Martin's famed establishment where he fitted his customers upon phrenological and scientific principles.[41] By early summer it was not cold but warm weather that required the purchase of a new hat since a cool head was conducive to health, and a light hat was very comfortable.[42]

Although the tide had swung in Britain's favour in India by the end of 1857 the military campaigning continued throughout 1858 and into early 1859. As news of British successes arrived in 1858 they afforded Martin fresh occasions to air his rampant nationalism and to repeat his unforgiving demands for retribution against the mutineers whom he dubbed "Infatuated miscreants," and for whom he demanded "no pusillanimous or mistaken philanthropy" be shown. Rather he wanted the British forced to "annihilate the last man of the mutinous Monsters in human form."[43] Fresh fighting around Lucknow in March 1858 brought forth ecstatic headlines from Martin a month later,[44] although he was less sanguine in May when he found himself in the not unaccustomed position of defending a British field commander against criticism for his conduct of operations.[45] Martin's wrath knew no bounds, however, in mid-July when he sounded forth against the bestowal upon Jung Bahadoor (Jang Bahadur), the *de facto* ruler of Nepal who had placed a force of Gurkhas on the side of the British, of the Grand Cross of the Order of the Bath (G.C.B.), an action that plainly offended Martin's sense of honour and romantic spirit. Under the headline "**DISGRACE TO THE NAME OF CHIVALRY**" Martin protested that Britain was forgetting herself:

> By apparently burying in oblivion the real meaning of her noble orders of honour and merit, instituted, gloriously fought for, and purchased by the life's-blood of her Forefathers. Britons you are acting like a degenerate race. Think of, look at it in your mind's eye, and steadily review the deeds of your Forefathers in the Twelfth and Thirteenth Centuries. See how you are defiling the orders of Chivalry which they instituted, and ever looked up to with holy reverence, and went through serious and solemn religious resolves to *obtain* and *maintain*. See what it cost them to institute, and how they valued and appreciated their insignia of Christian Honour and Christian Power, that you are so evidently trampling upon. Would they have polluted their Escutcheon by making such as you have lately done a G.C.B., or Grand Cross of the Order of the Bath? Never. Would they have considered that the claims of
>
> **JUNG BAHADOOR**
>
> of Nepal, who, it is reported, is a fifteen times' murderer, and who, it may well be supposed, has taken the British side in the Indian War as a simple act of policy - to save himself - and who, 'tis said, has lately retired to his native hills in dudgeon - possibly because his reward has not been in

> accordance with a dastard spirit....No, no! they would have found some more suitable honour for him (if any he deserved) - more in accordance with his cruel and bloodthirsty temperament, and more in accordance with the *Brutish* acts of the man, who only showed his enthusiasm in Britain's cause when her power was evidently in the ascendant, and may as easily and hurriedly become a *foe* as he *became a friend.*[46]

Martin's final comments on the Indian scene came in November 1858 and January 1859 when he urged Sir Colin Campbell, now Lord Clyde, to "strike and spare not", and to complete the work of finally subduing the rebels in a manner the Queen and country expected. He reminded his readers that his own "fame has been heard and spoken of amongst the gallant Highland Battalions, who are so nobly doing their duty to their country amidst the burning sands, and under the death-dealing sun strokes of the present Indian Campaign!"[47] Indeed, there is some independent evidence to support Martin's claim in this instance in the shape of a letter from Samuel Chalmers, an Aberdonian employed by the East India Company, writing from Mynpoorie to his mother in Aberdeen on June 4, 1858. Chalmers wrote, "How is Sam Martin? His advertisements break the monotony of many an idle hour in India."[48]

Martin did not confine his remarks in the latter part of 1858 solely to the Indian situation. He found space to report on Queen Victoria's official visit to Cherbourg, which he argued was perfectly justified as an act of courtesy in response to the invitation of Napoleon III, and which would help to allay previous ill feelings that had existed between the two nations. Martin displayed quiet unaccustomed feelings of friendship toward the French ruler, whom he characterized as demonstrating "good taste," and "manly and straightforward spirit." In conclusion, he assured the French that if ever they landed in Britain, either as friends or foes, they were sure of a warm reception.[49] Naturally he welcomed **"BRITAIN'S BELOVED QUEEN"** in September when she made her annual visit to Deeside. In his usual effusive prose Martin wrote:

> WELCOME. Amiable Lady! Welcome, Daughter of a Royal Race! Welcome, Pattern Mother! Welcome, Model Queen! whose every act is conducive to the welfare of your people, who respect, love, and adore you. Welcome again and again! heartily welcome to your Highland Home. Long, long may your Majesty be spared health to enjoy your annual visit to Balmoral.

"When Summer comes, the heather bell
Shall tempt thy feet to roam,
The cushat dove within the dell
Invite to Peace and Love.
For blythesome is the month of May,
And sweet the bonnie broom;
But sweeter far the rills that play
Around my Highland Home."

WELCOME!

OH, HEARTILY, SINCERELY WELCOME, BRITAIN'S BELOVED QUEEN, TO YOUR HIGHLAND HOME!!

WELCOME, Amiable Lady! Welcome, Daughter of a Royal Race! Welcome, Pattern Mother! Welcome, Model Queen! whose every act is conducive to the welfare of your people, who respect, love, and adore you. Welcome again and again! heartily welcome to your Highland Home. Long, long may your Majesty be spared health to enjoy your annual visit to Balmoral.

YOUR BODYGUARD IS SCOTLAND,

Whose sons would shed their life's blood to protect their Queen. Fathers, mothers, brothers, and sisters of those gallant men who have so lately done such good service to your Majesty and their country in the ever-to-be-remembered glorious achievements in India. These, and such as these, are they who greet and welcome you.

LOYAL, LEAL, TRUE-HEARTED SCOTCH,

whose blood ever flows freely in defence of their Queen and country. Your Majesty possibly had not time to notice that your Guard of Honour at Ballater was, and still is, a Company of the ever-to-be-remembered gallant

78th HIGHLANDERS,

stalwart Scotchmen, all Havelocks at heart to the extent of their ability in the time of need, and all anxious and willing to finish up the ball that their comrades have so gloriously opened in India. But your Majesty needs not to be reminded of the doings of

YOUR HIGHLANDERS.

They are, and will ever be, found in the brightest page of Britain's history. So thinks

MARTIN THE HATTER.

Therefore let the pipes of the brave 78th ascend to the summit of the lofty, heather-clad CRAIGENDARRAH; there, while admiring the far-famed scenery of their native land—land of poetry, birthplace of heroes—let the heart-stirring strains of the pipes that ever lead British armies to victory echo through the gigantic hills, lovely valleys, and fairy-like windings of the romantic Dee—thus sending forth the news to the admiring world that Britain's beloved Queen is again at Balmoral, in the midst of her faithful, gallant Highlanders.

MARTIN thinks that it is scarcely requisite to mention that

HER MAJESTY

did *not* call at his Establishment in passing through to Balmoral. But if her Majesty

Commands Martin to Attend at Balmoral to be Knighted,

Martin will be happy to obey, and would candidly confess to her Majesty that he was the first of the family that ever received such an honour; and when again fairly into the open air, He would give a jolly good cheer for her Majesty and himself—MARTIN the Hatter to the People.

Martin's Stock is very large at present. Magnificent SATIN HATS, New Shapes, 6/6, 8/6, 10/6, 12/6, 13/6, and 15/6. Best quality SATIN HAT, 18/.

PORTMANTEAUS; LEATHER HAT CASES; CARPET BAGS; UMBRELLAS; SHELL and FELT HATS; BALMORAL BONNETS; ORNAMENTS, &c. &c. very Cheap.

Observe!

SAMUEL MARTIN,

HATTER TO THE PEOPLE,

34, UNION STREET, ABERDEEN.

Established Twenty Years.

LONG LIFE TO THE QUEEN, PRINCE ALBERT, AND THE ROYAL FAMILY!

HURRAH! HURRAH!! HURRAH!!

One Cheer more—

H--U--R--R--A--H!

He continued:

MARTIN thinks that it is scarcely requisite to mention that

HER MAJESTY

did *not* call at his Establishment in passing through to Balmoral. But if her Majesty

Commands Martin to Attend at Balmoral to be Knighted,

Martin will be happy to obey, and would candidly confess to her Majesty that he was the first of the family that ever received such an honour; and when again fairly into the open air, He would give a jolly good cheer for her Majesty and himself - MARTIN the Hatter to the People.[50]

Martin was considerably less happy with the achievements, or rather the lack of achievements, by the Prime Minister, Lord Derby. He headed one advertisement "**DISAPPOINTED HOPES!**" referring to the fact that the government had failed to bring forward the expected new parliamentary reform bill or other measures to improve the political, commercial and social condition of the country.[51] He certainly observed, but did not comment upon, the fact that his old rival Steele & Co had expanded their business at 20 Union Street by adding "the adjoining Shop, which makes their present Premises about twice as large as they formerly were, thus giving them ample room for an immense variety of Stock; as also more room for the convenience and comfort of their Customers."[52]

As the excitement of the Indian Mutiny ebbed in early 1859 so another diplomatic crisis arose to provide Martin with an excuse to offer comment and advice to all who cared to read *The Herald.* For a variety of reasons, including a desire to upset the 1815 settlement set forth in the Treaty of Vienna after the Napoleonic Wars, the Emperor Napoleon III of France had become sympathetic to the cause of Italian unity, a cause that inevitably meant a clash with Austria. In July 1858 Napoleon III and the Piedmontese prime minister, Count Camillo Cavour, met secretly at Plombières, where it was agreed that France would aid Piedmont in a war against Austria provided that the Austrians could be provoked into some action that would make them appear to be the aggressor. As an obvious sign of friendship the Princess Clotilde of Piedmont married Prince Jérôme Bonaparte in early 1859, at which time an alliance between the two countries was also signed. That a war between Piedmont, aided by France, and Austria was impending soon became an open diplomatic secret and at the official New Year's Day reception at the Tuilleries in 1859 Napoleon III addressed the Austrian ambassador with a regret that relations between the two empires were not as good as they had been, words that were taken by European statesmen, and by Samuel Martin, as an indication of likely hostilities. On January 7 Victor Emmanuel II of Piedmont opened parliament at Turin with a speech from the throne in which he announced that he was not insensible to the cry of woe that reached him from so many parts of Italy. This was an obvious statement of the willingness of Piedmont to champion the cause of Italy, and it was enthusiastically received throughout the peninsula.

That Martin had been following events keenly is apparent from his advertisement published on January 15 in which he warned Britain to be prepared for hostilities which she might not be able to avoid. He wrote:

> GLOOMY APPEARANCE OF THE POLITICAL HORIZON,
> APPARENT CONTINENTAL WAR.
> **THE EMPEROR NAPOLEON**
> Spoke rather sensitively, but evidently more plain than pleasant, to Austria on New Year's Day. The Emperor of Austria, equally plain and amiable, returns the compliment, regretting political coolness, &c. &c. But there is ever danger in the wind when
> **DESPOTS TURN POLITE**
> THE KING OF SARDINIA SPEAKING BOLDLY
> but such boldness, on his part (though he is justly admired by Britain), would be very like foolishness, unless he is backed by his BIG POLITICAL BROTHER OF THE TUILLERIES. No! no! Sardinians, brave as you are (and no Power doubts it), your army of some 47,000 men, and somewhere about 100 guns, cannot cope with Austria's army of 470,000 men, and nearly 1200 guns. But the question is, is your BIG BROTHER prepared to back you and keep himself safe? Ay, that's the question, and he will do well to solve it to his entire satisfaction, before he opens the ball of WAR. He may well see the beginning, but possible events may make the end disastrous to himself! Let Napoleon beware![53]

Four weeks later Martin was still speculating as to whether the signs pointed to peace or war as both sides began to mobilize. In his opinion the proper balance of power had been "signed, sealed, and agreed to by the leading Powers of Europe nearly half a century ago" and should not now be thrown aside as waste paper. To secure Britain's position in such uncertain times he recommended that the navy should be strengthened, that the militia be expanded and that every town in Britain should raise a Volunteer Corps of young men or "embryo warriors" amounting to a total force of about 200,000. He added:

> ...Aberdeen could, doubtless, raise a Volunteer Corps of from 700 to 1000, and if the Queen should make
> **MARTIN THE HATTER the Commander,**
> He might possibly appear
> ON A WHITE CHARGER
> (not Lord Clyde's) on the Links, when putting these gallant youths through their manoeuvres.[54]

Napoleon III, facing political constraints at home and strong diplomatic pressure abroad, showed signs of backing down in March 1859, and was even prepared to accept a congress of the powers on the Italian question or a general demobilization. However, at this moment the Austrians made the mis-step that Napoleon III and Cavour had been waiting for by delivering an ultimatum on April 19 for Piedmont to disarm on pain of invasion. Cavour rejected the demand on April 26, from which date a state of war existed, and the Austrians crossed the Ticino on April 29. The first major encounter of the war was at Montebello on May 20 where the allies defeated the Austrians.

Martin welcomed Napoleon III's hesitation in March, claiming, "The War fever is cooling; the Emperor getting gradually brought to his senses by the power of the people."[55] By the end of April, however, he was able to run the headline:

> **THE BEGINNING OF A SERIOUS END!**
> APPARENT CONTINENTAL WAR!!
> CONGRESS AND ARBITRATION THROWN
> TO THE WINDS!!!

He went on to report that the Austrians had crossed the Ticino, "a river a little broader than the Dee at Aberdeen," which divided Austria and Piedmont, and that news of the first engagement was expected hourly. At such a moment a dissolution of the parliament at Westminster was most unfortunate, still it provided the opportunity for the electorate to return a Liberal majority and for the replacement of Lord Derby with a ministry headed by the staunch political veteran Lord Palmerston. It can have been no surprise to his readers that he added:

> ...MARTIN thinks that during the coming war he may possibly have occasion to make many remarks upon what may take place, and as his PEN and INTELLECT are as keen as ever, he is not likely to shrink from animadverting in political matters upon what he thinks deserves censure; but will ever be prepared to admire acts that appear conducive to the honour and dignity, and that are likely to strengthen the pristine power, of glorious Britain,
>
> **LAND OF FREEDOM!**[56]

Only a week after the event Samuel Martin was discoursing about the action at Montebello which he saw as a French victory and an Austrian defeat.[57]

Indeed, the war was very largely one of French victories and Austrian defeats, though the margins involved were often small and the casualty figures high on both sides. The two major battles were at Magenta on June 4 and Solferino on June 20, the carnage deeply affecting Napoleon III who for a number of reasons decided to call a halt to his Italian adventure at this point and signed an armistice with the Austrians at Villafranca on July 9 without consulting Piedmont.

Martin was not sure what to make of the passage of events. In late July he offered the opinion that both the rulers of France and Austria were playing deep games, that it was a humbug peace, and that the cause of Italian independence had been betrayed. He was appalled at the wanton sacrifice of human life by "blood-stained despots." He complained about "Upwards of Twenty-two Millions of brave people trifled with and betrayed, by the despotic, arrogant, insolent, aspirations and bravado of the Emperors of France and Austria, who may well be looked upon as scourges to the human race, and plague-spots on the earth. ITALY, garden of the earth! lovely, romantic ITALY! left by a deceptive Peace in a worse, because more precarious position, than when the War commenced."[58] In August, however, Martin was expressing a slightly different opinion of Napoleon III, whom he saw as "SATIATED, for a time, with human blood," and, therefore, unlikely to attack Britain. He appeared to recognize how affected by the sight and sound of battle Napoleon III had really been, heading his announcement:

WONDERFUL
EFFECTS OF SMELLING POWDER,
AND SEEING A BATTLE FIELD!
THE EAGLE TURNED A DOVE!!

- - - - - - - - -

THE EMPEROR OF FRANCE
DRAWING IT MILD,
ANXIOUS FOR PEACE!!![59]

Of course Martin had never been an enthusiast of Napoleon III, and he was willing to exploit Anglo-French friction and suspicion in late 1859 to advocate defensive precautions and to express scorn for the French leader, though he never shared the extreme fears of some that a real invasion threat from France existed in late 1859. The experiences of the Crimean War had encouraged both the British and the French navies to ponder the merits of ironclad warships, and the French had changed the design of four wooden warships to provide them with armoured protection. The first of these ships to be launched, in November 1859, was *La Gloire*, some thirteen months before the first British armoured warship the *Warrior*. Many people in Britain resented this French challenge to traditional British naval supremacy, and some even believed the new French ships would be able to support an invasion of Britain. Ever up to-date in his comments Samuel Martin headed his November 26, 1859, announcement, **"INVASION PANIC"**, but went on in confident tones:

> The British Navy in glorious trim; the Channel Fleet prepared for a moment's warning. Britain ready for the first onset, and lots of men-of-war building, to be armed with the famous ARMSTRONG GUNS, which, when handled by BRITISH BLUE JACKETS, will astonish the steel-plated sides of the much vaunted foreign ships of war. Foreigners may possibly require, for peculiar reasons (not to use harsher words), to place great dependence on the metal sides of their ships; but the *metal* that Britain can at all times depend upon is on the *decks* of her ships, in the firm, loyal hearts of her sailors and marines.

Ably protected by her navy and also by the new and virtually spontaneous formation of the Volunteer Rifle Corps which the government had authorized, Martin was able to claim that the country was safe from invasion:

The Eagle of France has been soaring too high,
Her wings will be clipped, if she attempts here to fly;
The British Lion's roused, and he'll ne'er stick at trifles,
Till the Eagle succumbs to the Volunteer Rifles.

According to Martin nearly five hundred riflemen had already been raised in Aberdeen with more companies forming daily, and the Volunteers who had lately performed their evolutions on the Links in their handsome uniforms had done so in a very satisfactory manner. He hoped, however, that the opportunity would be given for artisans and not just those with means to provide their own accoutrements. He ended with the rousing sentiments, "LONG LIFE TO THE QUEEN! CONFUSION TO HER ENEMIES!! AND SUCCESS TO THE RIFLE CORPS!!! HURRAH!!!!"[60]

Foreign crises did not occupy all of Martin's attention in 1859, there was plenty in the way of domestic politics for him to reflect upon. Martin was a supporter of parliamentary reform as he frequently made clear with approving comment as to the hard work and reliability of the lower classes. He reminded parliamentarians that the comfort and well-being of the working people was essential to the health of the nation, and he saw no reason why "industrious and educated mechanics who pay a Five Pound Rent" should not be enfranchised. If the framers of future reform bills were to consult him he believed he could make suggestions that would enlarge simple justice without endangering the country.[61]

It was on the question of reform of the electoral franchise that the second Derby ministry was defeated on March 31. Since the House of Commons had now overturned two ministries in little over a year a dissolution of parliament was not an unreasonable next step, and actually took place on April 23. The resultant general election saw Conservative gains, but they still lacked an overall majority so that a period of uncertainty followed during which Derby remained in office until defeated in a vote of confidence on June 10. A new government headed by the seventy-five year old Palmerston and including Lord John Russell as Foreign Secretary and William Gladstone as Chancellor of the Exchequer, was then formed.

The political confusion and uncertainty was reflected in Martin's advertisement on June 18:

POLITICS AND POLICY!

- - - - - - - - - -

MUCH NOISE, LITTLE WORK.
WISE HEADS (DOUBTLESS) BUT WEAK DOINGS.
WASTE OF TIME!
CHILD'S PLAY, WEAKNESS, ABSURDITY.
THE OLD MEN IN NEW PLACES.
DIFFICULTY IN FORMING A
NEW MINISTRY!!!
(BUT SAID TO BE FORMED AT LAST.)

- - - - - - - - - -

> TALENT, Ability, and Patriotism, frustrated by party spirit, petty jealousies, and anxiety for place and power.
> Precarious political state of Britain brought about possibly by want of unanimity among her Statesmen.

Martin, despite his attachment to the elderly Palmerston, went on to lament the lack of new and young blood in the new ministry and to call for a working and progressive government that would act with decision, energy, intellect and ability. If her Majesty were to solicit his advice upon matters of moment, or should the seals of office be offered to him, Martin believed he would not shrink from either responsibility, "satisfied that if he did not govern with transcendant ability, he would certainly govern in accordance with the dictates of common sense and with an anxious wish to do his duty and keep up the true dignity of the Country in Peace, and ever have her prepared for War."[62]

When not pronouncing upon foreign affairs and national politics Martin still found time to discuss more parochial matters. In late 1859 his two main local concerns were, as ever, the annual visit of the royal party to Balmoral, and city improvements, specifically the St Nicholas Churchyard wall and iron railing in Back Wynd.

On September 24 Martin informed the world that he had lately been to Ballater and had no doubt been seen in the vicinity of Balmoral, so that it might have been supposed that he was at last on his way to be knighted. He added:

> But although MARTIN was certainly nearer Royalty on Monday the 12th inst. than he ever had the honour of being before (except when sitting in Crathie Church on the Sunday preceding, about two yards on the right

> from Her Majesty), having passed her Majesty on horseback, or rather ponyback, opposite Balmoral, Her Majesty possibly not knowing MARTIN, would have no idea that such a loyal subject was at hand; and although
>
> SIR SAMUEL MARTIN,
> HATTER TO THE PEOPLE,
>
> Would sound uncommonly well, yet MARTIN has not as yet received any notice of it being her Majesty's intention to confer upon him any such honour. But honours deferred are often the more appreciated when received, so that the good time may be coming for MARTIN to be Knighted, but, if intended, the sooner it takes place the better, as honours lose a great deal of their value when received in old age.[63]

Any disappointment that Martin experienced because Queen Victoria did not see fit to honour him at this time, though it is believed that the royal family were amused by his pretensions,[64] was possibly overtaken by his concern, that developed into virtually a crusade, over the St Nicholas Churchyard wall and railing. The subject first appeared in the same advertisement that recounted Martin's close encounter with the Queen. Martin agreed that civic improvements were to be applauded, and possibly referring to himself he proceeded to explain that such changes certainly ought to have "a most pleasurable and satisfactory effect on the minds not only of natives of the city, but on others who are located in it, and who, looking upon it as their home, feel a natural pride in believing her magnificent edifices to be famed throughout Europe." However, when from want of good taste or other causes a change actually made things worse than they had been originally, appeared to be only half done and seemed likely in time to come to be an eyesore rather than an improvement, then "it cannot but cause a strong feeling of chagrin and disappointment." He agreed that it was often easier to find fault than to do better, but added:

> if (upon true architectural principles) it can be elucidated to MARTIN THE HATTER that the so-called improvement of taking down a portion of
>
> **THE CHURCHYARD WALL,**
>
> in the Back Wynd, and Railing in as at present, is likely to be as *chaste* and *complete* as it could be made, he will certainly be very much surprised; MARTIN would suggest that the whole of the granite wall (except about two feet high), up to Gaelic Lane, be taken down, and a LIGHT, FIRM, FANCY Railing, six or seven feet high, be run up to the harl'd or plastered wall, 'twould look better and be less expensive than the heavy, *clumsy*

railing now being put up, which, it will be seen, will greatly obstruct the view from Union Street into the Churchyard, which the *high wall was taken down to improve,* indeed the railing, at present putting up, looks more like what might be required round a COUNTY PRISON, than improvement or adornment, to one of the most CHASTE and BEAUTIFUL FACADES, perhaps in Britain....[65]

That Martin was not alone in his objections to these changes may be gauged from a news item in *The Herald* on October 8 which reported that in pursuance of the resolution adopted at their meeting the previous Monday, October 3, the Town Council had met in St Nicholas Churchyard on Tuesday morning, and after examining the new railing so far as it was completed, resolved to stay its further prosecution meantime. "The Council," it was reported, "were of opinion that the square pillars in the design were too heavy, and that by removing these, and substituting others of a lighter construction, in connection with the panels already erected, all the effect that can possibly be obtained, by enclosing the Churchyard with a railing at this part, would be secured." *The Herald* added that a wooden model was to be prepared before the new design was finally approved. The Council also agreed that a further portion of the wall should be taken down and the railing continued along Back Wynd as far as the north gable of the first house past the Advocate's Building. This latter decision not being made without a division of opinion within the Council.[66]

As feelings escalated *The Herald* published a critical editorial on the subject, on October 15, which began:

PUBLIC opinion has been unmistakeably pronounced against the iron railing recently erected at the south-west corner of the Churchyard. It has been condemned by the Town Council, and yet there it stands! What is to be done? Is this outrage against good taste to be doggedly abetted in defiance of the community? If there is any party who is secretly at the bottom of all this, he ought not to be permitted to screen himself under the irresponsible generality of membership of the Council or of the Churches Committee. The responsibility attached to all executive duty is obviously not transferable. The public interest imperatively demands that some one or other individual shall, in such a case, be directly accountable. How else can the public have anything like a satisfactory guarantee that their money shall be honestly and judiciously expended, and not foolishly squandered?

With respect to the railing in question we have good authority for

> stating that what Mr Smith, City Architect, originally suggested was the very thing the public want - a simple and inexpensive railing, just sufficient for the protection of the Churchyard; but this common-sense suggestion was scouted by a member or members of the Churches Committee, who insisted on having something more ornate and expensive.[67]

A week later Martin was suggesting sarcastically that he might have misunderstood the design or the effect intended upon passers' eyes by the railing. Perhaps the square pillars and knobs at the top were supposed to represent coffins and death's-heads, in which case they were quite up to the mark. Martin suggested, however, that to make the general appearance complete cross bones should be added under the knobs.[68] A month later he noted "The Coffin-like Pillars are still disfiguring the appearance of the Town Churchyard....*Could they not be made into Rifle Balls?"*[69] At the close of the year he expressed his happiness that arrangements were nearly complete for the removal of the "*melancholy*" railings,[70] but his pleasure was premature since he would not be able to record the actual removal of the offending railings until July 1861.

The end of the year found Martin expressing his usual thanks to the people for their kind support over the previous twelve months, and informing them that he enjoyed good health, that his intellect and energies were unimpaired, and that he was inclined to continue his advertising propensities and to continue to discourse upon public matters though avoiding harsh or unbecoming language or giving unnecessary offence. In his farewell to 1859 he stuck an unfamiliar note of melancholy, when in addressing the soon to pass away year he wrote:

> ...In your time you must have seen many phases in society, many happy and many mournful changes in family circles. Worldly enjoyments, overflowing upon some, while in others voids have been made in many happy homes by the grasping hand of Time and human frailties. Vacant seats painfully apparent round the once happy and joyous family fireside. The young called away amid their joyful aspirations; the middle-aged and the old, possibly making the vanities of this life their peculiar vocation, called forth in the middle of health, prosperity, and worldly position. Alas! such is human nature; but which should make mankind THINK. But adieu. adieu 1859! Farewell! Your time is short, and young 1860 has to be received in a becoming manner.[71]

A week later Martin welcomed 1860 in somewhat more optimistic mood, his only complaint being that Aberdeen day policemen no longer carried truncheons openly.[72] However, *The Herald* in the same number was able to report an unusual occurrence in the town involving an unnamed hatter's premises:

> On Tuesday evening, while some cattle were being driven along Union Street, one of their number, a white horned ox, walked deliberately into a hatter's shop. He went so far into the shop as the counter would allow him, and then stood gazing about, doubtless "taking stock," after his own fashion. The astonished shop-boy vehemently waved a *chapeau* in his face, and the patient steer, possibly considering that the place contained no article that would be a likely "fit" for him, quietly backed out into the street.[73]

It is impossible to know whose establishment the ox had favoured with his interest, though Martin might well have commented had it been his.

In 1860 the Chancellor of the Exchequer, William Gladstone, brought forward his Budget statement from April to February in order that the tax concessions in the Anglo-French Commercial Treaty newly negotiated by Richard Cobden, partly as a means of easing the tension between the two countries, could be incorporated. It was necessary, therefore, that the signing of the treaty and the Budget be co-ordinated. On February 10 Gladstone made a four hour speech explaining the tax changes which left a much reduced tariff list. To help pay for these concessions and for the proposed repeal, at a cost of £1,250,000 per annum, of the excise duty on paper, which many had long denounced as a tax on knowledge, Gladstone raised the income tax to 10d. On May 21 the House of Lords, in a move of dubious constitutionality, threw out the repeal of the paper duty, but since the Prime Minister, Lord Palmerston, was inclined to agree with the Lords the paper duty remained for another year, being repealed in 1861.

Only a week after Gladstone's statement Martin was expressing his hostility to both the Budget and the French Commercial Treaty, maintaining that their terms were inequitable. The tariffs on luxury items, which the poor could not afford anyway, had been reduced thus benefiting the wealthy, but high rates of duty had been retained on working class requisites and comforts especially tea and sugar. Martin wanted to sweep aside such unfairness, particularly the "glaring *one-sided* peculiarities" of income tax, which he described as "the most obnoxious tax of the age," claiming the commercial and working classes were carrying an undue tax burden, while the rich and the landed interests were advantaged. It was, perhaps, something akin to special pleading when he wrote:

> ...'Tis simply downright nonsense and farcical to tax *precarious incomes from people in business,* &c., at the same rate as from landed proprietors, whose incomes, as a rule, are the same, *no matter* how the commercial interests of the country may be affected; indeed the proposed *Budget* and *French Commercial Treaty* in their entirety are neither *just, generous* nor *consistent*, being devoid of the *three greatest elements of sound policy,* they should be altered and amended until made more in accordance with the wants, requisites, and enlightened ideas of the present age. But, indeed, looking at the Budget, mixed up as it appears to be, with the French Commercial Treaty, Britain seems to have put her foot in it by enabling a *dubious* friend to obtain the munitions of war (coal and iron) at a cheap rate for a comparatively paltry return (of what is called Free Trade) of a little cheaper French Wine, Silks, Kid Gloves, Pomatums, and Perfumes.... If there should be a
>
> CHANGE OF MINISTRY,
>
> AND IF
>
> **MARTIN THE HATTER**
>
> IS SOLICITED
>
> **TO BE CHANCELLOR OF THE EXCHEQUER,**
>
> if he accepts office, he will of course, be expected to bring in a Budget, and if he should be, in accordance with the fashion of the day (and which is quite within the bounds of possibility), complimented and eulogized upon his *oratory*, being then a great man, he would, of course, receive it gracefully; but whatever might be thought by the country of the general tenor of the Budget that he would bring in, MARTIN thinks that it would have the merit of being original, as he would study to place the taxation of the country upon a more equitable footing without any preference being shown to those in elevated aristocratic positions, unless allowing them the preference of paying taxes in *accordance* with their *high position and certain* income.[74]

A month later Martin was no happier, considering the Budget of 1860 as one of the most one-sided produced for many years on account of the "glaring advantages to the rich and affluent" given to the detriment of workers and tradesmen. Martin specifically rejected Gladstone's claim that the repeal of the paper duty would be more beneficial to the community at large than a reduction in the duties on tea and sugar.[75] Even after the repeal of the paper duty was rescinded Martin remained critical of the short-sightedness, absurdity and inconsistency of the Budget and the French Commercial Treaty and, indeed, "of the procrastinating style adopted in the House of Commons in carrying on the business of the country," as a result of which many useful bills were lost due to lack of parliamentary time.[76]

In fact the session of parliament which began on January 24, 1860, did not end until August 28 when it was prorogued until November 6. Despite its unusual length the common belief, shared by Martin, was that its achievements were meagre, and the Hatter to the People felt moved on this occasion to publish on September 1, only three days after the session ended, the text of the speech he would have given had he been deputed or ordered to prorogue parliament. Martin's speech was not much short of a thousand words and he poked some fun at the members and their dilatory habits. They had, he said, made treaties and carried a Budget that he hoped were well understood by them, since they appeared to be beyond the comprehension of the country generally. He continued:

> ...No doubt, the People were led to expect a Reform Bill and other useful bills to pass this Session, but, Gentlemen, 'tis quite possible that the People expected too much - perhaps, forgetting the labours connected with your positions. Let them think, Gentlemen, of the many nights that you have attended to the Business of the Country in the House - long tedious nights of debates, &c. &c. and although it has been thought in *times past* that Members occasionally fell asleep, not knowing what was going on until *roused by the call of "Divide,"* then in their somnambulative state Bills were passed by their *"Ayes"* which they would have *opposed* if *Wide Awake*. But, Gentlemen, these were the thoughts in *times past*, but, supposing such things possible, they are trivial matters not worth enlarging upon, for, if Members were *in the House,* they were certainly in the way of their duty, and 'tis well understood that *man cannot do without sleep.*[77]

Martin's attention did not remain entirely focused upon domestic politics in 1860 as the Italian drama continued to unfold. The Villafranca armistice in July 1859, and the definitive peace between France and Austria signed in November, left many problems unresolved. The nationalist spirit in Italy, once aroused, was not easily quenched, and Parma, Modena, Tuscany and the Romagna quickly made clear their desire to link with Piedmont whose only territorial gain in 1859 had been Lombardy. Early in 1860 Napoleon III began once more to support Italian unity, and he agreed new terms with Cavour whereby Piedmont could annex Parma and Modena, but if Piedmont also took Tuscany then France would require compensation in the shape of Nice and Savoy. In March 1860 the central Italian states voted virtually unanimously in plebicites in favour of union with Piedmont, and the same month Cavour honoured his bargaining by publicly agreeing to transfer Nice and Savoy to France.

Martin began 1860 with his anti-Napoleon III prejudices still firmly in place,[78] but the diplomatic deal over Nice and Savoy raised his ire to new heights. Under such headlines as **"THE WOLF IN SHEEP'S CLOTHING CASTING HIS COAT",** and **"DECEIT AND DUPLICITY"** Martin raged:

> THE Exile of yesterday, deep designing despot, desecrating the position and power that a complication of circumstances have placed him in, by evidently sinking all the finer feelings of human nature by selfish and unjust acts of aggression upon weaker POWERS who have *justice* and *right* on their side, aye - and even *treaties intended to protect them;* but all of which he sweeps away because they have not brute force sufficient to resist the ambitious aspirations of this human plague spot upon civilization, and juggling hindrance and drawback to the welfare of mankind.[79]

Nor did Napoleon III's image improve in Martin's eyes as the year progressed. By June the French Emperor had become "deep, selfish, mendacious...the man of yesterday...apparently at the bottom of the coming mischief."[80] Martin's hostility to the French Commercial Treaty and to Napoleon III's foreign intrigues were clearly mutually reinforcing.

Meantime Giuseppe Garibaldi had sailed with Piedmontese connivance from Genoa on May 5, 1860, and landed at Marsala in Sicily on May 11 with his thousand red shirts. Within a month the island had been won and the Neapolitan garrison retired to the mainland. Garibaldi crossed the Straits of Messina in August and drove the King of Naples, Francis II, out of his capital in early September. Piedmont, anxious to limit Garibaldi's gains, the growth of his personal prestige and to minimize the diplomatic complications his astounding successes might engender, invaded the Papal States. Victor Emmanuel II and Garibaldi met on October 26 when the romantic revolutionary leader surrendered his authority and his conquests to the King of Piedmont. As a result of these events Italy was united save for Rome and Venetia.

Samuel Martin shared the general British sympathy for the Italian cause and admiration for Garibaldi's exploits. He did not mention Garibaldi until September 1860, but left no doubts about his regard for this heroic figure:

> **GARIBALDI**
>
> going a-head in style. Honest motives is the best way to secure Victory. Thus has GARIBALDI, by his noble conduct, gained the confidence, and it may be said, the *Freedom* of Italy, and the admiration of the world.
>
> BOMBA SEEING ITALIAN FREEDOM COMING SO QUICK,
> TO SAVE HIS LIFE, WISELY CUT HIS STICK.
>
> - - - - - - - - - -
>
> THE TYRANT FLED FROM A PEOPLE BRAVE,
> WHO FOUGHT FOR FREEDOM OR THEIR GRAVE;
> GARIBALDI'S NOW ITALY'S HOPE AND POWER,
> AND THE DESPOT'S REIGN FOR EVER O'ER.
>
> - - - - - - - - - -
>
> Noble, gallant GARIBALDI, chivalrously are you doing your duty. Long will your name live in History as the Leader in Italian Freedom; freeing the long chain-bound Italians from the links of Slavery. Well have you earned British sympathy, *and you have experienced it.* Britain ever admires noble and chivalrous acts in friend or foe; but your righteous, straightforward conduct for the cause of the oppressed and iron-bound Italy, is double appreciated, *Timely, Noble, Gallant,* and *Unselfish*, in an arduous struggle for a brave but injured People. GARIBALDI, Britain admires you....But Britain is well aware, looking at your antecedent acts, that you know how to value her sympathy, and thus justify her in the eyes of Europe in the confidence that she appears to have in your honest endeavours for the freedom and welfare of the ill-used Italians. So, go ahead and prosper.
>
> NATIONS LOOK ON, AND SOME PEOPLE HOPE
> THAT YOU'LL SOON BE ABLE TO *CALL* ON THE POPE.[81]

By October 1860 the Italian situation had become more confused after Piedmont invaded the Papal States and a clash between the Piedmontese army and Garibaldi's forces seemed not impossible. Perplexity was plainly visible in Martin's advertisement published a week before Garibaldi and Victor Emmanuel II met and he feared that his hero had been betrayed by either Napoleon III or Piedmont. Referring to Garibaldi Martin stated that an honest man had been thwarted, a victorious man deceived and a hero outwitted. Napoleon III, still a wolf in sheep's clothing, was "deep, designing, inscrutable, unfathomable" and not to be trusted. Victor Emmanuel II was either a mere puppet of Napoleon or a free and brave man, but only time would show which. Piedmont was supporting Garibaldi but breaking treaties in the process and had invaded southern Italy without any declaration of war. This was a great crisis in Italian affairs, but whether Italy was to be independent, or merely going to exchange one master for another by becoming a mere province of France, was uncertain.[82] The happy turn of events in Italy naturally won Martin's approval.[83]

Given the Anglo-French tension of the period and Martin's deep interest in military matters it is no surprise that his encouragement of the volunteer movement included a five guinea contribution in January 1860 to the City of Aberdeen Artisan Volunteer Artillery And Rifle Corps.[84] Throughout the year he also included numerous reference to defence measures in general and the Volunteers in particular. In April he published a not uncritical account of the recent parade of the Aberdeen Rifle Volunteer Battalion,[85] but the review of Volunteers in Edinburgh in August by Queen Victoria led to an outburst of enthusiasm:

Twenty Thousand Scotch Volunteers in the Field

Ready for any emergency. Loyal Hearts and Steady Hands.

Sons of Brave Sires, whose deeds adorn the brightest page of British history. Well: oh, nobly have you acquitted yourselves. RIFLEMEN, your country thanks you heartily - oh, how heartily! - thanks for your gallant and chivalrous turn out in the hour of need. Men of the North - Sons of the Mountain Land - Scotia, Land of Heroes! the eyes of Europe were upon you, and although *some* may envy, yet all must admire a brave people who so unanimously and spontaneously stand forth for the defence of their country. Well may every man's heart who has a drop of true Scotch blood in his veins beat with heartfelt enthusiasm, delight, and satisfaction at the gallant display of his countrymen.

Scotchmen, your doings on the 7th August, 1860, will ever stand out in bold relief as one of the brightest days in the annals of Britain.[86]

Martin continued to manifest interest in the Volunteer Rifles in 1861, referring to the movement as the greatest institution of the age with its admirable and patriotic objectives. However, he also evinced doubts as to the future of the organization given an obvious slackening of both government and public concern. Martin asked, *"Is it to be a permanent institution, or is it to die an Unnatural Death from the want of sustenance from its natural parent, the Government, whose institutions it protects, and whose stability it secures?"* He went on to mention the lethargic state of the movement, to demand positive government action, and to recommend the encouragement of Ladies' Rifle Bazaars.[87] Notwithstanding Martin's advocacy the movement does seem to have faded from the scene.

Nevertheless, Martin did welcome one French invasion, the visit of the Empress Eugenie of France to Scotland though not to Aberdeen. Martin's dislike of Napoleon III had never extended to his wife who was depicted very favourably, probably because Martin claimed she had Scottish ancestors. Aberdonians, he felt were unlikely to have been upset by her failure to visit their city since they were so used to royalty, and any disappointment might well have been on her side as she had missed the chance to see "one of the HANDSOMEST AND MOST SUBSTANTIAL built Cities in Britain." Martin seized the opportunity, however, to speculate on what might have happened had the Empress included the city in her itinerary, using this device to renew his criticism of the St Nicholas Churchyard railing:

> Imaginary pictures are often very amusing; for instance, Fancy
>
> **THE PROVOST,**
>
> IN HIS AFFABLE, AGREEABLE, AND POLITE MANNER,
>
> RECEIVING EUGENIE AT THE RAILWAY STATION,
>
> and immediately Conducting Her Majesty to the WET FISH MARKET, which, from its *Locality, Extent,* and *Peculiar Conveniences*, is such as is not likely to be met with in many large towns, and from its vicinity to what may be considered the *principal approach from the South to Aberdeen*, it may well be supposed to have a most FLAVOURABLE effect upon the olfactory feelings of *Invalid* Visitors. Then fancy the Provost, as Her Majesty's Cicerone for the time being, Conducting Her Majesty up Market Street, then turning *left*, making a full Stop at the *Back Wynd*, then showing to the Empress, and very naturally *dilating* upon the *architectural beauties* of the much talked-of

> **CHURCHYARD RAILING,**
> and mentioning (what might have already entered Eugenie's head) the object of having COFFIN-like pillars stuck on end in a railing in an *attractive* and *most conspicuous* part of the town where men of taste might consider *Beauty*, with the *ordinary usefulness of a railing*, the *requisite* and *permanent* object in such a *locality*, that the happy design was possibly to show the *power* and *forethought* of *genius*, by *uprightly* representing the *Interior* of the Churchyard. Such information, doubtless, making a lasting and useful impression on Eugenie's *sensitive* mind....[88]

Of course, Martin was also able to comment on a real royal visit in 1860 when Queen Victoria and Prince Albert made their annual visit to Deeside. In August he recorded that he had been at Ballater a few weeks earlier, "but, having heard that her Majesty was coming to Scotland earlier than usual this season, he modestly returned to Aberdeen, thinking that it might be considered thrusting too much honour upon one locality for her MAJESTY and MARTIN to be in the vicinity at the same time," an event that might lead to the lovely village of Ballater being inconveniently overcrowded. Nevertheless, he intended to return to Ballater before the royal party left Balmoral, and if her Majesty felt inclined to consult him his time and advice would be at her disposal. Besides if she intended to knight him that year it would be as well if he were close at hand.[89] A few weeks later he repeated his intention to be in Ballater for a few days in the near future, the time of his arrival no doubt spreading rapidly. Though he would respectfully decline an offer to go shooting with Prince Albert he would enjoy accepting an invitation to dine at Balmoral.[90]

Martin's veritable crusade against the St Nicholas Churchyard railings was another hardy perennial in 1860. In addition to the introduction of the topic into the Empress Eugenie's fanciful tour of Aberdeen Martin made mention of the matter on several other occasions. In January he complained:

> THIS DEATH'S HEAD LOOKING RAIL,
> FIT FOR GUILLOTINE OR JAIL,
> IS NOT YET TAKEN DOWN -
> WANT OF TASTE IN THE TOWN.

He remarked that he had entered the Town Hall a few days earlier to view a portion of the new improved casting, which he heard was lying there for public approval, only to be told it had been removed.[91]

By June Martin's discontent with the situation had inspired him to verse:

Provost Anderson, it has been thought
 That you're the coming man -
For Aberdeen improvements
 To have some noble plan.

Could *you* not get this Railing down.
 And place it on the *Links*,
For Riflemen to practice at,
 By firing through the chinks.

'Tis fit for nothing else, my Lord;
 Men of taste look on't with scorn;
Then get a handsome railing up
 That would the town adorn.

If you could manage this, my Lord,
 You would many people please,
And when sitting in your Civic chair
 The fact might give you ease.[92]

Nearly four months later he tried again:

MARTIN. keep up the steam, it must come down,
The most unseemly sight in town;
Tho' some appear to think it pretty,
'Tis the ugliest Rail in the Granite City.

If the *Coffin Pillars* were removed,
The Railing would be much improved;
They really spoil the whole affair,
Which Men of Taste at once declare.

Some may think its *Beauty* would be seen,
If painted lively - perhaps, TEA GREEN;
While others, who don't want it down,
Might like to see it all done BROWN.

But to Men of Taste the matter's plain -
Run the Railing up to Gaelic Lane;
Then down the *Coffins*, up *Fluted* Pillars slight,
They would look handsome Painted White.

Then the Railing would be quite complete,
And truly an Ornament to Union Street;
Thus, do it chastely. 'Tis simply common-sense,
And, surely, *Aberdeen* can bear the Trifling Expense.[93]

If in the following nine months the rest of Aberdeen forgot about the offending railings Martin certainly did not. He returned to the subject with a vengeance in June 1861 when he offered his readers a poem of twelve stanzas and forty-eight lines on the topic. After several flattering references to the Provost, Alexander Anderson, Martin reached the eighth and most interesting verse in which he claimed that it was his publicity that was keeping the issue alive:

Indeed, it has been said of late,
    That 'tis a trifling matter,
Which none seem much to speak about
    Was it not for MARTIN THE HATTER.[94]

How much influence Martin's campaign actually had must be a matter of conjecture, but only five weeks later he was able to proclaim, in verse, naturally, that good taste was finally in the ascendant and the despised Churchyard railing was down at last, strongly hinting at his own role. On this occasion his poem consisted of only nine stanzas, the last two of which ran:

Thus, the *Coffin Pillars being removed,*
    Ends this amusing matter;
But the Public will, no doubt, give thanks
    To SAMUEL MARTIN THE HATTER.

So, seeing the New Rail's nearly up,
    Which fact deserves attention;
MARTIN early thanks the Council, for
    Carrying out his bright suggestion.[95]

If this particular crusade ended in triumph Martin was never short of alternative ideas and interests. At the beginning of 1861 he had followed his usual pattern of welcoming the new year while thanking the people for their continuing patronage.[96] Before January was out, however, and on the eve of a new session of parliament, he was heaping praises upon Lord Palmerston, whom he described as, "THE tried, the Experienced, the Veteran Pilot, he who has weathered and surmounted many a *Political* Storm (and has ever brought Britain's State Ship into a haven of safety)...." Martin exhorted Palmerston to proceed in his accustomed calm, steady, firm and consistent manner but to be prepared for all emergencies. Possibly in reaction to the contemporary political agitation for reductions in military and naval expenditures, which even divided the Cabinet, Martin argued that such costs were a necessary evil, especially in view of the unsettled foreign outlook.[97]

The Queen's Speech at the opening of parliament on February 5, 1861, contained no reference to a parliamentary reform bill, but Martin's speech, that he would have made to open the session if asked, published on February 9, was sympathetic to reform.[98] In April the Chancellor of the Exchequer introduced his Budget which reduced income tax back to 9d and repealed the paper duty postponed from the previous year. Gladstone claimed that the rise of a cheap press, aided by the abolition of the paper duty, would give the lower classes a renewed interest in public affairs and a fresh attachment to the nation's institutions.[99] Martin needed no fresh stimulus to renew his interest in current affairs, and was not impressed with the 1861 Budget to which he devoted an entire advertisement of many column inches. Martin admired the Chancellor's oratory and the dexterity of legislation that put money into the Peoples' pocket with one hand and took it out with the other, but he regarded the repeal of the paper duty as absurd. Tax cuts should have taken place on necessities like tea and sugar and not on paper, "*which will not perceivably benefit the masses of the people....*"[100] On this occasion Martin's shrewdness seems to have deserted him as apparently he did not foresee the effects the ending of this tax might have on the rise of a popular press.

This was a rare lapse on Martin's part as he was usually close to the pulse of public opinion and would have liked to think that, locally at least, he helped to shape that opinion. From mid-1856 to mid-1861 his business continued to thrive, no doubt helped by the retirement from the retail hat trade in Aberdeen of W.H. Miller & Co., 69 Union Street, in March 1861, on account of other engagements in London.[101] In this same period he continued to offer his thoughts on such diverse imperial and foreign distractions as the Indian Mutiny, the *Arrow* War, Italian unification, the war scare with France, on politics, economics and defence at the national level, as well as on a range of local issues. For the next several years, however, a good deal of Martin's attention was going to be focused across the Atlantic on the fratricidal struggle in the United States.

NOTES

1 *The Herald*, July 12, 1856, p4, col 3, and August 23, 1856, p4, col 2.

2 *The Herald*, July 12, 1856, p4, col 3.

3 *The Herald*, September 27, 1856, p4, col 3. Martin's colourful prose style was again in evidence on this occasion with his reference to, "Fathers and Brothers dragged ignominiously from their happy homes - made to suffer Corporal Punishment in its most degraded form - thrust into loathsome Dungeons of Pestilence, Suffering, and Disease - there left to die a miserable death, without a friend to hear their last sigh; and for what? - in many cases for Crimes, *so-called*, that in happy BRITAIN would not justify the interference of A POLICE OFFICER; but all done under Despotic rule by a Tyrant, who (if all be true that is attributed to him) is the greatest evil to a People, *whom it is his duty to protect*, abusing his power daily by using his Subjects worse than brutes, yet retaining the title of KING."

Martin's sentiments certainly reflected those of Gladstone, who in the winter of 1850-51 had visited the prisons of Naples and described the conditions under which the opponents of King "Bomba" Ferdinand II of the Two Sicilies were held as "the wholesale persecution of virtue...It is the awful profanation of public religion...It is the perfect prostitution of the judicial office...It is the savage and cowardly system of moral as well as physical torture...This is the negation of God erected into a system of government." See Philip Magnus, *Gladstone. A Biography* (1954), pp98-99.

4 *The Herald*, October 11, 1856, p4, col 2. This advertisement was one of the comparatively few that specifically referred to ladies' hats.

5 *The Herald*, December 13, 1856, p4, col 2.

6 *The Herald*, January 10, 1857, p4, col 2.

7 *The Herald*, February 14, 1857, p4, col 2.

8 For details of the original incident at Canton and the background see Douglas Hurd, *The Arrow War. An Anglo-Chinese Confusion 1856-1860* (1967), pp1-38. Martin's advertisement appeared in *The Herald*, January 10, 1857, p4, col 2.
9 *The Herald*, March 7, 1857, p4, col 2.
10 Douglas Hurd, *op. cit.*, pp39-73.
11 *The Herald*, July 3, 1841, p129, col 4.
12 *The Herald*, March 7, 1857, p4, col 2.
13 Douglas Hurd, *op. cit.*, pp74-76.
14 Douglas Hurd, *op. cit.*, pp79-81.
15 *The Herald*, April 11, 1857, p4, col 2.
16 *The Herald*, May 23, 1857, p4, col 2.
17 *The Herald*, September 24, 1859, p4, col 2. Referring to the fact that the British commander, Admiral Sir James Hope, had been wounded during the action, Martin wrote "TRULY 'HOPE' DEFERRED MAKETH THE HEART SICK. NO HOPE (EVIDENTLY) FOR CHINA. But that the Admiral, and officers, and men behaved gallantly, and fought like heroes, cannot be doubted...." For the details of this action see Douglas Hurd, *op. cit.*, pp179-88 wherein the author refers to Admiral Hope as "a gallant ass."
18 *The Herald*, May 2, 1857, p4, col 2.
19 For details regarding the causes and course of the Indian Mutiny see Christopher Hibbert, *The Great Mutiny. India 1857* (1978), R.C. Majumdar, *The Sepoy Mutiny And The Revolt Of 1857* (1957), and Michael Edwards, *Battles Of The Indian Mutiny* (1963).
20 See, for example, James Bryne "British Opinion And The Indian Revolt," in P.C. Joshi (ed), *Rebellion 1857, a symposium* (1957).
21 *The Herald*, June 20, 1857, p4, col 2.
22 *The Herald*, July 18, 1857, p4, col 2.
23 *The Herald*, August 29, 1857, carried a news item on the massacre on p3, col 4, and an editorial comment on p4, col 5. For detail and discussion of the military operations and of the killing of the European soldiers in June and of the women and children in July see Hibbert, *The Great Mutiny. India 1857,* pp168-266 and 327-66, R.C. Majumdar, *The Sepoy Mutiny And The Revolt Of 1857*, passim, and Michael Edwards, *Battles of the Indian Mutiny*, pp57-111.
24 *The Herald*, September 5, 1857, p4, col 2.
25 *The Herald*, October 10, 1857, p4, col 2.
26 *The Aberdeen Journal*, October 14, 1857, p4, col 1.
27 *The Aberdeen Journal*, October 14, 1857, p4, col 1.
28 *The Herald*, October 17, 1857, p5, cols 2-6. *The Aberdeen Journal*, October 21, 1857, p6, col 4, also described the decorations in detail but

selected Martin for special comment, remarking, "For simple beauty, the decorations of Mr Martin's (hatter) establishment were, perhaps, unmatched in the city." A.S. Cook, *Old-Time Traders and Their Ways*, (1902), p20, wrote of Samuel Martin, "His get-up was showy, but it was his style. Many will remember that on public occasions of rejoicings and processions that Sammy stood in the open wareroom window above the shop, which was gaily decorated, clothed in a red jacket and wideawake hat, in Garibaldi costume, playing on a silver bugle 'God Save the King,' to the great enjoyment and amusement of the onlookers."

29 *The Herald*, October 17, 1857, p4, col 2.

30 *The Herald*, October 24, 1857, p4, col 2.

31 *The Herald*, November 21, 1857, p4, col 2.

32 *The Herald*, December 5, 1857, p4, col 2.

33 *The Herald*, December 5, 1857, p4, col 2. Martin had already raised this subject in *The Herald* on October 17, 1857, p4, col 2. The topic had been discussed in the columns of *The Herald* on various occasions, for example on August 22, 1857, p2, col 4, and p6, col 1.

34 *The Herald*, January 2, 1858, p4, col 2. Martin added, "At this, the beginning of 1858, MARTIN thanks the People most heartily for their kind support during the past year - a year of great events in Europe, and a year of great satisfaction to MARTIN, as his trade for the year has quite come up to his expectations: and, as MARTIN has ample means to puchase his Goods at the best Markets, for Cash, and, being determined to continue selling good articles at moderate prices, he thinks that all are likely to be pleased who purchase at his famed Establishment."

35 *The Herald*, March 6, 1858, p4, col 3.

36 *The Herald*, January 30, 1858, p4, col 2.

37 *The Herald*, February 27, 1858, p4, col 2. The events in China at this time are covered in Douglas Hurd, *The Arrow War. An Anglo-Chinese Confusion 1856-60*, pp109-29.

38 Herbert F.C. Bell, *Lord Palmerston*, Vol II, p183, describes the adverse result as "a snap vote secured by political manoeuvring, and through an appeal by its opponents to popular passions...."

39 *The Herald*, February 27, 1858, p4, col 2.

40 *The Herald*, March 13, 1858, p4, col 2. *The Herald* of the same date, p5, col 5, remarked, "The weather for the past eight days has in this quarter been of a very stormy character - snow falling every day, with strong northerly gales, and severe frost. People of good memory will tell you that exactly twenty years ago - 1838 - there had been a fine open winter, such as we have experienced this year, and that it was followed by a snowstorm of six weeks' duration, after the 1st of March. We are glad to think, from the appearance of the weather of yesterday, that the coincidence will not be

complete. A mild southerly wind prevailed, the snow was disappearing, and this morning rain was falling fast." On March 20, 1858, p6, col 1, *The Herald* published a brief description of the eclipse which lasted from 11h 37m 1s a.m. till 2h 7m 2s on March 15 and obscured 9/10ths of the sun.

41 *The Herald*, March 20, 1858, p4, col 2.

42 *The Herald*, June 26, 1858, p4, col 2. Martin assured his customers that he was, "Ever on the alert, and anxious to please all who purchase at his famed Establishment," and that he had "lately got to hand a magnificent Assortment of *Extraordinary Light* and *Well-ventilated* HATS, suitable for summer wear, weighing from 4½ oz. to 5½ oz.; and, when it is kept in view that the weight of an ordinary Hat is from 6½ to 8 oz., it may well be supposed that the removal of from 2 to 3 oz. weight from the head will remove a corresponding weight from the mind" and thus keep the body in a serene state during the very warm weather.

43 *The Herald*, March 13, 1858, p4, col 2.

44 *The Herald*, April 17, 1858, p4, col 2. Martin's headlines included the phrases "SLASHING NEWS FROM INDIA!", "Highlanders Never Show their Backs to Foes", and "Forward, Highlanders, to Victory!!"

45 *The Herald*, May 22, 1858, p4, col 2. Martin wrote in part "...great want of British Soldiers for the work to be done, for although a braver army never fought the battles of their country than the British Army in India has proved itself to be, yet, from the smallness of their numbers compared with the enemy, their victories have been obtained, to a great extent, by the admirable ability and strategy of their commanders; and to such an extent has this been obliged to be carried out, that, strange and startling as it may appear, insinuations and doubts are actually thrown out upon the ability of Sir COLIN CAMPBELL as a Commander, because he allowed so many of the Rebels to escape from Lucknow. A braver Commander than Sir COLIN, or one that has served his country more in her time of need, 'tis scarcely too much to say, never drew a British sword. But Sir COLIN cannot perform miracles. Thus to military men, or others who understand military matters, 'tis as plain as common sense can make it that Sir COLIN, with the army at his command, could not have taken Lucknow and annihilated or taken prisoners all the garrison - thus was obliged to let a portion of the Rebels retreat into the open country, there to be dealt with as his army and tactics would permit."

46 *The Herald*, July 17, 1858, p4, col 3.

47 *The Herald*, November 20, 1858, p4, col 2. Martin's ability to mix bloodthirsty prose with his sales pitch was once again demonstrated on this occasion, the contrast in styles being the more apparent as he was addressing himself, quite unusually, to a female clientele, "**LADIES**,

MARTIN has a magnificent display of FELT HATS, Trimmed and Untrimmed, *charming* Goods, *becoming* Shapes, beautiful Qualities, and which, from his immense trade, he is enabled and determined to Sell at very moderate prices. MARTIN HAS JUST UNPACKED A LARGE LOT FROM LONDON, bought upon the best terms, and which he can well suppose are likely to please those who appreciate good taste and stylish got up goods, particularly when it is kept in view that the fine appearance or *tout ensemble* of a superior Felt Hat may at once be spoiled by a *too elaborate* or *vulgar* style of trimming. Very pretty, stylish, and chaste Trimmed Felt Hats, 7s. 6d., 8s. 6d., 9s. 6d., 10s. 6d., and 13s. 6d. each, and a very superior quality, indeed, as 18s. 6d." See also *The Herald*, January 15, 1859, p4, col 2.

48 Letters of Smauel Chalmers, MS 2884/1/3/1-2, Letter No. 197, June 4, 1858, in Letters and Papers of the Family of Alexander Wallace Chalmers, deposited in the Special Collections of Aberdeen University Library. I am again indebted to Dr Marjory Harper of the Department of History & Economic History at Aberdeen University for bringing this reference to my attention.

49 *The Herald*, August 14, 1858, p4, col 2.

50 *The Herald*, September 11, 1858, p4, col 2.

51 *The Herald*, October 9, 1858, p4, col 2.

52 *The Herald*, August 28, 1858, p4, col 3.

53 *The Herald*, January 15, 1859, p4 col 2. Martin did not forget at this time to give thanks to "the People, most heartily for their kind support during the past year, and at this the beginning of 1859, it may possibly be very gratifying to the People to know that MARTIN'S mental faculties are bright as ever."

54 *The Herald*, February 12, 1859, p4, col 2. Martin returned to his idea of a Volunteer Rifle Corps more than once, see, for example, *The Herald*, May 28, 1859, p4, col 2.

55 *The Herald*, March 26, 1859, p4, col 2.

56 *The Herald*, April 30, 1859, p4, col 2.

57 *The Herald*, May 28, 1859, p4, col 2.

58 *The Herald*, July 23, 1859, p4, col 2.

59 *The Herald*, August 20, 1859, p4, col 2.

60 *The Herald*, November 20, 1859, p4, col 2. *The Herald* had carried an announcement of a public meeting on April 30 regarding the formation of a Volunteer Rifle Corps in Aberdeen on June 4, 1859, p3, col 3, and on p4, col 3 the Committee of Aberdeen Volunteer Rifle Corps advised the public that they were prepared to receive the names of those who wished to enrol. An editorial on the subject appeared on p4, col 6.

61 *The Herald*, March 26, 1859, p4, col 2.

62 *The Herald*, June 18, 1859, p4, col 2.

63 *The Herald*, September 24, 1859, p4, col 2. On September 17, 1859, p5, col 5, *The Herald* reported that on Sunday, September 11, the day Martin was in Crathie Church, the Queen, the Prince Consort, the Prince of Wales, Princess Alice and other members of the Court attended public worship at Crathie. The Rev. Dr. Cook had preached a very earnest and religious sermon from 1 Corinthians iv, verses 5 and 6. The church was very well filled on this occasion. On Monday, September 12, the weather being very fine, the Queen, the Prince Consort and Princess Alice "went out through the road to Crathinard village, and viewed the scenery around, the Queen using her sketching pencil different times."

64 *The Daily Free Press*, January 9, 1888, p4, col 6, in its obituary for Samuel Martin commented that "There were pretty good grounds for believing that the way he used to poetically point to a forthcoming 'knighthood' for his own humble self was frequently matter of mirthful comment within Balmoral Castle."

65 *The Herald*, September 24, 1859, p4, col 2.

66 *The Herald*, October 8, 1859, p5, col 4.

67 *The Herald*, October 15, 1859, p4, cols 5-6.

68 *The Herald*, October 22, 1859, p4, col 2.

69 *The Herald*, November 26, 1859, p4, col 2.

70 *The Herald*, December 31, 1859, p4, col 2.

71 *The Herald*, December 31, 1859, p4, col 2.

72 *The Herald*, January 7, 1860, p4, col 2. Martin deplored the fact that the policemen now carried small batons up their sleeve, which made them look as though they had rheumatism, or stuffed them into a coat pocket, "causing a most unbecoming protuberance, *second only to another extreme of fashion of the day.*"

73 *The Herald*, January 7, 1860, p5, col 2.

74 *The Herald*, February 18, 1860, p4, col 2.

75 *The Herald*, March 17, 1860, p4, col 2. With regard to the proposed repeal of the paper duty Martin asked, "Will the working-classes be enabled to purchase a Book hitherto charged One Shilling for Eleven Pence, will they get a Three Pence-halfpenny Newspaper for Three Pence, will they get a Penny Newspaper for Three Farthings, will they get a Halfpenny Sheet of Writing Paper for a Farthing, or will they, when making ordinary purchases perceive the Articles purchased *cheaper*, because wrapped in Paper with the Three-halfpence a pound weight duty off? Pshaw! 'tis a mere farce."

76 *The Herald*, July 28, 1860, p4, col 2.

77 *The Herald*, September 1, 1860, p4, col 2.

78 *The Herald*, January 21, 1860, p4, col 2.

79 *The Herald*, April 7, 1860, p4, col 2.
80 *The Herald*, June 2, 1860, p4, col 2.
81 *The Herald*, September 22, 1860, p4, col 2.
82 *The Herald*, October 20, 1860, p4, col 2. Martin remarked "When British Statesmen can 'make a Silk Purse out of a *Sow's* ear,' they will likely make Napoleon a *sincere* friend."
83 *The Herald*, November 17, 1860, p4, col 2. Much of this advertisement was devoted to comments concerning the Lord Mayor's Banquet in London and the speeches of British politicians and the French and Piedmontese ambassadors.
84 *The Herald*, January 21, 1860, p4, col 1. A week earlier *The Herald*, January 14, 1860, p4, col 2, listed Martin as having given a subscription of 10s 0d to the Public Soup Kitchen.
85 *The Herald*, April 7, 1860, p4, col 2.
86 *The Herald*, August 11, 1860, p4, col 2. There were further references to the Volunteers on October 20, 1860, p4, col 2, and December 29, 1860, p4, col 2.
87 *The Herald*, February 23, 1861, p4, col 2.
88 *The Herald*, December 1, 1860, p4, col 2.
89 *The Herald*, August 11, 1860, p4, col 2.
90 *The Herald*, September 1, 1860, p4, col 2.
91 *The Herald*, January 21, 1860, p4, col 2. Martin's advertisements were always full of priceless local detail, and on this occasion he wrote: "MARTIN felt a sort of awe when in the Hall (looking on the Old Portraits, which appear really very good) - thinking on the effects of time, and the many scenes that had possibly taken place there....yet, all must pass away! and, glancing at the *Carpet*, MARTIN felt inclined to exclaim, Yes, your *(W)hole* appearance indicates that *gaps* will manifest themselves, and that all things *wear* away."
92 *The Herald*, June 2, 1860, p4, col 2.
93 *The Herald*, September 22, 1860, p4, col 2.
94 *The Herald*, June 22, 1861, p4, col 2.
95 *The Herald*, July 27, 1861, p4, col 2.
96 *The Herald*, January 5, 1861, p4, col 2.
97 *The Herald*, January 21, 1861, p4, col 2.
98 *The Herald*, February 9, 1861, p4, col 2. This proposed speech was even longer than his prorogation address the previous September, running to around a thousand words or a hundred lines of advertising copy.
99 Philip Magnus, *Gladstone. A Biography,* pp151-52.
100 *The Herald*, April 20, 1861, p4, col 2.
101 *The Herald*, March 30, 1861, p4, col 3.

CHAPTER FOUR

MARTIN AND THE AMERICAN CIVIL WAR. 1861-1865.

In view of the fact that Samuel Martin took such a keen interest in foreign affairs, and was ever willing to give the readers of *The Aberdeen Herald* the benefit of his opinions, it is somewhat surprising that Anglo-American relations attracted his attention only once before 1861, when, in 1855-56, he had commented upon the ill-fated attempt to recruit Americans to fight in the Crimea.[1] Perhaps Martin was too absorbed by British domestic affairs and too focused upon European and Imperial matters to spare time and space in his advertisements to discourse upon the dramatic events taking place across the Atlantic in the 1850s. In these years the United States experienced a series of sectional crises culminating in the bitterly fought presidential election of 1860 and the consequent secession of the Lower South states following the victory of the Republican candidate, Abraham Lincoln. None of these developments called forth any comment from the practical hatter, and it was not until March 23, 1861, that Martin drew the notice of his audience to the American imbroglio.

Less than three weeks after the event, which allowing for the time it still took for news to cross the Atlantic still made his observations topical, Martin referred to President Lincoln's inaugural address, which he saw as "Sensible, and Manly" and plainly demonstrating:

> that the Southerners have no just cause for their late movement in attempting to throw off their allegiance to the United States' Union, to which it plainly appears they are yet legally bound, as the President distinctly says, that "each State has the right to order and control its own domestic institutions," and distinctly states that he had no wish supposing he had the power (which he has not) to interfere with the arrangement or internal management of the Slave States - IF THEY WISH TO REMAIN SLAVE STATES - thus, it may be asked, what can be the object of the recent doings of the Southerners, knowing, as they ought to know, that the President has no legal power, and no wish to interfere with the internal management or arrangements of Slave States? Thus, seeing that they have no *just* reason in their attempt to dissolve the Union, it makes their acts of late *very like*, if *not actual treason*, their bombast mere moonshine, and themselves the laughing-stock of Europe. But it would simply appear, that

not liking the *democratic principles* of the New President, Lincoln, they may have an *idea* that *he would* possibly interfere with the Slave States. If so, they have evidently made themselves look very ridiculous, for an *idea*. But evil intentions are often surmounted by *good acts*, thus the present American movement *may*, and likely *will*, be

The Stepping Stone to razing the Foundation of Slavery.

And the sooner the better will likely be the opinion of all right thinking minds. But the Southerns evidently don't like the New President LINCOLN - they don't like the *man*, and are thus dubious of his acts; but their narrow prejudices are evidently in a fair way to hurt themselves most; indeed, they appear at present, in their *regard* for President LINCOLN, to be imitating the old saying of -

"I DO NOT LIKE THEE DOCTOR FELL,
THE REASON WHY I CANNOT TELL."

But, if the American misunderstanding *can* be sett'ed WITHOUT Bloodshed, so much the better.

SO THINKS

MARTIN THE HATTER.[2]

In his comments Martin had certainly perceived the major points of Lincoln's address - his desire to avoid strife and the fact that he had no power or immediate wish to abolish slavery - as well as the South's neurosis about its so-called peculiar institution. Martin's abhorrence of slavery would certainly have been a fair reflection of British public opinion.

Martin did not return to the American situation until May 25, 1861, when he made some tongue in cheek remarks about the firing of the first shot of the Civil War at Fort Sumter, in Charleston harbour, South Carolina, on April 12-13. The presence there of a Federal garrison was of negligible military account but of great symbolic importance to both sides. After a bombardment, that lasted some thirty-three hours, inflicted serious damage on the structure but caused no fatalities, the Union commander, Major Robert Anderson surrendered. Martin could not resist writing, "THERE has been no more *bloody* actions nor deeds of Heroism displayed as yet to the admiring world, *since* the *glorious and ever to be remembered taking of* FORT SUMTER, where both sides fought heroically *(really like Heroes of Romance)* for Forty hours, and *Nobody was hurt,* MAJOR ANDERSON giving in about *dinner* time, and *dining* with the Commander of the Enemy in the evening. *New feature in warfare, much to be commended, Long may it continue."* He suggested Britain and France might learn a lot from this new style of warfare where a fire brigade might be of more use than modern weapons.[3]

Following the fall of Fort Sumter President Lincoln called 75,000 state militia into federal service for ninety days to suppress what he called an insurrection. This action drove four Upper South slave states to join the Confederacy and both sides girded themselves for armed conflict. During the period of relative inactivity which followed, while both sides organized their ill prepared forces, hard news of military action was scarce. Thus Martin on June 22, 1861, was reduced to such remarks as that both sides were equally matched in bombast and that great preparations were afoot for a deadly conflict of words. He also made sarcastic comment about a well known incident when young and dashing Colonel Elmer Ellsworth, commander of a picturesque regiment of Zouaves in the northern army, a unit largely recruited from the New York City Fire Department, sprang up the stairs of the Marshall House in Alexandria, Virginia, just across the Potomac from Washington, D.C., to take down the Confederate flag. Ellsworth was shot by a young southerner who was then instantly killed by Ellsworth's men. Martin's flippant description of the incident would not have won approval in America, where both sides now had a martyred hero, and where flags North and South flew at half mast.[4]

Unaware that the first large scale battle of the American Civil War had taken place at Bull Run (or Manassas) on July 21, 1861, Samuel Martin on July 27 was still making mock of the war and the supposed lack of action, pointing out that the armies were out in all weathers marching and counter-marching, and not afraid to catch cold. He gave more attention on this occasion to expressing his gratification that the St Nicholas Churchyard railings were down at last than to the war in America.[5]

On August 10 Martin was able to report on the first battle of Bull Run, which had degenerated into a northern rout. Thus he headed his advertisement:

> "He that Fights and runs away
> May live to Fight another day."

Martin referred to the "DISASTROUS DEFEAT AND TOTAL ROUT OF THE NORTHERN ARMY," and the vulnerable position of Washington, D.C. His suggestion that each side had suffered about 1,000 dead was more than double the actual figures, and though the northern withdrawal had become a panic his remark that ten thousand more might possibly die of fright was unkind. He went on to express his own disdain for the North's fighting abilities, perhaps reflecting a more general British attitude:

> The Cannon's loud roar, to the North Volunteers,
> Deprived them of courage, but strengthened their fears,
> And each of his comrade being doubtful, all feels
> 'T will be safest at once to take to their heels.
>
> THIS GREAT BATTLE MAKES IT APPARENT that whatever difference of opinion there may have been as to the *Yankies* being up to the use of their ARMS, there can be no doubt that the *Northerners* are *thoroughly up to the use of their* LEGS.
>
> The *North* at Bull's RUN have sadly found out
> The Southerners have *whipped* them of *that* there's no doubt;
> But there may be *more* gory fields and serious disaster,
> Before LINCOLN or DAVIS knows who's to be master.[6]

Martin returned to the subject of the war and the apparent inaction in both October,[7] and November.[8] However, in the latter month events across the Atlantic produced a new crisis in Anglo-American relations. Earlier in the year there had already been a sharp disagreement between the two countries when, on May 13, Britain had issued a declaration of neutrality in the American Civil War, thus granting belligerent rights, but not full diplomatic recognition, to the Confederacy. Now, on November 8, 1861, a Federal warship, the *U.S.S. San Jacinto*, stopped and boarded a British mailsteamer, the *Trent*, bound from Havana to St Thomas. Under protest James M. Mason of Virginia and John Slidell of Louisiana, Confederate commissioners to London and Paris, were removed from the deck of the *Trent* and taken to Boston. Whereas the captain of the *U.S.S. San Jacinto* would have been justified in taking the *Trent* into an American port for a court to adjudicate on the status of its cargo and passengers, he had breached international law by removing Mason and Slidell while at sea. News of this escapade was greeted rapturously in the northern states where the capture of two leading rebels was seen as a

"He that Fights and runs away,
May live to Fight another day."

HORRORS OF CIVIL WAR.

GREAT NEWS FROM AMERICA.
THE FIGHTING'S BEGUN IN EARNEST,
GENERAL BEAUREGARD,
GOING A-HEAD.

UNEXPECTED NEWS.

DISASTROUS DEFEAT AND TOTAL ROUT OF THE NORTHERN ARMY AT BULL'S RUN (*a very appropriate name doubtless*, BUT MEN RUN *THIS* TIME) BY THE SOUTHERNERS.

ALARMING STATE OF THE *NORTHERN* CAPITAL.

Great Consternation at Washington.

The Southerners chasing their Enemies (a confused mass—all discipline being at an end in the Northern Army), in their ignoble flight—anxiety for individual Safety being evidently the *main point* with *these much talked-of and Blustering Veterans.* The Southerners Capturing all their Stores, Rifled Cannon, and Small Arms in great abundance. *The very articles they were most in want of*, and only stopping in the pursuit of the *rabble* at FAIRFAX, a small *Village*, about Twenty Miles from Washington.

SUPPOSED LOSS—ABOUT 1000 MEN KILLED ON EACH SIDE, AND, PERHAPS,
TEN THOUSAND MEN MAY POSSIBLY DIE OF FRIGHT.
HORRIBLE POSITION OF A GREAT COUNTRY.

Possible Cause and State of Mind during the Panic.

The Cannon's loud roar, to the *North* Volunteers,
Deprived them of *courage*, but *strengthened* their fears,
And each of his comrade being doubtful, all feels
'T will be safest *at once* to take to their heels.

THIS GREAT BATTLE MAKES IT APPARENT that whatever difference of opinion there may have been as to the *Yankies* being up to the use of their ARMS, there can be no doubt that the *Northerners* are *thoroughly up to the use of their* LEGS.

The *North* at Bull's RUN have sadly found out
The Southerns have *whipped* them of *that* there's no doubt;
But there may be *more* gory fields and serious disaster,
Before LINCOLN or DAVIS knows who's to be master.

SO THINKS
MARTIN THE HATTER.

MARTIN'S Stock of HATS, CAPS, &c. &c. is very large at present.

Best Quality, London-made Satin HATS, 18/ each.

Magnificent SATIN HATS, New Shapes, Light, Durable, and Easy Fitting, 6/6, 8/6, 10/6, 12/6, 13/6, and 15/6 each.

SHELL, FELT, and STRAW HATS; SHOOTING, FISHING, DEER-STALKING, and SMOKING CAPS; KNAPSACKS, SHOULDER BAGS, PORTMANTEAUS, LEATHER HAT CASES, &c. &c. &c. very Cheap.

Observe!
SAMUEL MARTIN,
HATTER TO THE PEOPLE,
34, UNION STREET (WAREHOUSE ABOVE SHOP),
ABERDEEN.

Established Twenty-three Years.

welcome ray of sunshine in an otherwise gloomy wartime outlook. Captain Charles Wilkes of the *U.S.S. San Jacinto* became an instant hero. News of the affair, and what was seen as an insult to the British flag, arrived in Britain on November 28 where it precipitated an outburst of bellicose resentment among politicians, press and public. Prime Minister Lord Palmerston exploded at a cabinet meeting, "You may stand for this but damned if I will!" The Royal Navy dispatched additional warships to reinforce the North Atlantic Squadron, troops were readied to sail for Canada, and talk of war was common on both sides of the Atlantic. In fact, calmer heads soon prevailed in both Washington and London since neither country had any conceivable advantage to be gained from a war. Meantime, however, on December 14, Martin's advertisement, which ran to sixteen column inches, burst upon the Aberdeen scene full of patriotic indignation. Never, Martin proclaimed, would the British flag be insulted with impunity, and never was the country better prepared for war:

> NEVER! was there a more enthusiastic War Spirit in the country. NEVER! was Britain better prepared to maintain her position and NEVER! did she go to War in a more righteous cause than she will do in the apparent coming War with the *North* American States....
>
> WELL DONE
>
> **LORD PALMERSTON**
>
> GALLANT, ADMIRABLE PRIME MINISTER OF BRITAIN,
>
> You have the feelings of the *country* with you in the Noble Stand you have made in your determination to *uphold the Honour of the British flag*, for the recent *cowardly* SAN JACINTO affair. Well may every man at *home* or *abroad*, who has one drop of true British Blood in his Veins be proud and delighted that your *Lordship* is at the head of British affairs at this (certainly not *alarming*, but nevertheless) momentous crisis. SEEING THAT THE HONOUR OF BRITAIN IS SAFE IN YOUR HANDS,
>
> **GO A-HEAD MY LORD,**
>
> Carry out your present policy thoroughly. *No compromise, reparation in full as demanded.* BRITISH HONOUR UNTARNISHED OR WELCOME WAR.

Martin hoped for peace, but if the "blustering Northern Yankees" forgot their "comparative pigmy and contemptible position" and provoked war with Britain then all her naval resources should be employed against the upstarts. He concluded his tirade with ten stanzas of anti-Federal verse:

The Yankees North have bounced too far,
    The British Lion won't stand it;
He's raised his mane, and, *If* War, its plain
    The Northerners will be pounded.
        Prepare for action, Ships of War,
            Thrash the Yankees, when *North* sent;
        Let your war-cry ever be -
            Britain's Honour - "Mind the Trent."

The San Jacinto's cowardly act,
    In boarding the Steamer Trent,
Appears to please the Northerners now,
    But the fact they'll soon repent.
        Prepare for action, &c.

SLIDELL and MASON they have secured
    In prison there's no doubt;
But, British cannon, when *they* roar,
    Will get these prisoners out.
        Prepare for action, &c.

Northern bombast soon will end -
    Britain's stood it rather long;
With Washington smashed about their ears,
    They'll find that Britain's ever strong.
        Prepare for action, &c.

The North's attempt to subdue the South,
    With great pretensions started,
They soon found out they couldn't do -
    So the North and South's now parted.
        Prepare for action, &c.

And, while the War's been going on,
    Honourably Neutral Britain's been;
But which the North's inclined to doubt,
    Which shows their Statesmen precious Green.
        Prepare for action, &c.

To avoid the War it was easily seen
To be Britain's wish, *provided*
The North would keep a civil tongue
Unless on War decided.
Prepare for action, &c.

But her *insolence* is getting worse,
And her advisers but deceive her
If they think she'll not be overhauled
For her set on the British steamer.
Prepare for action, &c.

So Yankees North you'll soon be smashed
About this awkward business,
Unless you make an apology
And at once give up your prisoners.
Prepare for action, &c.

And you'd better make your mind up soon
Nor dilly-dally longer,
As every day you *now* put off
Makes the British Lion stronger.
Prepare for action, &c.[9]

Despite Samuel Martin's ardent spirits the two nations had been anxious to avoid a serious breach, and President Lincoln was well aware that one war at a time was sufficient. Accordingly, on December 26, 1861, Lincoln ordered the release of Mason and Slidell and the United States issued a statement that could be interpreted as an apology. Martin certainly did so, and clearly felt no compunction not to exult over what he clearly saw as a great British diplomatic triumph and a humiliating American retreat. His advertisement on January 11, 1862, made no attempt to spare American feelings, but rather rejoiced at their discomfort. Martin wrote in bold headlines of the white feather being displayed and insisted that American impudence, arrogance, insolence and bombast had succumbed to British pressure, the prisoners had been released and an ample apology made. The Yankees had been forced to swallow a bitter pill, they had been humbled, subdued and humiliated and the star-spangled banner left in the dust. No generous feelings or wish for reconciliation flowed from Martin's pen as he continued:

> **SERVE THEM RIGHT!**
> They deserve no pity until they learn to keep Civil tongues in their heads to a power that could annihilate them. BRITAIN HAS NOBLY AND GENEROUSLY DONE HER DUTY in this American affair, and shown to the World that HER POSITION to maintain Peace is ever to be prepared for War, and thus save human life. *Reasoning* and *Arbitration* may all be well enough with *reasonable* people; but a *righteous cause* and *Armstrong Guns,* with British Blue Jackets to man them, will ever be found the *best* line of argument with *Northern* Yankees.

Martin concluded with seven verses of rhyme that continued to rub salt into northern wounds.[10]

Any initial sympathy Martin had felt for the Union cause was obviously badly undermined by the *Trent* affair, and thereafter his sympathies were often with the South. Later in January 1862 he was claiming the Federal blockade of the southern coast to be ineffective and consequently not valid in international law. He wrote of the manifest inability of the North to subdue the South and called for the European powers to recognize Confederate independence.[11]

In March Martin recorded the Federal capture of Roanoke Island off the coast of North Carolina by General Burnside, but also noted the inactivity of the main northern army in the East commanded by General George B. McClellan, sometimes known as "Young Napoleon," whom Martin felt gave the appearance of being backward in going forward. Martin went on to comment on the lack of any apparent progress in the war and to state:

> But the matter appears plain. If the North does not subdue the SOUTH soon, it will be apparent that they cannot do so; then, *if they cannot*, let them henceforth be separate people, independent of each other, and it may ultimately prove better for both North and South, and will likely be more satisfactory to Europe, as it will end the present *heathenish, diabolical, blood-thirsty*, and *fratricidal* War - a blot upon the intellect of the Nineteenth Century.[12]

Somewhat surprisingly Martin did not return to the subject of the American conflict again until May 24. Surprising because on March 8 and 9, 1862, at Hampton Roads at the mouth of the James River there occurred one of the most famous naval encounters of the nineteenth century, which Martin, as an eager student of maritime warfare, might well have been expected to take note of. On March 8 the Confederate ironclad *Virginia*, (formerly the *Merrimack*), sallied forth in an attempt to break the Union blockade and quickly dispersed the northern vessels, sinking the wooden sailing ships *Cumberland* and *Congress*. Fortunately for the North that same evening the Union iron gun-boat the *Monitor* arrived on the scene, and the next day the two iron vessels, the progenitors of modern warships, fought an inconclusive duel. Martin's ignoring of these events is the more difficult to explain since the details of the vessels and the battles were covered thoroughly in the Aberdeen press. Both *The Aberdeen Journal* and *The Herald* carried accounts of the naval engagement as soon as the news was available, and both included comments in their editorial columns, noting that this was the first encounter between ironclad warships.[13] In a lengthy editorial entitled "MAILED SHIPS" *The Aberdeen Journal* wrote perceptively, "The sea-fight of Hampton Roads was as momentous in its consequences as the Battle of Trafalgar. In some respects, more so. In the one, the French navy was destroyed, but the other has sealed the fate of all the navies of the world."[14] *The Herald* published an article on "IRON SHIPS - THE MONITOR AND THE MERRIMAC," which included detailed drawings of the two vessels, and claimed, "The appearance of the Monitor and Merrimac on the warlike scene of action in America has raised such a fluffer of excitement among our naval architects, and created such general interest in the question of iron ships throughout the country, that we need no further excuse for laying before our readers the excellent drawings given above."[15]

Martin did, however, mention the capture of New Orleans by the Federal forces in late April, though without any comment on the military significance of that event. The loss in early May of Yorktown in Virginia and the abandonment of Williamsburg by the Confederates marking the beginning of the Peninsula Campaign was drawn to the attention of Martin's readers, but the main thrust of his remarks at this time was still the lack of any decisive action and the need for European intervention or mediation.[16]

Martin did not comment directly on the first major encounters of the Peninsula Campaign - Fair Oaks and Seven Pines on May 31 and June 1 - but he was critical of General McClellan's lack of decision and admiring of the Confederate military leadership including "Stonewall" Jackson.[17] The decisive Seven Days' Battles, from June 25 to July 1, when General McClellan was forced to retreat from outside Richmond by the daring attacks of the new Confederate commander, Robert E. Lee, did elicit gushing admiration for the southerners and yet more distain for the Union army. Martin stated, with no attempt to conceal his feelings:

> MACLELLAN and his army taking to their heels, hotly pursued by the Southerners. Ha! Ha! Ha! Hurrah, the biter bit, follow them up Southerners, don't give them time to rally, warm the Hides of the Northern Braggarts 'twill do them good. The Northerners appear to wish it to be understood that their *retrograde* movement was a deep stroke of strategy, *pshaw! tell that to the Marines....* [18]

With the failure of the Peninsula Campaign the scene of operations returned once more to northern Virginia, where the two armies met again at the second battle of Bull Run on August 29 and 30, 1862. On the Union side General McClellan had been replaced by General Pope who suffered a humiliating defeat at the hands of the Confederates led by Generals Lee and Jackson. Martin's contempt of the northern troops, but respect for the southerners, was once more conspicuous:

> **Another Great Battle at Bull's Run**
> On the 29th August last.
> SECOND EDITION, DOUBTLESS ILLUSTRATED WITH *CUTS.*
>
> Both sides, as usual in American warfare, claiming the victory - the Federals apparently losing ground daily.
>
> THE BLUSTERERS CATCHING A TARTAR
> **Jackson's the Boy for bewitching them.**
> HA! HA!! HA!!! HURRAH.
>
> Go-a-head *Stonewall, you're the boy for a* dash,
> The *Federal* Commanders you know how to thrash;
> Go on as you're doing, you've plenty of scope,
> And *polish* them off as you lately did POPE.[19]

General Pope's inept performance led to his replacement by McClellan who commanded the Federal army in the Antietam Campaign that culminated in the great battle of September 17, 1862, the bloodiest single day of the entire war. The battle was indecisive, and McClellan missed a possible opportunity to inflict severe punishment on the Confederates as they withdrew. Martin was certainly correct in his facts when he wrote:

GREAT BATTLE OF THE 17th SEPTEMBER LAST.

DREADFUL SLAUGHTER

A Sort of drawn Battle, *as usual* - the victory, if such it can be called, claimed by the Federals, as *they*, 'tis said, remained in the best position *after* the battle. Supposed to be about

TEN THOUSAND MEN
KILLED AND WOUNDED
ON EACH SIDE.

Martin admitted McClellan and his army had done well, but warned the Federal military leader not to be too elated as the southern commanders were capable and likely to restore the situation. Martin again expressed the opinion that Britain and France should seize the first chance to offer mediation to end what was *"Brutish, Bloodthirsty, Fratricidal,* and *Disgusting War."*[20] Ironically, it was the turn of events in favour of the North at Antietam, and President Lincoln's announcement of the Preliminary Emancipation Proclamation five days later on September 22, that deterred any European attempt at mediation.

After Antietam the northern and southern armies did not engage in any offensive actions for several weeks despite the pressure President Lincoln tried to put on McClellan to move. Martin was again quite right when he wrote on November 8, 1862, "Fault found with GENERAL MACLELLAN for want of strategy; indeed his supposed lethargy appears to have been openly discussed, so much so, 'tis reported, that he is likely to be, if he is not already, superseded by a GENERAL HOOKER." Martin continued in verse:

MAC, to advance, seems inclined to refuse,
Because his brave men are in want of new shoes,
Their clothing's worn out, which each man much feels,
But the main thing with them seems the use of their *heels*.

Once more, as in the Crimean War and Indian Mutiny, Martin leapt to the defence of commanding officers, this time those serving the Union cause, whom he felt were subject to ignorant criticism. He noted, however, that anyone who could measure up to northern expectations would need to be a miracle of perfection. By contrast Martin wrote about "the Wide-awake *Confederate Commanders* and their well-disciplined armies, where *General* and men evidently keep their respective positions, and having confidence in each other, work together like a piece of machinery...."[21]

Martin was right in anticipating yet another change in Union commander, General McClellan being relieved of his command for a second time on November 7, but his replacement was not General Joseph Hooker but Ambrose E. Burnside, a fact that Martin corrected in an advertisement devoted to news from America on December 6, adding, "New Besoms Sweep Clean."[22] On December 13, 1862, Burnside's army was crushingly defeated by the Confederates, commanded by Robert E.Lee, at Fredericksburg, suffering appalling casualties. Martin reported the news at the beginning of January 1863 with such headlines as **"THE NORTHERN BRAGGARTS WHIPPED AGAIN," "WELL DONE CONFEDERATES!"** and **"DEFEAT, RETREAT, AND FLIGHT OF THE POTOMAC ARMY."** He wrote of the dreadful slaughter at Fredericksburg, and wrongly attributed Burnside's ill judged advance as due to political pressures. On this occasion his verses were somewhat better than usual:

The Rappahannock's been crossed, But Burnside's defeated;
Serves him quite right, as he seemed too conceited.
He took the command with decision and boldly,
But the Potomac army received him but coldly.

They possibly thought that MAC, was the man
To lead them to glory, tho' by a slow plan;
So when MAC, was marched *off*, and BURNSIDE marched *on*,
Their hopes of great victories seemed to have gone.

The army felt hurt, as they thought it was slander
That caused them to lose their much loved commander;
And tho' willing to think that BURNSIDE was smart,
The change, at the time, made the army lose heart.

AMERICAN NEWS.

THE NORTHERN BRAGGARTS WHIPPED AGAIN.

WELL DONE CONFEDERATES!
PRACTICE MAKES PERFECTION.
YOU'RE DOING YOUR WORK NOBLY.

BATTLE OF FREDERICKSBURG.

(A Small Town, or rather *was* a small Town (having been almost battered to the ground by Federal Artillery), on the South side of the Rappahannock river, in Virginia, containing about from Four to Five thousand inhabitants, and situated in a beautiful Valley, about Sixty miles from Richmond by Railway, and has Railway communication with Washington.)

DEFEAT, RETREAT, AND FLIGHT OF THE POTOMAC ARMY.

DREADFUL SLAUGHTER, DISGUSTING SIGHTS.

THE Plains of Fredericksburg, truly like a Slaughter-house, 20 to 25 thousand Federals, 'tis said, killed and wounded, having been mowed down like grass, and mutilated horribly, by the well served artillery of the Confederates, and the Rappahannock river studded with bloated and bursting corpses, by the well trained Confederate riflemen. Panic stricken state of the Federal army, demoralized, dispirited, disheartened, repulsed at all quarters by the superior tactics of the Confederates, and the scattered remains of the once great army ignominously chased to their former position on the opposite side of the Rappahannock from Fredericksburg, and by an enemy that they felt inclined to despise, but which is daily proving too many for them.

LOUD AND VEHEMENT FAULT-FINDING WITH THE FEDERAL GOVERNMENT.

Fearful responsibility on their heads, if the glaring military blunders that has so continuously taken place during the war, and which has caused the sacrifice of so many brave men's lives, can be attributed to *their* incapacity for the position they hold. 'Tis said that General Burnside was decidedly opposed to attacking the admirably arranged Confederate entrenchments at Fredericksburg, well-knowing, from his military knowledge, that he had little, if any, chance of succeeding, *but was peremtorily ordered to do so by his Government*. Shame! shame!! that a Commander's reputation should be trifled with, and thousands of brave men's lives sacrificed (for, that the Federals fought bravely, there seems to be no doubt) by the shallow-brained acts of civilians in office assuming military knowledge in preference to military Men, evidently showing their unfitness for Office by inability to comprehend the magnitude of their political responsibilities.

Pshaw! such men should retire. They might possibly find themselves more in their element sitting by their firesides *nursing sucklings*.

Magnificent tactics and manœuvres by the Confederates. Burnside evidently caught in a trap, and his army uselessly (for the Federals) sacrificed in thousands, like so many vermin, by the tiers of Confederate cannon in their semicircle front of nearly *twenty miles*—and cannon *well served* by brave disciplined and well trained soldiers.

The Rappahannock's been crossed, But Burnside's defeated;
Serves him quite right, as he seemed too conceited.
He took the command with decision and boldly,
But the Potomac army received him but coldly.

They possibly thought that MAC. was the man
To lead them to glory, tho' by a slow plan;
So when MAC. was marched *off*, and BURNSIDE marched *on*,
Their hopes of great victories seemed to have gone.

The army felt hurt, as they thought it was slander
That caused them to lose their much loved commander;
And tho' willing to think that BURNSIDE was smart,
The change, at the time, made the army lose heart.

But the trumpet's loud blast bids divisions advance,
Thus, to make up for *Bull's Runs* they had a fair chance,
But at double quick time—and urged to go faster—
Their gallantry ends in defeat and disaster.

The South gained the day on the thirteenth of December,
A day that the North will sadly remember;
For tho' BURNSIDE is brave, he's let all the world see
He's no match in tactics for JACKSON or LEE.

The doings of the Confederates are manifestly gaining on the sympathies of Europe, which can hardly be wondered at, as there is a natural inherent feeling in mankind to admire bravery either in friend or foe. But really the sooner the North makes arrangements for separating from the South, the sooner they will likely have peace of mind, as *their* glory in warfare is apparently fearfully costly *to them* in human life—indeed, it looks very like as if they had taken a much larger job in hand than they are able to manage *to their own* satisfaction.

SO THINKS

MARTIN THE HATTER.

MARTIN's Stock of HATS, CAPS, &c. &c. is very large at present.

Best Quality, London-made Satin HATS, 18/ each.

Magnificent Satin HATS, Light, Easy Fitting, and Durable, 6/6, 8/6, 9/6, 10/6, 12/6, 13/6, 15/6, and 16/6 each.

UMBRELLAS, PORTMANTEAUS, LEATHER HAT CASES, &c. &c. VERY CHEAP.

Observe!

SAMUEL MARTIN,
HATTER TO THE PEOPLE,
34, UNION STREET (WAREHOUSE ABOVE SHOP),
ABERDEEN.

Established Twenty-FOUR Years.

But the trumpet's loud blast bids divisions advance,
Thus, to make up for *Bull's Runs* they had a fair chance,
But at double quick time - and urged to go faster -
Their gallantry ends in defeat and disaster.

The South gained the day on the thirteenth of December,
A day that the North will sadly remember;
For tho' BURNSIDE is brave, he's let all the world see
He's no match in tactics for JACKSON or LEE.[23]

The heavy losses suffered in the Civil War, especially by the North, repeatedly led Martin to hope for a peaceful settlement,[24] and he appears not to have realised that the nature of the war had changed with President Lincoln's emancipation proclamations of September 1862 and January 1863, neither of which he mentioned.

The early months of 1863 saw another period of tension in Anglo-American relations. There was in the United States simmering resentment over the activities of British owned blockade runners and the building in Britain of the famed Confederate ship *Alabama*, even though the Foreign Enlistments Act of 1819 had not technically been breached, as the depredations against northern owned shipping rose steadily. On the other hand feelings ran high in Britain over the detention by the Union authorities of British ships for alleged violations of the blockade. In February 1863 the *Peterhoff* was seized in the Caribbean, even though she was bound for Matamoros in Mexico, and an American prize court upheld the seizure on the grounds that her cargo of war supplies was obviously going to be transshipped by land into the Confederacy. Moreover, the Confederacy was still contracting to build or purchase additional ships in Britain, either for commerce raiding or to break the Federal blockade of southern coasts. Naturally the North made every attempt via diplomacy to block these endeavours and threatened counter-measures against such ships. On April 5 the British government ordered the seizure of the *Alexandra*, a commerce raider intended for southern service, which helped to defuse the situation, although no resolution regarding the fate of the so-called "Laird rams" was achieved until that September.

As it happened *The Aberdeen Journal* made more mention of the deterioration in Anglo-American relations than did *The Herald*. The subject made an appearance in the editorial columns of *The Aberdeen Journal* in every number in April 1863. At the beginning of the month there was a reference to a debate in Parliament on the "much-agitated question of the construction in British ports of vessels of war for the Confederate States of America," and at the end of April the paper reported that, "The seizure of British ships by American cruisers is creating an intense feeling in the public mind, and that feeling has extended to both Houses of Parliament. The question was discussed very calmly in the Lords, and taken up very hotly in the Commons."[25] This background probably explains Martin's sudden intemperate outburst against the United States in April, when all his anti-American prejudices and assumptions found full rein. Martin claimed that Britain, "well knowing her power, continues, *as yet*, to look on the Northerns in their present deplorable condition with commiseration and noble magnanimity, well knowing that she has really done nothing to deserve the ill-feeling which they have so continuously displayed towards her of late," and protested that British forebearance and philanthropy had been met by insolence, arrogance and impudence. American conduct might well lead to war, and in that event Martin trusted British forces would:

> Mow down the ranks of their rapidly-made rabble regiments with the RIFLE, annihilate in scores their *farcical-looking* and *ludicrous-acting officers*. Surely such men and officers will never be allowed to stand before the well-disciplined and gallant rank and file and officers of the BRITISH ARMY. Never! Never!! Chase them from the battle-fields, where only well-drilled soldiers should ever appear, trample them under foot, send them flying to their cities to mind merchandise, which may suit their abilities better than trying to be soldiers; and if it is to be war, spare them not. Spread their carcasses over the land, and let those that run away hurry home to manufacture penny whistles and wooden nutmegs.
>
> **BRITAIN, BE READY.**
>
> The time is apparently fast approaching when your iron-sided ships of war may possibly have an opportunity of practising and showing their power upon the house-roof-looking iron-clad gun-boats of the Northern Yankees, which appear to have neither stem nor stern, and often 'tis said refuse to obey their helm.[26]

Happily, the diplomatic situation did not degenerate even further, so that Martin's prognosis was never put to the test.

Meantime, after the disaster at Fredericksburg General Burnside was in his turn replaced, and command of the northern Army of the Potomac passed to General Hooker, who fought the battle of Chancellorsville in early May 1863. Once again the Confederates were victorious under General Lee's daring direction. Martin believed the North and the "bombastical Hooker" had been *"outwitted, outgeneralled,* and *humiliatingly defeated"* by the superior military knowledge and tactics of the Confederate officers, and the North had lost its last chance of victory:

> ...Thus the Northern President seems to be in a mess of bungling, and should make the best of a bad job. Abraham, Old Boy, try and find out some good excuse for giving up the War. Steep your brains, old fellow; 'tis evident that you are not able to subdue the South. You've doubtless done your best, though some people may think that matters might have turned out different if the Northern Presidency had been in some other man's hands.[27]

By mid 1863 the fortunes of war changed again with the double Union triumph in early July of the Confederate surrender at Vicksburg, the capture of which gave the Federals control of the Mississippi Valley and cut off the Trans-Mississippi southwest, and the northern victory at Gettysburg. Martin's first comments on Gettysburg were of a southern success and of panic and consternation in the North. Given the actual military situation Martin's observations were, on this occasion, singularly at variance with reality:

> ...the Southerns have *already* shown to the world by their *indubitable courage, noble magnanimity of mind, singleness of purpose, admirable perseverence under difficulties almost incredible, determined bravery,* and masterly strategic movements, that they have *fairly earned* and are *entitled* to their *independence* - having shown to the eyes of admiring Europe that they are a people possessed of attributes *not only* for governing but for *maintaining* their *independence* as a Nation of the Earth.[28]

Martin quickly revised his appreciation of the situation as more accurate intelligence became available, but chided the North for not following up its success at Gettysburg and noted that Lee had retired in good order.[29]

After Gettysburg the war in the eastern theatre in 1863 settled down to a renewed stalemate, followed in 1864 by a war of attrition. Not surprisingly, therefore, Martin turned his attention to the western theatre in late 1863. On September 9 Federal forces occupied Chattanooga, Tennessee, but when they moved further south they were severely defeated on September 19 and 20 at Chickamauga and forced to fall back on Chattanooga where they were virtually besieged. Martin made mention of the actions around Chattanooga on October 24, but it was not clear from his text to what stage of the campaign he was referring.[30]

From October 1863 until May 1864 Martin's readers had to go elsewhere to find news and comment on the American Civil War. This hiatus was probably not so strange, as Martin had found other topics of interest to divert and entertain his audience, namely the European diplomatic situation and the war between Denmark and Prussia abroad, and plans to erect a statue to Queen Victoria in Aberdeen at home.

Martin was genuinely shocked by the "manifest unnecessary loss of human life," "the awful Sacrifice" and "butchery" witnessed in 1864, especially as he saw no prospect of victory for either side.[31] In August Martin was able to report on what has been described as the most awesome spectacle of the war, the explosion that was the prelude to what became known as the Battle of the Crater. In an attempt to break the Confederate defences around Petersburg, that in turn defended the southern capital of Richmond, the Federals drove a tunnel more than five hundred feet under a rebel battery, filled the excavation with four tons of explosives, and detonated it on the morning of July 30. The earth literally erupted, killing three hundred Confederate soldiers and creating a huge crater. Unfortunately, the Union infantry attack designed to follow up this explosion went disastrously wrong, and the Confederates rallied swiftly to inflict enormous losses on the attackers. Martin's description was a reasonably accurate account of the effects of the explosion and the awful mêlée that followed, but his following remarks are of interest. He wrote:

> The Darkies were as usual placed at the front, and they, well knowing their comrades' often practiced style of fighting, after firing one volley at *their then exasperated foes*, took to their heels, the *Whites* not being slow in running after them, *doubtless to bring them back to their duty*, but not before they lost six or seven thousand men in killed and wounded.

This is the first, albeit condescending, remark by Martin referring to the use by the North of coloured troops. In fact the original battle plan had called for the Union infantry attack to be led by coloured troops, but fearful that such action would lead to the accusation that black soldiers were being used as cannon fodder, the plans were changed at the last minute, a factor which contributed to the débâcle that followed. In this engagement, as in many others, the coloured troops fought with bravery and distinction.[32]

By September 1864 Martin was interesting himself and those who read his advertisements in the pending American presidential election. Neither General McClellan, who had reemerged as the Democratic Party nominee on a peace platform, an odd situation given McClellan's military background, nor Abraham Lincoln, who was seeking re-election, received Martin's endorsement. The Aberdeen sage wrote:

> That there is a strong feeling in the minds of many American people that Old ABE has not shown himself the man for the position might well be supposed. If, for no other reason than the apparent fact that he appears to have little, if any more than ordinary, political talent; indeed, some of his enactments show an intellectual capacity little fitted for his elevated position. Doubtless he has shown a great aptitude for anecdotes and jokes; but when the welfare of a Continent containing millions of human beings depends upon SERIOUS ANSWERS TO SERIOUS QUESTIONS AT SERIOUS TIMES, anecdotes and jokes may be so much out of place as almost to become *crimes*.[33]

Martin hoped for a bold, good man to come upon the American scene, one fit to fill the presidential office, but had to admit by late October that Lincoln was gaining and McClellan losing ground in the race for the White House.[34] Lincoln's re-election was headlined by Martin in November,[35] and owed much to the improved military prospects of the North.

Although Martin was still expressing optimism about the Confederacy's political and military situation at that time,[36] it was only a month before he found himself describing, with severe disapproval, General Sherman's famed march across the southern state of Georgia from Atlanta to the sea. According to Martin the northern army was:

> ADDING fresh laurels to their great fame as marauders, by their sagaciously planned and fearlessly carried out attacks upon old men and women.

> Farm steadings burning in all directions, the flames lighting up the Country for Miles by night, and the smoke well nigh Suffocating all around during the day; roofless houses in hundreds, their late happy, but defenceless inmates sent adrift homeless to wander, perish with Cold, or Starve in the open Country, it matters not which to the admirable Federal Spoilers, they're not particular. The ruins of barn-yards, dairies, cow-houses, hen-roosts, and pigstys, lying in heaps around, having been gloriously attacked and levelled with the ground by the spirited invaders. Hay, Corn, and Straw stacks Smouldering at all Corners, having been ruthlessly set fire to and destroyed by the gallant fellows, because not Wanted for immediate use. Officers and men t'would appear outvieing each other in their fiendish work, showing admirable zeal and activity in bringing up their Battalions and Cannon against helpless Citizens and plough-boys. This, it seems has been, and continues to be, the work of the Federals in Georgia, and it may well be supposed that such doings would not be tolerated, were they not in strict accordance with the orders of the Federal Government, nor so devilishly carried out by officers or men were they not led to believe that they were performing the *pleasant* duty under the full sanction of their precious President, and in accordance with Sherman's ideas of subjugating the Southerns.[37]

The new year, 1865, saw northern successes in all directions, Fort Fisher, which guarded the entrance to the Cape Fear River and the city of Wilmington, North Carolina, and last significant southern port that blockade runners could still use, was captured at the second attempt on January 15, after an embarrassing failure by the notorious General Butler in late December 1864. Sherman was now advancing through the Carolinas and threatening General Lee's rear, and the South was reported to be extending peace overtures.[38] Even at this stage, with the Confederacy on the edge of defeat and disintegration, Samuel Martin still lavished praise on the southern military performance.[39]

Given the drama in America it was perhaps surprising that Martin's copy on April 22 should be devoted to the subject of hats! General Lee surrendered to General Grant on April 9, 1865, and other southern armies soon laid down their arms. On April 14 President Abraham Lincoln, while attending the theatre was shot by John Wilkes Booth and died the next morning. Lincoln was succeeded in office by Vice-President Andrew Johnson, who in his youth had been apprenticed to a tailor. Martin did not report the end of the war, Lincoln's assassination and rumours of Jefferson Davis' complicity until June 3, but then did so in verse:

The Northern President's may act well enough,
But Johnson, late Tailor, seems made of queer stuff;
He fain would look large but he's cross in the grain,
And would crush gallant Davis with a murderer's stain.

But the Knight of the Thimble, Needle, and Thread,
In wreaking his vengeance is fast going a-head;
To destroy a good man his evident aim is,
But he'd better not injure Jefferson Davis.

To mix up brave Jeff with Abe's assassination,
Looks like a dodge to create a sensation;
So Andy keep quiet, your Jefferson's Jailor,
And that's a great honour for a Jolly old Tailor.

Doubtless, the old saying's well known in the North,
That in making a coat cut according to cloth;
Thus, in steering States' ship, use your helm like a sailor,
And don't run aground, you Jolly old Tailor.

Abe, done well, and would have gone on quite smooth,
Had he not met his death by the player Wilkes Booth;
But America sinks if discretion should fail her,
So act with discernment, you Jolly old Tailor.

Tho' Jeff's shown the world he's a northern disturber,
'Tis a different matter to charge him with murder,
So Andy, be *aisy* and hear Jeff's disclaimer,
Don't be harsh to a foe, you Jolly old Tailor.

Hanging and quartering are not pleasant sights,
But David can claim a Belligerent's rights;
He fought for the South, and tho' freedom's a failure,
Show mercy, tho' strong, you Jolly old Tailor.

And tho' Davis's back is now at the wall,
'Tis too bad to charge him with old Abe's fall,
But Jeff's in a mess, and t'will be no easy matter
To get safely out, so thinks MARTIN THE HATTER.[40]

While Martin's advertisements appeared in *The Herald* every week without fail, the actual text changed approximately every four weeks. Between March 1861, when he first commented on the threatening situation in the United States, and June 1865, when he made his final observations, Martin published forty-eight different advertisements, and of these no less than forty-one were devoted in whole, or in substantial part, to the American scene. The public of Aberdeen could not complain that their local oracle was reluctant to speculate on the trans-Atlantic fratricidal struggle. Yet, despite the fact that Martin obviously followed events in the United States closely, it would be difficult to argue that this was the practical hatter at his most perceptive and most entertaining. Martin shared, and indeed epitomized, many of the prejudices, condescensions, suspicions, resentments and jealousies that the press, the politicians and the people of Britain felt in relation to the United States. Martin's chauvinism, his excessive patriotism, were clearly revealed in his arrogant tone and the unconcealed distain and even contempt he showed for the northern states at least. His reaction to the *Trent* affair and to the diplomatic crisis of early 1863 was bombastic, and showed him engaging in the kind of verbal excesses for which he condemned the North. He constantly cast doubts on Federal political and military leadership, and on the ability, if not the courage, of Federal troops. In doing so, and in suggesting that the Yankees were good only at the pursuit of profit, he unconsciously echoed exactly what the South had always maintained about the North. On the other hand Martin was a consistent admirer of the Confederacy's attempt to establish its independence, and he heaped as much praise upon southern generals, especially Jackson and Lee, as he did opprobrium on their northern counterparts. Martin's jingoism and vainglorious comments about the British army and Royal Navy in comparison to American forces serves only to reveal his narrow patriotism and his failure to appreciate the new styles of military and naval warfare that were emerging during this conflict. In fact Martin often employed a light-hearted tone in reference to events in America that the seriousness of the conflict and the enormous casualty rate, 620,000 dead, did not justify. Although initially Martin condemned slavery there is little evidence that he appreciated what was at stake in the American Civil War, and he made no mention of Lincoln's emancipation proclamations. Given that President Abraham Lincoln's greatness was not always appreciated in his own day and even by his own people it is hardly fair to condemn an Aberdeen hatter for a similar lack of insight.

The value of Martin's advertisements at this time is the light they shed on public interest in American affairs. Martin knew what his readers' tastes were, and his announcements both revealed and reinforced these popular prejudices.

NOTES

1 See Chapter Two, pp30-31.

2 *The Herald*, March 23, 1861, p4, col 2.

3 *The Herald*, May 25, 1861, p4 col 2. Martin was right that the bombardment was bloodless. Between them the two sides fired about 4,000 to 5,000 shells, but as the garrison of the Fort quickly retired from the ramparts no one was fatally injured, though a horse on neighbouring Morris Island was killed by an errant shot. The only death occurred on April 14, after the surrender on April 13, when during the ceremonies marking the evacuation of the fort an accidental explosion killed one of the garrison and injured five others, one of whom died later.

4 *The Herald*, June 22, 1861, p4, col 2. Martin also stated:

But MARTIN, the Hatter, hopes that North and South
Will soon come to their senses,
And Each and all will soon march home,
And pay their war expenses.

He also referred to his magnificent assortment of satin hats, splendid for summer wear, his scientific knowledge of his business and his far-famed establishment.

An account of the Ellsworth incident is given in Allan Nevins, *The War for the Union, Vol I, The Improvised War 1861-1862* (1959), pp145-46.

5 *The Herald*, July 27, 1861, p4, col 2.

6 *The Herald*, August 10, 1861, p4, col 2.

7 *The Herald*, October 5, 1861, p4, col 2.

8 *The Herald*, November 23, 1861, p4, col 2. Martin wrote sarcastically:

The American War is now at its height,
But, both sides appear most unwilling to fight;
With Armies in motion each other to shun -
Doubtless, afraid of another "Bull's Run."

The North threatens Boldly, and so does the South
But the *Pluck* of them all seems to lie in their mouth,

Peace suits *them* best - for, if War has its charms,
Americans don't show it by the deeds of their *arms*.

9 *The Herald*, December 14, 1861, p4, col 2. For full detail of this particular Anglo-American crisis see Norman B. Ferris, *The Trent Affair*, (1977).

10 *The Herald*, January 11, 1862, p4, col 2.

11 *The Herald*, January 25, 1862, p4, col 2.

12 *The Herald*, March 1, 1862, p4, col 2.

13 *The Aberdeen Journal* published a short account of the fight of March 8 and 9 on March 26, 1862, p3, col 4, and made reference to it in its editorial "THE WAR IN AMERICA" on p8, col 1. *The Journal* carried a more detailed account of the engagement on April 2, p6, cols 3-4. *The Herald* printed an account of a "Naval Battle - Iron-Clad Ships," on March 29, 1862, p3, cols 4-5, and in an editorial that week, p6, col 1, remarked "By far the most interesting part of the news, however, is the naval engagement at the mouth of James River."

See also William C. Davis, *Duel Between the First Ironclads* (1975).

14 *The Aberdeen Journal*, April 9, 1862, p8, cols 1-2.

15 *The Herald*, April 12, 1862, p7, cols 2-4.

16 *The Herald*, May 24, 1862, p4, col 2.

17 *The Herald*, July 5, 1862, p4, col 2.

18 *The Herald*, July 19, 1862, p4, col 2.

19 *The Herald*, September 13, 1862, p4, col 2.

20 *The Herald*, October 4, 1862, p4, col 2.

21 *The Herald*, November 8, 1862, p4, col 2.

22 *The Herald*, December 6, 1862, p4, col 2. Martin celebrated Burnside's appointment with four verses of more than usually indifferent quality. Aware of his own limitations Burnside had, in fact, already twice declined command of the Army of the Potomac, and he accepted the third offer reluctantly.

23 *The Herald*, January 3, 1863, p4, col 2. Burnside's lasting contribution to history is the word "sideburns," as a consequence of his famous mutton-chop whiskers.

24 *The Herald*, February 7, 1863, p4, col 2, where Martin offered eight stanzas on the subject of the war's stalemate and the need for mediation. He added:

But if the North and South Americans are determined to persist in *fighting it out*, they might, for variety, put a little more romance and chivalry into their war. Let them take a look into the history of chivalrous Scotland; then let their *two brave, hair-splitting, if not wood-splitting* Presidents be armed *cap-a-pie*, and choose fifty followers each, mounted upon fiery chargers, and let them appear in the tented field determined on death or victory; and when the brazen trumpet sounds the charge, let them meet mid-way in the deadly strife - those that gain the victory dictating terms of peace to the side of their conquered foes. But Americans, perhaps, prefer their present systematic way of murdering each other *cooly* in thousands by the sword and disease to having any fixed *principle* either in their *fighting or what they are fighting for.*

Martin made a similar suggestion for Lincoln and Davis to meet in single combat to decide the outcome of the war in *The Herald*, June 18, 1864, p4, col 2.

25 *The Aberdeen Journal*, April 1, 1863, p8, col 2; April 8, 1863, p8, col 1; April 15, 1863, p8, col 1; April 15, 1863, p8, cols 1-2; and April 29, 1863, p8, col 1. On April 25, 1863, p3, col 6, *The Herald* carried reports from the *New York Evening Post* and *New York Herald* that Secretary of State Seward was sending despatches to the American Minister in London, Charles Francis Adams, containing strong remonstrances to the British government over war vessels being fitted out for the Confederacy in Britain and hinting at reprisals.

26 *The Herald*, April 25, 1863, p4, col 2. The iron-clad monitors Martin refers to certainly were unwieldy, but effective in some circumstances.

27 *The Herald*, May 23, 1863, p4, col 2.

28 *The Herald*, July 18, 1863, p4, col 2.

29 *The Herald*, July 25, 1863, p4, col 2. Also *The Herald*, August 15, 1863, p4, col 2.

30 *The Herald*, October 24, 1863, p4, col 2. This advertisement also contained some disapproving comments regarding President Lincoln, whom Martin accused of talking much but doing little. Rather interestingly Martin included a reference to the visit of the Russian fleet to New York in 1863, though he was sceptical about the sudden Russian demonstration of support for the United States, as well he might be since the Russian fleet's courtesy call had more to do with European affairs and rivalries than the American situation. See Gerald Carson, "God Bless The Russians," *Timeline*, Vol 3, August-September 1986, pp2-17.

31 *The Herald*, June 18, 1864, p4, col 2, and July 16, 1864, p4, col 2.

32 *The Herald*, August 20, 1864, p4, col 2.

33 *The Herald*, September 17, 1864, p4, col 2.

34 *The Herald*, October 22, 1864, p4, col 2.

35 *The Herald*, November 26, 1864, p4, col 2.

36 *The Herald*, November 26, 1864, p4, col 2, refers to Jefferson Davis's bold defiance and to General Lee's thwarting of Grant's attempts to advance on Richmond.

37 *The Herald*, December 31, 1864, p4, col 2.

38 *The Herald*, February 4, 1864. Martin described General Benjamin Butler as **"The Ladies of New Orleans Favourite,"** a reference to the fact that as Union military commander of New Orleans, May-December 1862, the controversial Butler made himself obnoxious to the South, in particular by his notorious order that any woman who continued to insult northern soldiers "shall be regarded and held liable to be treated as a woman of the town plying her avocation." In the First attack on Fort Fisher the Union troops were commanded by Butler and the fleet by Admiral David Porter. For the second attack Butler was replaced by General Alfred Terry. Braxton Bragg was the senior Confederate officer in the area, though not actually the garrison commander in Fort Fisher. An understanding of these responsibilities makes clear Martin's comment:

'Tis said that the ADMIRAL was disgusted after keeping up a continuous fire so long that BUTLER did not attack at the proper time and take the *Fort at once*, while BUTLER 'twould appear seems to think that he would have taken the *Fort* in glorious style if the ADMIRAL *had done his duty*. Thus it seems they have been amusing themselves with crimination and re-crimination, but

PORTER was strong and frothed for a while
Yet BRAG defended Fort Fisher in style,
BUTLER'S nerve fail'd in the hour of his need
If not frighten'd at heart he looked like it in deed.

But, PORTER annoyed at his recent retreat
Got TERRY to put him again on his feet,
Thus PORTER and TERRY have carried the day,
And that is the end of Fort Fisher affray.

39 *The Herald*, March 18, 1865, p4, col 2.

40 *The Herald*, June 3, 1865, p4, col 2.

CHAPTER FIVE

ROYAL EVENTS AND ROYAL STATUES. 1861-1866.

The American Civil War did not absorb all of Samuel Martin's attention in the years 1861-1865. As ever he found the comings and going of the royal family and state occasions provided opportunities for him to manifest his loyalty, and there were always events on the Continent to divert his readers. It should never be forgotten that Martin was a businessman, and his advertisements not only amused the good citizens of Aberdeen, they also kept his name and his shop in the public eye. When Martin had opened his business in 1838 the population of Aberdeen had been in the region of 65,000, but according to the "Seventh Decennial Enumeration," held in 1861, the figure had risen to nearly 74,000.[1] The number of potential customers had thus increased substantially, and Martin made every effort to attract their attention.

The annual visit of the court to Balmoral in September 1861 drew forth from Martin his usual expressions of fidelity together with praise for the scenic beauty of Deeside, where:

> The cloud-capped mountains seen afar
> Lead travellers on to Lochnagar,
> While wood and water both combine
> Other scenes to make sublime.

Martin admitted there was no news as yet to suggest that the Queen intended to bestow a knighthood on him that year, but that happy event might not be too far away.

> And should the knightly sword on Martin fall,
>   He might feel a little dizziness,
> But would accept the honour for
>   Minding his own business.
>
> And would wear the honour with an air
>   In accordance with his station,
> Which to the Queen might ever be
>   A source of consolation.

But Knight or not, the fact's quite plain,
As that the Town-House has a steeple,
That Martin's fame's spread far and wide -
The Hatter to the People.[2]

Martin's admiration for the monarchy and other British domestic institutions led him to hold up the British constitution as an example to the United States. Queen Victoria warranted special praise, always happy in the midst of her subjects, as recently at Fettercairn. Martin continued, "Long, long may HER MAJESTY, Prince Albert, and all the members of the Royal Family be spared health, and may HER MAJESTY ever find herself *happy* and at HOME in her autumnal trips to, and *around*, the heather-clad hills of her lovely Highland Residence, at Balmoral."[3] Regrettably, Martin's good wishes for the health of all members of the royal family were to be confounded in the near future.

In the midst of the *Trent* affair, before the United States agreed to release Mason and Slidell, Prince Albert, whose moderating influence had helped to soften the language used in the British despatches, was suddenly taken ill and he died on December 14, 1861. Across the nation there arose the desire to erect some tangible memorials to Prince Albert, and Aberdeen was not backward in this feeling. Lord Provost Alexander Anderson convened a public meeting, held only six weeks after Prince Albert's death, on January 23, 1862, for the purpose of "promoting a Memorial to the late lamented Prince Consort." The meeting was described as enthusiastic and influential, the problem faced being not to raise sufficient money for a memorial, but to agree how to spend it, whether on a simple statue or for the foundation and support of an institution bearing the prince's name. However, it was ascertained that the Queen preferred a statue, and Baron Marochetti was given the commission.[4] That Martin approved of the decisions taken may be deduced from the fact that his name appeared in the press on April 12 as having given two guineas toward the funds for raising a "Memorial Of His Late Royal Highness the Prince Consort."[5] On October 13 Victoria emerged from the seclusion into which she had withdrawn on Prince Albert's death to unveil the statue, then situated at the north-west corner of Union Bridge. Despite appalling weather a dense crowd turned out to pay their respects.[6]

Meantime, Martin took the opportunity to assail the Budget in April

1862. He still found the reduction of the paper duty as ill-advised as he had in 1861, wanted taxes reduced on sugar, tea, and beer, complained of the "inquisitorial Income Tax" kept at ninepence in the pound, and offered his own substitute proposals designed to lower the tax burden on the industrial classes.[7] One part of the country where working people were in distress, due to the shortage of raw cotton caused by the American Civil War, was the cotton manufacturing area of Lancashire, and Martin showed that his concern was real, and not just verbal, by contributing five guineas to the Relief Fund for Distress in Lancashire.[8]

Martin was able to show concern for another group of people in a different kind of distress in early 1863, though this time his support could only be verbal. Once again Martin, no admirer of Russia, mirrored British public opinion in voicing his sympathy for the Poles in their rebellion against a tyrannical Czar. Martin described the Poles as a brave people goaded into desperate actions by Russian repression.[9] Unfortunately for the Poles the balance of power in Europe and the self interest of the major nations was such that no one went beyound mere remonstrance over the situation.

On a happier note, on March 10, 1863, the Prince of Wales married Princess Alexandra of Denmark, and Samuel Martin exhorted Scotland and Aberdeen to demonstrate their devotion and duty to their queen and country. He wrote:

> **ABERDONIANS,**
>
> GET THE STEAM UP AND KEEP IT UP,
>
> enter *heartily, enthusiastically,* and with *life* and *true British spirit* into the festivities, and the displays on Tuesday, 10th March, ever keep in mind that it is from acts that conclusions are drawn, remember that HER MAJESTY and the PRINCE OF WALES have often been, and 'tis to be hoped, often will be among you, thus, your doings on *Tuesday* should stand *peculiarly conspicuous,* and may be remarked and commented upon in *foreign lands by you countrymen far from the land of their forefathers, its heath and its heather,* their hearts glowing with true Scottish pride and satisfaction on hearing that their friends at home have so nobly done their duty. Then, ABERDONIANS, stand forth, and stand forth in style, put true patriotic spirit into your rejoicing on *Tuesday,* show to the world that *Spirit, Bravery,* and *Loyalty,* are ever to be found in the *Granite City.*

Martin went on unabashed to describe Queen Victoria as a model

Queen, wife, mother and widow, the Prince of Wales as, "strongly imbued with his mother's virtues, his mind doubtless strengthened by her example," and Princess Alexandra as possessing many virtues and an amiable disposition.[10]

On the day itself Martin obviously did his best to enter into the spirit of the occasion. *The Herald* reported:

> Union Street was the favourite resort of the numerous wanderers during forenoon. It was a gay sight, but not nearly so gay as we have seen it on that ever-memorable occasion when the Queen passed through Aberdeen to Haddo. Still, the display was extensive. Samuel Martin, Hatter to the People, again attracted numbers to look in at his upper window, in front of which he had a neatly assorted collection of flags; and, just seen inside, was the gentleman himself, dressed *à la* Garibaldi, lustily blowing loyal tunes out of a bugle.11

In May Martin was able to wish long life to the happy couple,[12] and at the beginning of June there was the Queen's birthday to commemorate. Both *The Aberdeen Journal* and *The Herald* devoted space to local responses, *The Journal* noting that the occasion was "celebrated most loyally and becomingly by all classes here on Saturday last," while *The Herald* commented that the day "was observed with every proper demonstration of quiet loyalty." Government offices were closed, flags waved from the Town House and the shops of all the royal tradesmen, while the shipping in the harbour was dressed in gay colours. *The Herald* added, "Mr Martin, Hatter to the People, though not technically a 'Royal' tradesman, being an extremely 'loyal' one, hung out also during the day his very tastefully arranged group of neat bannerets."[13]

Fresh opportunity for a demonstration of Martin's affection for the royal family followed very closely with a visit by the recently married Prince and Princess of Wales to Scotland in August 1863. Martin gave vent to his loyal feelings in his familiar poetical style under the title "The Prince and Princess of Wales among the 'Birks of Abergeldie.' "

> Long Life to the PRINCE and the PRINCESS of WALES;
> May they enjoy the world's pleasures, and miss all its gales;
> May they ne'er be inclined to give each other pain; -
> So welcome to Scotland, Britain's loved Dane.

The sons of Old Scotia, the land of the heather,
All wish 'midst the "Birks" you may enjoy the fine weather;
They're anxious to please you - their love you'll retain -
So welcome to DEESIDE, Britain's loved Dane.

You're very much loved, and may have heard of the matter
That you're highly esteemed by MARTIN THE HATTER;
He thinks you are good, and he'd be greatly to blame
If he *did not esteem* Britain's loved Dane.

But while loving you much, Scotland still loves another,
And that, dear young PRINCESS, is your husband's kind mother.
Yes; the Scotch Love the PRINCE and YOU handsome Dane,
But wish that VICTORIA may be long spared to reign.

In all the positions she ever has been
She has ever shown herself a thorough good QUEEN;
Then Hurrah for VICTORIA! long, long may she reign!
Good health to HER, the PRINCE, and YOU, pretty Dane.[14]

Only a month later Martin again burst forth in his own brand of verse, this time to welcome Queen Victoria herself to Balmoral.[15]

At this point a simmering diplomatic crisis in Europe came to the boil, a crisis made more difficult for Britain by the recent royal wedding uniting the British and Danish royal families. The crisis concerned the relationship of the crown of Denmark with the twin duchies of Schleswig and Holstein which dated back to the Middle Ages. In November 1863 Frederick VII of Denmark died without a direct heir and the crown passed to Christian of Glücksburg, a member of a collateral branch of the family, but Christian's claim to the duchies was disputed by Frederick of Augustenburg who had support from some of the German princes and people. The details need not concern us here except to note that they were extremely complicated and open to different interpretations. Palmerston once joked that only three people had ever really mastered the Schleswig-Holstein question, and one was dead, one insane, while the third had forgotten it., Palmerston had written to Russell, the Foreign Secretary, on April 5, 1860, that the whole affair was "more intricate than any Sphynx's riddle, and more difficult to unravel than any Gordian knot."[16] However, the dispute had the potential to escalate into a general European war.

On November 5, 1863, Napoleon III proposed a European Congress to consider not only the Schleswig-Holstein crisis and the Polish question, but also a revision of the treaties of 1815. The French suggestion allowed Samuel Martin to reiterate his distain for Napoleon III, whom he referred to as pompous, conceited and arrogant. He continued:

> **THE EMPEROR OF FRANCE**
>
> Calls loudly for a European Congress. *Modesty in the extreme!* Yes NAPOLEON THE THIRD calls for a Congress, possibly with an idea of remodelling the Map of Europe in accordance with *his* ideas, ripping up old sores which even *Napoleon salve* may not be able to heal if once again opened, yes! the man of yesterday, whom a breath of political wind in a manner *blew* into his present position and which he may lose by a *returning breeze*; whose main objects have ever apparently been *Political Superiority and anxiety to form a Dynasty*, and not appearing over-scrupulous in attaining them, *if* attained. Yes, Napoleon calls for a Congress!

Martin made it clear he was against any such Congress and advised Lord Palmerston accordingly.[17] However, by the time of Martin's declaration the British government had already decided to reject the French proposal, and did so in brusque terms. Martin was, naturally, delighted that the scheme for a Congress had been knocked on the head, and he headlined his advertisement on December 26, 1863 **"ALL'S WELL THAT ENDS WELL."** He added modestly that he had thought from the first that any Congress would have done more harm than good, and that British statesmen seemed to have taken the same point of view.[18]

The complicated diplomatic situation grew more threatening in early 1864 with many of the parties involved playing a double game. Martin was aware that affairs were serious, and on January 23 he headed his latest announcement:

FIX BAYONETS! SHOULDER ARMS!!

EYES FRONT!!! STEADY!!!!

- - - - - - - - - - - - - -

GLOOMY APPEARANCE ON THE CONTINENT.
THE SEVERAL POWERS APPARENTLY SUSPICIOUSLY
WATCHING EACH OTHERS MOVEMENTS.

Martin believed, with some cause, that while trying to look as though they were anxious for peace, the powers were actually preparing for a war that was likely to break out very soon. Should this happen then *"Let Britain at once buckle on her armour* (No dilly-dallying, the time has come for *acts*, the *time* and *feeling* for *Conferences* is past), and at any rate be prepared, if *not* to strike, to show her power by being prepared to avoid any blow that may be aimed at her; for however *willing*, Britain will likely find *She's* not *able* to avoid being mixed up with the coming fray."[19]

In fact, Prussian and Austrian troops invaded Schleswig on February 1. Denmark promptly appealed to Britain where public opinion was strongly opposed to the action taken by Prussia and Austria. However, although some of Lord Palmerston's statements in 1863 had perhaps encouraged the Danes to believe Britain would stand by them, he was unable to live up to any implied promises and for once was left looking a sorry figure. With the British government both unwilling and unable to take any action Danish military resistance was quickly overcome.

In April Martin was looking forward to an international conference to settle the Danish question, but remained suspicious of Napoleon III's motives, comparing the French eagle to a vulture. He still recommended that Britain take a strong line in protecting her own interests, and felt she might yet have to draw her sword to aid the gallant Danes.[20] Martin might have been disillusioned had he known that Queen Victoria opposed aid for Denmark, favouring policies she believed consistent with the wishes of her late husband.

As it happened a conference on the Danish problem opened in London on April 25, but broke up on June 25 having reached no conclusions. Martin complained in May that the conference was dragging on without result, hinting it was Napoleon III's fault. He acknowledged that the British Lion had lately been looking somewhat sheepish, and lacked his usual sagacity and foresight, but was now rapidly recovering from his lethargy.[21]

A new conference opened on July 25, a preliminary peace was signed on August 1 by which the King of Denmark renounced all his rights in the duchies in favour of the Emperor of Austria and the King of Prussia, and a definitive peace treaty was signed in Vienna on October 30. Thus ended a rather sad affair, although it turned out to be one that planted the seeds of disunity between Austria and Prussia and helped lead to war between them in 1866.

During the months when the Danish problem was attracting public attention nationally, another, and happier issue, was absorbing the interest of Aberdonians. After a series of preliminary discussions and suggestion, a meeting of those favourable to the erection of a statue of Queen Victoria in Aberdeen was held in Trinity Hall, Union Street, on Tuesday, January 19, 1864, with Councillor Leslie in the chair. At the meeting three resolutions were passed:

> I. - That, in consideration of the happy and prosperous reign of her Majesty Queen Victoria over these realms, of the influences which her Majesty's presence have so often brought to bear on the City and County, and of the many marked honours which her Majesty has seen fit to confer on this part of her kingdom, we, her Majesty's loyal subjects in the City and County humbly desire to commemorate the reign of her Majesty; and that the deep and loyal feelings of our attachment to her Majesty's person may be handed down to our posterity, as the loving tribute of a grateful people to a virtuous and beloved Sovereign, it is resolved to erect a statue of Her Most Gracious Majesty in a conspicuous part of this City.
>
> II. - That, in order to the successful carrying out of the said movement, this meeting resolve to open subscription lists in such a form that it may be within the power of all classes in the City and County to assist in the furtherance of this laudable object.
>
> III. - That with the view to encourage native talent, it is agreed to intrust the work to Mr Alexander Brodie; and the following gentlemen have consented to act as a Committee (with power to add to their number) for forwarding the object, by raising subscriptions, &c. (Here followed the names of a large Committee.)[22]

Such a project was certain to enjoy Samuel Martin's hearty endorsement, and when the subscription lists were opened his name appeared for the sum of three guineas.[23] In fact, he had already devoted an entire advertisement on February 27, 1864, to the project. It began with reams of praise for Victoria and reference to her close relationship with Aberdeen and its people and their mutual affection, and concluded, as might be expected, in verse:

> Up with the Statue to Britain's loved Queen;
> Let it be handsome, complete, and well seen;
> Let the site be well chosen, the best that's in town,
> For a more beloved Queen ne'er wore a crown.

WELL DONE! ABERDEEN!!

RIGHT AGAIN.

GO A-HEAD

WITH THE STATUE TO THE QUEEN.

KEEP THE STEAM UP, DON'T FAG.

DO IT IN STYLE, REMEMBER, "WHAT'S WORTH DOING IS WORTH DOING WELL."

HURRAH! FOR BRITAIN'S BELOVED QUEEN!!

NEVER was there a QUEEN on the British Throne that deserved the Love of her Subjects more than Good QUEEN VICTORIA.

NEVER was there a QUEEN on the British Throne that's done more to please her people by her kindly, amiable, and QUEENLY, aye, womanly feelings and conciliatory considerations for their welfare than good QUEEN VICTORIA.

NEVER was there a QUEEN on the British Throne who apparently more appreciates the knowledge that her Subjects are aware that their comfort and well-being are among the greatest Solaces to her bereaved heart.

NEVER was there a QUEEN on the British Throne who so well deserved the Love and Respect of *the People of Aberdeen* than good QUEEN VICTORIA, having honoured Aberdeen more by her recent acts than she ever honoured any other city in the realm, thus openly showing her partiality for the locality, and her peculiarly marked anxiety to please the inhabitants of the *Granite City*—and not on'y doing so, but giving loud expression to her gratified feelings, and her just appreciation of the truly Loyal and becoming manner in which she was received by the Aberdonians on a late momentous occasion—the becoming behaviour of the Vast Crowd that lined the streets on that occasion being in the highest degree gratifying, and feelingly appreciated by Her Majesty, *because being in strict accordance with Her Majesty's expressed wishes.*

ABERDONIANS, reciprocate these kindly feelings of your beloved QUEEN, surely one of the greatest worldly pleasures is the knowledge and pleasure of reciprocating good acts; and, oh! surely that exquisite pleasure must be greatly enhanced by the knowledge that such kind acts (in a manner nourishment to the life's blood) are in the highest degree valued and appreciated by the recipient, but when *that* recipient is a *Crowned Head*, and *that* Crowned Head *a Widowed* QUEEN, and *that Widowed Queen* VICTORIA, Britain's *adored* QUEEN, who lives in the hearts of her subjects. Oh, well may the feelings be excited to an admirable degree by touching the hearts of loyal subjects to do *their duty* not only in *words* but in *deeds*, and take delight in having an opportunity of not only showing the blessings enjoyed under *good* VICTORIA's reign, but also showing to the eyes of Europe that *Scotchmen's hearts and hands are ever where they ought to be when there's a duty to do to their* QUEEN or COUNTRY.

Forward, then, Aberdonians, to your Duty,

Keeping in view the sympathetic feelings that Her Majesty has on so many occasions shown towards the *working* classes of the country, it well becomes *them*, when they have an opportunity, to show that they are aware of Her Majesty's kindly disposition towards them. Thus, at the present time, *the Working Classes of Aberdeen and Aberdeenshire* have a gratifying opportunity, by the length of their Subscription List to the QUEEN's Statue, (which list, by the way, after being closed, should be neatly printed and circulated amongst the Subscribers; an extra neat got-up copy being handed to the QUEEN) to show Her Majesty how thoroughly her genuine goodness of heart and kindly disposition is understood by them, and having the *will*, avail themselves of this opportunity of causing their widowed QUEEN pleasurable emotions from the fact of knowing how much She is respected and has endeared herself to the hearts of *all classes* of her subjects, and at the same time making the STATUE as much as possible what it *should be*,

"THE PEOPLE'S" STATUE TO THEIR BELOVED QUEEN.

SO ABERDONIANS GO-A-HEAD WITH THE STATUE,

('twould be the very opposite to a compliment to HER MAJESTY *not* NOW to go on heartily with it). Remember

THE OBJECT'S GOOD.

THE PLEASURE PECULIARLY DEVOLVES UPON YOU.

Do your duty, and do it well.

As to the Site for the STATUE, 'twould look very well to arch over the *North-east* corner of St. Nicholas Street there, with the Pedestal placed in the centre of Granite Plainstones, 'twould be in a most commanding and attractive position, and with a handsome *Fancy and Gilt-topped or brightly Bronzed* railing round the corner,

THE "PEOPLE'S" STATUE TO GOOD QUEEN VICTORIA WOULD BE NEAT AND COMPLETE.

SO THINKS

MARTIN THE HATTER.

SO,

Up with the Statue to Britain's loved QUEEN;
Let it be handsome, complete, and well seen;
Let the Site be well chosen, the best that's in town,
For a more beloved QUEEN ne'er wore a crown.

In choosing the Site there should be no delay,
For on *that* much depends both style and display,
But there's no occasion to choose it in haste,
If a *little* delay shows "The People's" good taste.

Somewhere in Union Street would be the best place,
If about *there* could be got a good space;
But it must be conspicuous and easy to view,
Without these essentials it may please but a few.

St. Nicholas Street corner really would be
A very nice Site, "The People" may see,
Couldn't be better, tho' they gave a small bounty,
And would likely be pleasing to THE TOWN AND COUNTY.

And tho' *not* made of Granite there's no need to garble,
T'will look very well of Sicilian Marble.
The QUEEN, God bless her, is a nice canty bodie,
And the *Statue* may please if done by *A. Brodie.*

So up with the Statue, let all Scotland see
There's spirit and taste on the banks of the Dee;
Little more need be said on this p'easant matter,
But up with the Statue, says MARTIN THE HATTER.

MARTIN's Stock of HATS, CAPS, &c. &c. is very large at present.

Best Quality, London-made Satin HATS, 18/ each.

Splendid Satin HATS, Very Pretty, New Shapes, Light, Durable, and easy Fitting, 6/6, 8/6, 10/6, 12/6, 13/6, 14/6, 15/6, and 16/6 each.

UMBRELLAS, LEATHER HAT CASES, PORTMANTEAUS, &c. &c. very Cheap.

Observe!

SAMUEL MARTIN,

HATTER TO THE PEOPLE,

34, UNION STREET (WAREHOUSE ABOVE SHOP),

ABERDEEN.

Established Twenty-FIVE Years.

In choosing the Site there should be no delay,
For on *that* much depends both style and display,
But there's no occasion to choose it in haste,
If a *little* delay shows "The People's" good taste.

Somewhere in Union Street would be the best place,
If about *there* could be got a good space;
But it must be conspicuous and easy to view,
Without these essentials it may please but a few.

St Nicholas Street corner really would be
A very nice Site, "The People" may see,
Couldn't be better, tho' they gave a small bounty,
And would likely be pleasing to THE TOWN AND COUNTY.

And tho' *not* made of Granite there's no need to garble,
T'will look very well of Sicilian Marble.
The QUEEN, God bless her, is a nice canty bodie,
And the *Statue* may please if done by *A. Brodie.*

So up with the Statue, let all Scotland see
There's spirit and taste on the banks of the Dee;
Little more need be said on this pleasant matter;
But up with the Statue, says MARTIN THE HATTER.[24]

During the course of 1864 Martin had found one other source of speculation to amuse his readers. April 1864 was the tercentenary of the birth of William Shakespeare, and noting the occasion Martin wondered if it would become fashionable to celebrate the three hundredth anniversaries of the births of famous men. Thus, it seemed quite possible that his own tercentenary might be held in 2114. Unfortunately the present generation would be unable to witness this, which was a pity as they would be denied the discussion at that time as to whether Martin or Shakespeare was the greatest and most useful man of his age. Meantime, he would continue to sell hats as cheap as ever, "satisfied that the master minds of the year 2114 will have pleasure in holding the Tercentenary to him in a becoming style, showing him *up* to the eyes of the world at that time for *what he was*, and handing his memory *down* to posterity as one of the brightest shining lights amidst the many brilliant meteors of the go-ahead Nineteenth Century."[25]

For all his deviations on local, national and international affairs, Martin always remained a salesman, and he occasionally felt obliged to return to the subject of his business. He did so on December 31, 1864, when, at the end of another year of prosperity, he once more thanked the people for their support, and wished them all a happy new year. He also remarked that Old Father Time had laid his hand but gently on him, except, perhaps, for a few grey hairs. Otherwise he retained the faculties of body and mind.[26] Martin's commercial success was maintained in 1864 despite the appearance in the advertising columns of *The Herald* for a few weeks of announcements by E. Webb, 15 Market Street, advising the public of the availability of the new shape Prince of Wales hats. Webb had the audacity to claim to be "THE ONLY PRACTICAL HATTER IN ABERDEEN."[27]

Early 1865 brought the unexpected, and by now comparatively rare, sight of an advertisement by Martin that concentrated on his line of trade. He pointed out what an unpleasant sight a shabby hat was, how unnecessary in an age of prosperity and how men should emulate the example of the ladies who always displayed good taste.[28]

In both June and October 1865 Martin welcomed the Queen to Balmoral, in nine verses on the latter occasion.[29] However, when Victoria returned in June 1866 his muse worked even harder and produced eleven verses, although the last five were in praise of Deeside:

To people in business or other employment,
'Tis a treat up Deeside for country enjoyment.
The atmosphere's clear, being famed far and wide.
For its strengthening powers. The Bonnie Deeside.

Those that have *Shootings*, plump Grouse may soon scatter,
Pleasant amusement thinks MARTIN THE HATTER,
There's beautiful walks and mineral wells,
Viands are plenty, and there's first-rate Hotels.

You'll see HUNTERS and FISHERS and two landlord COOKS,
And you may fish in the River if ye prefer it to brooks,
The roads are all good, and there's no tolls to pay,
And you'll get up by Rail two or three times a-day.

In going by road, 'tis pleasant to feel
The sweet balmy air of Kincardine O'Neil,
And if you're inclined for Comforts within,
Refreshments are good at Kincardine Inn.

Talk of Swiss Scenery, of Scenes up the Rhine,
Of travelling cheaply and drinking good wine,
For Scenery and Comfort no need go so far,
There's plenty of both twixt ABERDEEN and BRAEMAR.[30]

On the occasion of the Queen's second visit to Balmoral in 1866, in August that year, Martin again lavished praise on the beauty of Deeside, but concluded by waxing philosophical:

There's "Sermons in Stones," aye! and sermons in trees,
There's Sermons in all things, if the mind so decrees;
The whole world's a Sermon, and Nature's the text,
Man's blessings are great, 'tis his mind that's perplexed.[31]

No doubt Martin took a keen interest in the progress of the Queen's statue. In September 1864 Victoria sat for the sculptor, Alexander Brodie,[32] and in June 1866 it was reported that work had begun on the preparation of the site at the juncture of Union Street and St Nicholas Street.[33] The actual ceremonial attending the inauguration of the statue took place on September 20, 1866, when the Prince of Wales performed the unveiling and later received the freedom of the burgh. Naturally, the events of the day were described in detail by the local press,[34] and *The Herald*, as so often on these royal occasions, making a point of commenting on Samuel Martin's personal and noteworthy contribution to the scene:

> The appearance of Union Street was especially good - gay and jubilant but without anything meritorious....Mr Samuel Martin, hatter to the people, was also prominent in his loyal demonstrations. There was not much in the ordinary way of display. There were flags; and a banner hung down the wall above the shop window appropriately announced - "Glad to see your Royal Highness. God Bless the Queen." There was a sort of bower of bliss in the first floor window, in the shape of a cluster of "ladyes fair," and in the centre Martin himself stood ready to proclaim his loyalty.[35]

The dramatic and tragic events in America had figured prominently in Martin's advertisements in the years 1861-1865 or even 1866, but had not prevented Martin from lightening the day of those Aberdonians who read *The Herald* with references to Continental affairs and the activities of the royal family. Martin reflected public opinion in his sympathy with the Poles in 1863 and continued Russophobia, and his support for Denmark and disapproval of the actions of Austria and Prussia over the Schleswig-Holstein affair struck another popular chord. Meantime, he seems to have sold a great many hats while maintaining his reputation as one of Aberdeen's most colourful characters.

NOTES

1 Population statistics for the City of Aberdeen, including St Machar, based on the census returns 1801-1861, are to be found in *The Herald*, May 18, 1861, p4, cols 2-3.

2 *The Herald*, September 7, 1861, p4, col 2.

3 *The Herald*, October 5, 1861, p4, col 2. As was only to be expected Martin added the verse:

MARTIN, *lately,* at CRATHIE passed the QUEEN,
And, altho' he was *not* knighted,
He saw HER MAJESTY looking well,
At which he felt delighted.

It is rather more difficult to see why he also wrote at this time:

Life, at best is like a running stream;
But some live on *milk*, while others get the *cream*.

4 *The Herald*, January 25, 1862, p5, col 2, and October 17, 1863, p6, col 1.

5 *The Herald*, April 12, 1862, p1, col 4.

6 The events of the day were described in *The Herald*, October 17, 1863, p5, cols 1-3, including the knighting, not of Samuel Martin, but of the Lord Provost of Aberdeen. Editorial comment may be found in *The Herald*, p5, cols 2-3, wherein the paper admitted, "The prevailing feeling as regards the Statue - why should it not be spoken out? - is one of decided disappointment. It does not realize the popular ideal of the Prince Consort, and does not reasonably approach that ideal. The Prince Consort probably never in his life assumed the spread-eagle attitude Baron Marochetti has adopted; and at all events, even the admirers of the figure will not venture to say that such an attitude is characteristic. We rather think that the venerated Prince would have shrunk from being thus seen in public -

certainly he would not have chosen to have his memory thus perpetuated. The military trappings and ribbands and bell-pull tassels and ornamental frippery are all alien to what we know of the quiet though earnest thoughtfulness and chastened unobtrusive dignity of the Prince." At all events at a later date, 1914, the controversial statue was removed, maybe the word is banished, to the far end of Union Terrace where it now resides in the shadow of the Wallace Statue. The site on the north-west corner of the Union Bridge is now occupied by the statue of King Edward VII.

7 *The Herald*, April 19, 1862, p4, col 2. Martin argued the industrial classes should be taxed "more in accordance with their circumstances."

8 *The Herald*, November 22, 1862, p1, col 3.

9 *The Herald*, March 14, 1863, p4, col 2.

10 *The Herald*, March 7, 1863, p4, col 2.

11 *The Herald*, March 14, 1863, p6, col 1. *The Herald* p6, col 6, included an S. Martin on the list of guests at the public Ball and Supper held in the Music Hall on March 10.

12 *The Herald*, May 23, 1863, p4, col 2.

13 *The Aberdeen Journal*, June 10, 1863, p4, col 6. *The Herald*,.June 13, 1863, p5, col 5. Presumably Martin did not attend the dinner of the royal tradesmen in the Royal Hotel thereby missing a bill of fare which included "some splendid haunches of venison, forwarded by the royal command...and served on a scale of liberality and good taste...the wines being also unexceptionable." He would also have missed Mr Ross' comic songs.

14 *The Herald,* August 15, 1863, p4, col 2.

15 *The Herald*, September 19, 1863, p4, col 2.

16 See Herbert C.F. Bell, *Lord Palmerston*, Vol II, p362. For background relating to the dispute and to public opinion see David F. Krein, *The Last Palmerston Government. Foreign Policy, Domestic Politics, and the Genesis of "Splendid Isolation"*, (1978), and Keith A.P. Sandiford, *Great Britain and the Schleswig-Holstein Question 1848-64: a study in diplomacy, politics, and public opinion* (1975).

17 *The Herald*, November 21, 1863, p4, col 2.

18 *The Herald*, December 26, 1863, p4, col 2.

19 *The Herald*, January 23, 1864, p4, col 2. Quite astutely Martin warned Prussia and Austria to watch their own back doors, as Hungary and Venetia might find Denmark's distress their opportunity to profit. Indeed Austria's room for diplomatic manoeuvre was restricted by what might happen in her own restive provinces.

20 *The Herald*, April 2, 1864, p4, col 2. Martin added:

Then Britain be firm, let Peace be your aim;
Let your wishes be known wide and far,

But, if Honour's at stake, you've no choice to make,
But put on your Armour for War.

21 *The Herald*, May 7, 1864, p4, col 2.

22 *The Aberdeen Journal*, January 20, 1864, p5, col 1, and September 26, 1866, p6, col 2. Also *The Herald*, January 23, 1864, p6, col 6 and p7 col 1.

23 *The Herald*, March 12, 1864, p1, col 3-5.

24 *The Herald*, February 27, 1864, p4, col 2. The reference in the fourth stanza to "The Town And County" may have been either a deliberate or unconscious use of double meaning, referring to the pleasure of both the city and county of Aberdeen, but more likely to the Town and County Bank which was then located at the corner of Union and St Nicholas Street. Martin also upstaged the modest official announcement, which appeared alongside his advertisement, regarding the proposed statue and opening of the subscription lists.

25 *The Herald*, May 7, 1864, p4, col 2.

26 *The Herald*, December 31, 1864, p4, col 2.

27 *The Herald*, March 5, 1864, p4, col 1. Webb's announcements appeared from March to May 1864.

28 *The Herald*, April 22, 1865, p4, col 2.

29 *The Herald*, June 3, 1865, p4, col 2, and October 21, 1865, p4, col 2. Martin added on November 4, 1865, p4, col 2, under the headline, "RECENT GREAT EVENTS," that "MARTIN THE HATTER saw 'the QUEEN' on Deeside, and the QUEEN saw MARTIN. He was delighted to see HER MAJESTY looking so well, and doubtless HER MAJESTY was equally well pleased to see MARTIN in his usual good health."

30 *The Herald*, June 16, 1866, p4, col 2. The references to HUNTERS, FISHERS and COOKS were to the proprietors of hostelries on Deeside. The building of the Deeside Railway had, of course, made the area infinitely more accessible to Aberdonians and to tourists as the line "And you'll get up by rail two or three times a-day" indicates. On July 7, 1866, coincidentally alongside Martin's announcement, the Deeside Railway Company ran its own advertisement for special cheap excursion trains during the Aberdeen annual holiday. There were similar announcements by the Great North of Scotland Railway and the Scottish North-Eastern Railway.

31 *The Herald*, August 25, 1866, p4, col 2.

32 *The Herald*, October 1, 1864, p5, col 3.

33 *The Herald*, June 16, 1866, p5, col 2, and September 8, 1866, p5, col 6.

34 *The Herald*, September 22, 1866, p4, col 6, and p5, cols 3-5. *The Aberdeen Journal*, September 26, 1866, p6, cols 2-5, and p8, col 3.

35 *The Herald*, September 22, 1866, p5, col 3. The subsequent history of the queen's statue might, or might not, have met with Martin's approval. In

January 1888, the month of Martin's death, the statue, which had not weathered well, was moved to its present location in the vestibule of the Town House. On November 9, 1893, a new statue of Victoria in bronze was unveiled at the junction of St Nicholas Street and Union Street. This second statue of Victoria was subsequently moved to Queen's Cross.

CHAPTER SIX

POLITICS AND REFORM. 1865-1868.

On July 7, 1865, parliament was dissolved and a general election followed. Martin, as was to be expected, endorsed the elderly Lord Palmerston and the Liberal cause. His advertisement in *The Herald* on July 22 began, however, with an exercise in alliteration rather more than political comment:

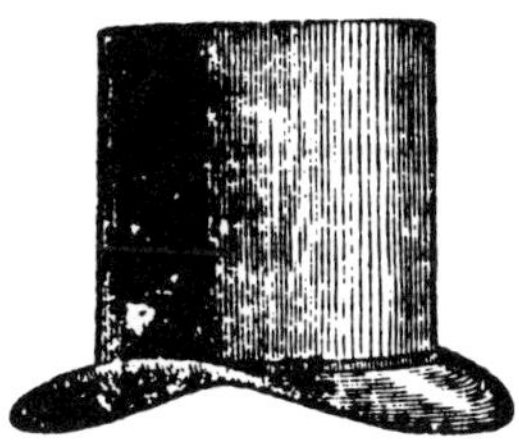

LOOKING

At the **P**rudential **P**olitical **P**olicy, and the **P**onderous **P**reponderating **P**eculiarly **P**leasant **P**rosperous **P**osition of the **P**rogressive **P**arties in **P**olitics, **P**rompting and **P**ointing to the **P**alatial **P**ositions of the **P**owerful, and to the **P**enetrating **P**ropensities of a **P**rominently **P**rudential **P**eople, **P**ertinaciously **P**erforming **P**erilous **P**erformances, with **P**ersuasive **P**rudence and **P**ertinacity, without **P**erturbation, **P**etulance, or **P**omposity, **P**hilosophically **P**ortrays a **P**hilanthropic **P**icture of a **P**eaceful **P**ersevering **P**eople, **P**rodigiously, **P**ungently, **P**otentially, and **P**roverbially happy in being **P**rovidentially **P**laced under the **P**rotection of a **P**re-eminently **P**ure **P**otentate.

Having caught the readers' eyes Martin assigned the electoral success of the government to the economic prosperity of the country, to the removal of obnoxious taxes during Palmerston's term of office and to a disposition by the voters to let well alone. Adding a local touch, Martin wrote:

> So, go-ahead Liberals, you're gaining the day,
> Keep up the steam, your talents display,
> Aberdonians, as usual maintaining their rights,
> *Their* duty have done and returned Colonel Sykes.[1]

In September British and French naval squadrons fraternized at Cherbourg, Brest and Portsmouth, a demonstration that the newly re-elected Palmerston hoped would help to ensure peace in Europe while also serving to deter any American ambitions by creating an appearance of European solidarity. Martin's insertion in *The Herald* on September 9, 1865, had a rather surprised and somewhat sceptical tone, though he added:

> But hurrah! for the FRENCH AND BRITISH JACK TARS;
> Wherever they meet may they part without scars.
> If true to each other, their foes they would scatter;
> They should cultivate Peace. So thinks MARTIN THE HATTER.[2]

In fact Palmerston had been seriously ill for some time, and, in addition, he was over eighty. He died on October 18, 1865, according to one biographer, "a hero to the mass of his fellow-countrymen."[3] He was certainly a hero to Samuel Martin whose favourite politician and patriot he had long been. In his advertisement for October 21 Martin included a eulogy edged in black:

> Weep! all ye Nations of the earth, the greatest man's away,
> His duty done to all mankind, he could no longer stay;
> Noble PALMERSTON, British Honour he ever had at heart,
> And now that he's received his call we find it hard to part.[4]

Of course, the death of Palmerston in office necessitated the choice of a new Prime Minister, and two weeks later Martin was able to comment on the selection of Lord John Russell to head the new ministry with Gladstone as Chancellor of the Exchequer and Leader of the House. Martin's advertisement said:

MARTIN THE HATTER.

NOT YET

SENT FOR.

But possibly "Her Majesty" may have an idea that though MARTIN *may* be the coming man for PRIME MINISTER, yet out of courtesy to an old friend, she would like EARL RUSSELL to try it first, but should he and the Ministry get to loggerheads as to a Reform Bill and other ticklish matters

"ALL MEN ACT THE PLAYER'S PART."

THE NEW MINISTRY.

INDICATION OF THE

MEMBERS WORKING

HARMONIOUSLY.

BUT AS TO THEIR DOING SO LONG REMAINS TO BE SEEN.

AS,

"Dissensions, like small streams, are first begun,
Scarce seen they rise, but gather as they run."

DIFFERENCES OF OPINION AS TO WHO SHOULD BE PREMIER.

"As in a theatre, the eyes of men,
After a well-graced actor leaves the stage,
Are idly bent on him that enters next."

BUT

Earl Russell has obtained the Honour.

Mr. GLADSTONE to remain Chancellor of the Exchequer, with the additional position (no trifling job) of being Leader of the House of Commons—a family of large boys, "Men are but children of a larger growth," often rather unmanageable.

MARTIN THE HATTER.

NOT YET

SENT FOR.

But possibly "Her Majesty" may have an idea that though MARTIN *may* be the coming man for PRIME MINISTER, yet, out of courtesy to an old friend, she would like EARL RUSSELL to try it first, but should he and the Ministry get to loggerheads as to a Reform Bill and other ticklish matters likely soon to be brought before the New Parliament, and the Country gets into a fix, and when it is plainly seen that Smart men, quick work, and Bold measures are expected, then, if "Her Majesty" should think so, that's the time to bring forward MARTIN. MARTIN has no reason to doubt but that "Her Majesty" knows that he will be found at 34, UNION STREET, Aberdeen, minding his own business. And, it is an old remark that a man that manages his own business *well* enjoys something like the germs to attain Legislative honours; and as MARTIN intends to keep his business, and has ever managed it *well*, and in the course of doing so, has never been either backward or timid in speaking on political matters, thus it may be inferred showing a good deal of Legislative knowledge. Hurrah! If he was *offered* and *accepted* a place in the Ministry, he might very likely have no objection to draw out his Legislative knowledge to its full extent, which *might* be a great blessing to the country, as a man may have his abilities hid from his country *if he never attains his proper position to show them.* But MARTIN would like a position where his income would *not be less* than Two or Three Thousand Pounds Sterling a-year, *and not much work*, as his philosophy has often caused him to observe that it is not always the men that work hardest that prosper most, and as Mr. GLADSTONE is apparently going to fill *Two* positions, clearly showing the powers and abilities of eminent men, MARTIN *naturally* thinks that He might also, "if not likewise" fill *Two* positions; but MARTIN wishes it to be distinctly understood that as he takes a pleasure in his business, and intends to stick to it, whatever Legislative position "Her Majesty" might be inclined to thrust upon him, whether PRIME MINISTER OR FOREIGN SECRETARY, MARTIN must ever be allowed to retain his proud title of HATTER TO THE PEOPLE.

MARTIN'S Stock of HATS, CAPS, &c. &c. is very large at present.

Best Quality, London-made SATIN HATS, 18/ each.

MAGNIFICENT SATIN HATS, NEW SHAPES,

6/6, 8/6, 10/6, 12/6, 13/6, 14/6, 15/6, and 16/6. Each.

FELT and SHELL HATS, NEW SHAPES, LEATHER HAT CASES, PORTMANTEAUS, UMBRELLAS, &c. & very Cheap.

Observe!

SAMUEL MARTIN.

HATTER TO THE PEOPLE,

34, UNION STREET (WAREHOUSE ABOVE SHOP),

ABERDEEN.

ESTABLISHED TWENTY-SEVEN YEARS.

RECENT GREAT EVENTS.

MARTIN THE HATTER saw "The QUEEN" on Deeside, and the QUEEN saw MARTIN. He was delighted to see HER MAJESTY looking so well, and doubtless HER MAJESTY was equally well pleased to see MARTIN in his usual good health.

likely soon to be brought before the New Parliament, and the Country gets into a fix, and when it is plainly seen that Smart men, quick work, and Bold measures are expected, then, if "Her Majesty" should think so, that's the time to bring forward MARTIN. MARTIN has no reason to doubt but that "Her Majesty" knows that he will be found at 34, UNION STREET, Aberdeen, minding his own business.

If Mr Gladstone was to be allowed to fill two positions, then if offered the post of Prime Minister or Foreign Secretary, Martin would also retain the proud title of Hatter to the People.[5]

At the end of the year, in reviewing the previous twelve months, Martin mused on the passing of great men, but consoled his readers with the thought that the country was never without men of talent, "She has her RUSSELL, her GLADSTONE, her GRANVILLE, her CLARENDON, her ARGYLE, and her MARTIN (THE HATTER), all men capable of throwing the brightest lustre around all legislative enactments emanating from them, in whatever position HER MAJESTY might see fit to place them." He thus managed to bracket his own name with those of five members of the cabinet. In bidding farewell to the old year Martin insisted that the country could no longer be governed by legislation that might have been adequate twenty or thirty years earlier, but was now hopelessly out of date. This may be taken as a fairly clear endorsement by him of the contemporary demand for electoral reform, as it was over thirty years since the last measure in 1832.[6]

Although reform of the franchise had not been the main issue in the general election of 1865, the question had been before the country for a number of years and it was widely assumed that the new ministry headed by Lord John Russell would address the problem. By 1865 there were great anomalies throughout the nation regarding the right to vote and the distribution of seats. Public meetings and debates in parliament generated a good deal of excitement, but it took time for particular schemes to emerge. Thus, in early March 1866 Martin produced an advertisement headlined **"DOINGS IN PARLIAMENT"** and expressing disappointment at the delay in producing any reform bill. (Gladstone actually introduced a reform bill on March 12). He then published ten verses on the subject of which the following are the first, fourth, seventh and tenth stanzas:

REFORM! Reform's the order of the day,
And, if required, no need for delay;
Earl Russell's inclined to please Mr Bright,
Then lower the Franchise if found to be right.

Procrastination, it seems and political strife
Is the way that M.P.'s now pass their life;
They battle away, raising many a storm,
But still appear anxious to stave off Reform.

The People, Earl Russell seems anxious to please,
But, about a Reform Bill seems ill at his ease;
He's pledged to the matter, of that there's no doubt,
But *details* he finds very hard to bring out.

Then Hurrah for "the People," if they get Reform
T'will likely be after the present snow storm;
Lowering hard taxes would be a great matter,
And please many people - so thinks MARTIN THE HATTER.

Continuing the theme of bad weather Martin derived some pleasure from the thought that the recent severe storms would take the shine off a good many hats, and thus soon increase his sales.[7]

By the end of April the chances of a reform bill passing had diminished rather than increased, giving Martin more reason to complain. He called for Lord John Russell to take a tighter grip of the situation, and noted that as so many M.P.s had been paying the working class compliments, that in itself suggested the franchise ought to be extended. Indeed, Martin wondered if some M.P.s were sincere in their commitment to reform.[8]

Almost at once Martin had a fresh opportunity to display his own political preference and enthusiasm. In May a parliamentary election took place in the County of Aberdeen due to the resignation of the Conservative member, William Leslie, on account of family illness. Mr Dingwall Fordyce stood in the Liberal interest and Sir James Elphinstone for the Conservatives. *The Herald* recorded the scene:

> ABERDEEN - Here there was excitement in abundance and that not confined to voters papers. The farmers came rattling into town in cobs, or gigs, or on horseback, gave their votes, and strolled through the city,

> waiting for the result; but, besides these, every lad and tradesman hustled and jostled to see what the state of the poll was as every fresh statement was published. Yellow favours - the Whig colour - were in great request throughout the day, and various placards in favour of the Liberal candidate were posted up during the day. The Majority from the first was in favour of Mr Fordyce, and continued steadily to increase as the day advanced. Among other displays yesterday, Mr Samuel Martin, hatter to the people, showed his zeal for the liberal cause by having several neat little banners floating from his windows, and a larger one commending the county voters in these words - "Well done, Aberdeenshire! Hurrah!" From the other window shot a poll with a branch of crape at the end, and a black cloth depending from it with an inscription expressive of mourning for the Tory cause - now presumed to be dead in the county. Mr Martin himself appeared occasionally at the window with a curious shaped hat - something after the fashion of a Parsee's head cover - with "Reform" printed over the front.[9]

This Liberal success was quickly overshadowed by the resignation of the Russell ministry on June 26 following a defeat on the reform bill in the House of Commons. Lord Derby immediately formed a minority Conservative government, with Disraeli as Chancellor and Leader of the House of Commons. Martin was not impressed by the new ministry which, he felt, looked remarkably like those of 1852 and 1859, writing "indeed, to use a homely saying, 'tis just **CAULD KAIL HET AGAIN."** In view of the dangerous state of the Continent, the Austro-Prussian War broke out on June 18, Martin wanted ministerial positions filled by men of ability regardless of their political leanings. Moreover, having observed the startling victories of the Prussian army, especially at Sadowa or Koniggratz only four days earlier, Martin demanded:

> ...at once arm the BRITISH ARMY and RIFLEMEN with that splendid weapon, the Breech-loading Needle-gun; let no mistaken economy cause this momentous matter to be overlooked and regretted *when too* late. Britain is not doing her duty to herself if she ever neglects having the best weapons in the hands of those who so well know how to handle them before their enemies; t'will be well to see to this matter *soon*, putting off may be dangerous; the weapon has proved itself to be the most deadly weapon of modern times, and to put off in matters of this kind is to endanger the very vitals of the country.[10]

Four months later Martin was making the same plea and backing the idea of an increase in pay for the services.[11]

When the time came to bid farewell to 1866 Martin felt it had not been a good year in national and international affairs with the failure to pass any reform bill, the Austro-Prussian War and the mistaken economy of the government in not spending more on defence. On the other hand his own affairs has prospered and he continued to enjoy good health.[12] He looked forward in 1867, despite the sharp weather in January, to better things, noting that this was an age of technological improvement. A properly thought out and well drafted reform bill was needed, not one so mutilated in committees as to be useless. Capital and labour both deserved to be given their proper status and recognition, and should be encouraged to work in harmony.[13]

When parliament met in February 1867 the details of any reform bill were still undecided, and a great deal of political mnoeuvring followed. Thus, Martin wrote on February 23, under the headline **"REFORM"**:

> "TO BE, OR NOT TO BE, that is the question;
> Whether 'tis nobler in the mind to suffer"
> The pangs and sorrows of disappointed hopes,
> At no Reform, or by a vote "no confidence,"
> Count the House and oust the Tory Ministry,
> Ah! t'would perhaps be well.

Martin also offered his readers no less than eighteen rhyming couplets, one for each of the leading members of the Derby administration, including Lord Carnarvon, Secretary for the Colonies, General Peel, Secretary for War, and Lord Cranborne, Secretary for India, all of whom actually resigned on March 2, over differences within the cabinet concerning the details of any reform measure. Nevertheless, Martin's advertisement continued to run unchanged until March 30. He wrote:

> The Colonial Secretary must keep people from starving,
> And thus show benevolence, the *Earl of Carnarvon.*
>
> \- - - - - - - - - - - - - -
>
> War, to avoid and fill his office with zeal,
> Seeme to be the wish of old *General Peel.*
>
> \- - - - - - - - - - - - - -

PROGRESS.

"The most superficial glance at the present condition of European States shows that those Nations which linger in the race cannot hope to escape the partial diminution, and, perhaps, final annihilation of their resources. It is with Nations as with Nature, which knows no pause in ever-increasing movement, development, and production—a curse ever cleaving to **standing still.**"

REFORM.

"TO BE, OR NOT TO BE,
that is the question;
Whether 'tis nobler in the mind to suffer"
The pangs and sorrows of disappointed hopes,
At no Reform, or by a vote "no confidence,"
Count the House and oust the Tory Ministry.
Ah! t'would perhaps be well.

The *Thirteen* resolutions all may deplore,
Luck ! in odd numbers, oh ! say it no more.

Let those that work hardest pay the smallest taxation,
'T would be *really* Reform and sound legislation.

This is the Ministry *their talents* wont hide,
'Tis a pity they're not on the Liberal side.

Derby looks firm, not inclined to go out,
But may be forced by Earl Russell or a *touch of the gout.*

D'Israeli looks calm, gentle, and kind,
But there's danger a-head when *he* draws it mild.

The Chancellor's smooth, and gets on with accord,
There's no doubt he's clever, old *Lord Chelmsford.*

The President means well, and quite above sham,
He's active and lively the *Duke of Buckingham.*

The Lord Privy Seal does'nt do things in a hurry,
But he works very well, the *Earl of Malmesbury.*

The Home Secretary's willing to please, on the whole,
He ever means well, *Sir S. H. Walpole.*

The Foreign Secretary ever shows himself manly,
There's fame in the distance for gallant *Lord Stanley.*

The Colonial Secretary must keep people from starving,
And thus show benevolence, the *Earl of Carnarvon.*

War, to avoid and fill his office with zeal,
Seems to be the wish of old *General Peel.*

India's Secretary o'er famines may mourn,
Do your best to avoid them *Viscount Cranborne.*

Admiralty's Lord his duty wont shun,
So keep up the Navy, *Sir J. Pakington.*

The Board of Trade President wont let things rot,
He has an eye to his business, *Sir Stafford Northcote.*

The Commissioner of Works, firm to Tory banners,
Will doubtless do his duty well gentle *Lord John Manners.*

The poor have a friend neither backward nor tardy
He's a go-ahead sort of Gentleman *Gathorne Hardy.*

Lancaster's fair Duchy will be managed quite even
The Work's to be done by the smart *Earl of Devon.*

The Post Office Matters, as all might suppose,
Will be managed quite well by the *Duke of Montrose.*

Ireland's Secretary's clever, so report says,
But to keep *Fenians* quiet may be hard for Lord Naas.

THE LEADERS OF THE OPPOSITION
MAY SOON WITH TORY'S CHANGE POSITION.

RUSSELL and GLADSTONE, LOWE and JOHN BRIGHT
Eager for REFORM if the thing be done right.
May THEY soon pass A BILL and thus end the matter
T'would please many PEOPLE *and* MARTIN THE HATTER.

India's Secretary o'er famines may mourn,
Do your best to avoid them *Viscount Cranborne.*[14]

Six weeks later Martin was still deploring the failure of the government to pass a reform bill, condemning the "FIDDLE FADDLE STYLE" of the ministry, and lamenting the lack of political leadership in the country. He repeated his own opinion that the true source of national greatness was the welfare of the people, and that a reform bill enlarging the franchise was required as a matter of justice. If the existing political leaders did not meet the legitimate demands of the people then, Martin believed future leaders might well be drawn from humbler backgrounds. He added that he might himself "bring some *new* and useful ideas before Parliament were he a member of the House of Commons," and he would carry with him a fair amount of common sense to guide him if he were to become a member of the House of Lords. Indeed more common sense and less party spirit would benefit both houses and produce better legislation.[15]

In fact the Reform Act of 1867 became law on August 15, adding nearly a million new voters in place of the 400,000 who would have been enfranchised by Gladstone's 1866 bill. Provision was also made for a redistribution of seats in the House of Commons to take account of population changes since 1832. The Conservatives had blocked the Liberal measure as being too extreme, but then passed a more radical act themselves, thereby taking the famous "leap in the dark," and stealing their opponents thunder. Samuel Martin, however, was not impressed. He denounced the act as "infirm" rather than "reform," and protested, "PSHAW! the Bill is but a Half-Measure after all, not at all settling the Reform question, or the just rights of the people, but merely *another put off.* What might have been good parts of the Bill, made useless by the strictures that follow, in short, **'MUCKLE NOISE BUT LITTLE WOO'."** Martin characterized the act as belonging to a "mongrel breed, full of inconsistencies, difficult to understand," and a means of throwing dust into the eyes of the populace.[16]

In September Martin speculated, a little prematurely as it happened, on the retirement of Lord Derby. This would create a nice situation for a middle-aged man, and Martin explained the qualifications required of any successor:

- strong physical energies, fair amount of mental abilities, a physiognomy that would give no indication of the workings of the mind (without this requisite the chances of filling the position are small indeed), a volubility of language at all times ready, large amount of self-esteem and philosophy, a thorough knowledge of human nature, ingenious in argument, admirable in phraseology

BOLD AND LOGICAL IN DEBATE,

And an aptness that, at all times, would be ready to upset the arguments of opponents, if not by sound reasoning, by sarcasm (which often *takes* in large assemblies where ready *wit* and *sharp answers pass* for intellectuality, and often enable men to look thoroughly conversant on a subject under discussion, when they may simply be *picking up* information from the arguments of their opposers), a brightness ('tis so called), of intellect that would, on the spur of the moment, be able to throw such a haze around well-understood opinions, that, by a kind of subtle reasoning, would show, *apparently* plain,

THAT WHAT WAS GENERALLY WELL UNDERSTOOD YESTERDAY MEANS THE VERY OPPOSITE TO-DAY.

Martin, however, was sure the people of Aberdeen and Aberdeenshire would be delighted to learn that he was not himself a candidate for the premiership, and if offered the office by the Queen he would politely decline rather than cause any jealousy among others.[17]

At least on this occasion Martin did refer to his business and to the very large stock of hats, caps, etc., at prices ranging from eight shillings and sixpence to eighteen shillings. In satin hats the best selling shapes were the "Baron," the "Anglesey," and the "Beaufort," in felt hats the "Tyrol," the "Planter," and the "Cambridge," and in shell hats numbers "6," "24," and "33." All these styles were tastefully displayed in Martin's attractive windows. He also advertised leather hat cases, knapsacks and umbrellas. In his next announcement Martin went further and included a short history of the umbrella in Scotland.[18] Certainly, he claimed in December that trade was good and his practice of selling his wares at moderate prices enabled him to keep up his large business and to enjoy many of the comforts of life.[19]

His penchant for advertising and self promotion was also evident at the beginning of 1868 when he combined pleas for civic improvements, especially the cleaning of streets, a Scotch reform bill and provision for the redistribution of parliamentary seats north of the border (and a request

A RETIRING MAN.

LORD DERBY,

TIS' SAID, IS GOING TO GIVE UP POLITICAL LIFE.
HIS LORDSHIP MIGHT BE INCLINED TO EXCLAIM,

"I fly from care and strife,
And gently tread the downward path of life;
No more expose myself to fortune's sport,
The noise of war or whispers of a court;
In letter'd solitude, unenvied reign,
Admire the hills but live upon the plain."

OPENING FOR A PREMIER.

THE PRESENT PREMIER
LIKELY TO VACATE
SOON.

A NICE SITUATION
FOR A
MIDDLE-AGED MAN

WHO has the following qualifications—strong physical energies, fair amount of mental abilities, a physiognomy that would give no indication of the workings of the mind (without this requisite the chances of filling the position are small indeed), a volubility of language at all times ready, large amount of self-esteem and philosophy, a thorough knowledge of human nature, ingenuous in argument, admirable in phraseology,

BOLD AND LOGICAL IN DEBATE,

And an aptness that, at all times, would be ready to upset the arguments of opponents, if not by sound reasoning, by sarcasm (which often *takes* in large assemblies where ready *wit* and *sharp answers pass* for intellectuality, and often enable men to look thoroughly conversant on a subject under discussion, when they may simply be *picking up* information from the arguments of their opposers), a brightness ('tis so called), of intellect that would, on the spur of a moment, be able to throw such a haze around well-understood political opinions, that, by a kind of subtle reasoning, would show, *apparently* plain,

THAT WHAT WAS GENERALLY WELL UNDERSTOOD YESTERDAY MEANS THE VERY OPPOSITE TO-DAY.

A recklessness of results *in manner* without really meaning it (highly dispiriting to opponents), but which comes under the name of *good generalship*, by bringing round matters exactly as you wanted them by superior tact and *political* ability. A man with something like the above abilities might almost make the PREMIERSHIP a permanent situation, at any rate for a year or two, particularly if of an easy mind—

LOOKING UPON ALL SHADES OF POLITICS COOLLY WHILE HE'S IN OFFICE,

and reserving his right of opinion *that the politics* that enables him to *retain* office are at any rate right, *time being*. And if at last shov'd out of office, such a man's philosophy will console him with the knowledge that, in politics, as in other matters, the *blunders* of one generation are often remedied by the abilities of the next, and, while living upon the loaves and fishes *made in office*, may, while in comfort, exclaim—

"It is in vain
(I see) to argue 'gainst the grain,
Or like the Stars, incline men to
What they're averse themselves to do;
For when disputes are wearied out,
'Tis int'rest still resolves the doubt."

The people of Aberdeen and Aberdeenshire will, doubtless, be delighted to hear that

MARTIN THE HATTER

IS *NOT* A CANDIDATE FOR THE PREMIERSHIP.

Indeed, if HER MAJESTY (God bless her) was to offer MARTIN the position, he would politely decline it, as his accepting it would likely cause petty jealousies among LORDS, DUKES, &c. as they might consider it was infringing upon what they call their prerogative. Then

HURRAH! FOR THE QUEEN, AND HURRAH!! FOR THE PEOPLE.

THE PEOPLE'S COMFORT IS THE NATION'S SAFETY.

SO THINKS

MARTIN, THE HATTER.

MARTIN'S Stock of HATS, CAPS, &c. &c. is very large at present.

MAGNIFICENT SATIN HATS,

THE NEW SHAPES.

8/6, 10/6, 12/6, 15/6, 16/6, and 17/ Each.

Best Quality, London-made SATIN HATS, 18/ each.

The Shapes that MARTIN is Selling most of at present are

IN SATIN HATS—

THE "BARON," THE "ANGLESEY," AND THE "BEAUFORT."

IN FELT HATS—

THE "TYROL," THE "PLANTER," AND THE "CAMBRIDGE."

IN SHELL HATS—

NUMBERS "6," "24," AND "33," THESE SHAPES,

ARE TASTEFULLY DISPLAYED IN MARTIN'S ATTRACTIVE WINDOWS.

LEATHER HAT CASES, UMBRELLAS, KNAPSACKS, &c. VERY CHEAP.

Observe!

SAMUEL MARTIN.

HATTER TO THE PEOPLE,

34, UNION STREET (WAREHOUSE ABOVE SHOP),

ABERDEEN.

ESTABLISHED TWENTY-NINE YEARS.

for an increase in the number of Scottish M.P.s) with an acrostic:

M any pleasures in Dress we often may find,
A s articles vary in cut and in kind;
R eally well pleased with people we meet,
T o see how well dressed from the head to the feet.
I n Dress there's philosophy, no doubt about that,
N o articles so nice as a good-looking Hat.

H ow pleasant to view, so smart and so neat,
A man with a good Hat looks on the street;
T is pleasing to think the people all know
T hat to buy a nice Hat they've not far to go;
E very one's well aware - no need to flatter -
R esort to 34, Union St. - mind MARTIN the hatter.[20]

In fact, due to ill health, Lord Derby resigned as Prime Minister in February 1868 and was replaced by Benjamin Disraeli. So far as Samuel Martin was concerned 1868 had not begun well, and his advertisement in March contained the word **HUMILIATION** encased in a black box. Martin's response to the idea of Disraeli as Prime Minister was "Oh! Oh!! AND A GROAN!!!" and he asked the question, "WHO would have thought that the QUEEN, the LORDS, or the COMMONS, would have submitted to this; but surely it can only be for a short time ('tis so laughable) - merely to fill a *gap* until our legitimate Legislators put matters in order...." Martin's explanation of the situation was that:

Being troubled so often with attacks of the gout,
Noble Lord Derby was obliged to go out;
Disraeli stept forward, quite healthy, tho' thin,
What troubles *him* most is how to keep in.

Martin admitted that Disraeli has a fair amount of political and literary skill and might even be called clever, but he was inconsistent and fell far short of the ability and tone of his predecessors in office.[21]

As Disraeli still headed a minority government a general elction could not be delayed for long, and the Liberal leader, William E. Gladstone, forced the issue to some extent in March 1868 by openly proclaiming in the Commons that the time had come to disestablish the minority Church of Ireland. At the end of April Gladstone carried resolutions to this effect through the Commons, and Disraeli responded by declaring that a general election would take place in the autumn when the new electoral registers had been prepared.

Samuel Martin welcomed Gladstone's move and demanded justice for Ireland and equality of treatment for her with England and Scotland and the elimination of Irish grievances. "Then will THE SHAMROCK, THE ROSE, and THE THISTLE entwine with an heartiness pleasant to look upon, for the Comfort of our good Mother THE QUEEN, and the general stability and happiness of her Subjects in ENGLAND, IRELAND, AND SCOTLAND."[22]

Martin did not return to domestic politics until late October 1868, a month before the general election, when he voiced the opinion, probable as much based on hope as on anything else, that Gladstone was gaining and Disraeli losing ground. Martin called optimistically for progress in politics so that government would be free of personal or party aggrandisement and legislation framed not as part of some partisan manoeuvre but for general improvement. He also suggested a mode of selecting candidates for constituencies based on a list of qualifications that included the ability to ignore the question at hand and to amuse audiences rather than inform them.[23] On this occasion Martin's advertisement actually ran the full length of a column in *The Herald*.

The November general election was a triumph for Gladstone and the Liberals who had a majority of 112 in the Commons. If Samuel Martin made any public display of his political loyalty and his pleasure at the election results locally or nationally by decorating his shop or rendering tunes on his trumpet the Aberdeen press failed to take note on this occasion. Even so, it was little wonder that Samuel Martin was in good humour at the end of the year. He included in his advertisement for December 19 the Shakespearean quotation:

> "All the world's a stage,
> And all the men and women merely players;
> They have their exits and their entrances,
> And one man in his time plays many parts."

He went on:

> AND it may be said that MARTIN THE HATTER has, and continues to play his parts, and 'tis to be hoped plays them well, as a sort of *Philosopher, Politician,* and HATTER, incongruous parts it may be thought, but the *World* must judge of their truthfulness. But, whatever opinion may be expressed as to MARTIN'S right to claim playing the two former parts, there can be no doubt (as the fact is glaringly apparent) that he has played his part well as HATTER TO THE PEOPLE....It is now close upon *Thirty-One* Years since MARTIN showed the light of his countenance to the *Aberdonians*, a happy era in *his life*, and doubtless in the highest degree *pleasant* and *gratifying* to the *Aberdonians* themselves, as, during that time, MARTIN has sold to them many thousands of Hats, Caps, &c, making their heads warm, and keeping their minds serene, thus assisting vastly in sending Hundreds of *Aberdonians* forth to the world as *Shining Lights* in the *Arts*, the *Sciences*.... [24]

While Martin had devoted a good deal of attention in the years 1865 to 1868 to domestic politics, including as they did two general elections and the changes of leadership in both political parties, to say nothing of the manoeuvres culminating in the reform act of 1867, he still found time and space to pay his respects to the royal family and to sing the praises of Deeside, often combining these two tasks.[25] Indeed, Martin often acted as an enthusiastic one man publicity and public relations agency for Deeside, and there can be no doubting the sincerity of his comments, as in August 1866:

> Oh! what a pleasure at this time of year,
> Health to improve and spirits to cheer,
> Is a trip up to Ballater, then to Braemar -
> Getting up's easy, and its not very far.
>
> The scenery's grand, the air, oh! its charming,
> Deeside being famed for excellent farming;
> The mountains stupendous, and sweet heathery plains -
> Travelling's pleasant, there's well-arranged trains.
>
> 'Tis a land of romance, the hills look like iron -
> A land full of poetry, as shown by Lord Byron.
> Lovely phases of Nature you'll see wide and far,
> And grandest of sights snow-clad Lochnagar.

Such scenery's delightful, oh! what pleasure to see,
The sweet lying valley and the swift running Dee;
'Tis a sight mid'st its pleasures might cause happy tears,
And be a theme of delight for many long years.

Some rush to the Continent spare time to employ,
Thinking foreign scenery they're sure to enjoy;
Whereas, by taking a Guide-book in hand,
They'd find glorious scenery in their own native land.

Scotch Highland scenery is romantic and bold,
Before seeing it all you'd grow very old;
And altho' foreign scenery none need deride,
There's not much that's better than Bonnie Deeside.[26]

Martin's admiration for both the Queen and Deeside continued to be attested to in print during 1867,[27] and in May 1868, on the occasion of Victoria's first visit that year to Balmoral, he published no less than sixteen verses on the subject. Evidence of Martin's personal familiarity with the territory, and with the local hostelries, is to be found in the last six verses, which amounted to free publicity for favoured landlords:

BERRY is anxious to please,
  RAINNIE is equally so,
For a dinner and glass of good wine
  Banchory's a good place to go.

BARCLAY is pleasant to meet,
  There's a genial smile on his face,
To enjoy the sweet county air,
  Kincardine's a very nice place.

COOK'S at Aboyne is most pleasant,
  The Landlady, kind as a mother;
At Ballater, too, you will find
  The Landlady there such another.

Then as you step on to Inver,
  Admiring the scenery still,
The Inn is close by the road,
  Good viands you'll get from CARGILL.

HUNTER (Braemar), has a nice billiard room,
    And cheroots and cigars if you're smok'y,
FISHER also has comforts within,
    And a lawn for playing at Croquet.

Inns are first rate, society good,
    There can't be a doubt of the latter.
HER MAJESTY visits twice in the year,
    And so does MARTIN THE HATTER.[28]

The visits of the prince and Princess of Wales in August and of the Queen in September were also both recorded at length and in verse.[29]

Although domestic politics provided plenty of incident for Martin to record and to comment upon for the edification of his readers, there were, of course, selected foreign episodes as well. Martin clearly picked and chose which Continental or overseas events to introduce into his advertisements. His comments on the Austro-Prussian War of 1866 were surprisingly limited and given over mainly to concern about British preparedness, yet he devoted an entire advertisement in May 1867 to the question of the future of Luxemburg.[30] When that particular question was settled peacefully if not amicably Martin was able to report that the Continent was comparatively quiet, at least for the moment, though he considered the treaty signed in London regarding Luxemburg to be "a farce."[31]

At the beginning of November Martin was able to applaud one of his old heroes, Giuseppe Garibaldi, when the Italian patriot began a march on Rome, not yet part of a united Italy, in a vain attempt to capture the city. Martin was correct in observing that "gallant GARIBALDI'S success will likely be *short-lived*," as French intervention led to Garibaldi's defeat and temporary captivity.[32]

At the end of 1867 a magnificent villain presented himself to the British public in general and to Samuel Martin in particular. The unfortunate victim of national wrath was the Emperor Theodore of Abyssinia. Prior to the opening of the Suez Canal in November 1869 Abyssinia was an extremely remote area, and communications from the interior of the country to London via the port of Massawa could, and did, take months. In consequence the area was shrouded in mystery and romance, and was in addition the scene of religious confrontations between the forces of Christianity and Islam, and a field of intrigue between Britain and France. Theodore, (or Tewodros) formerly known as Kassa, came to power in 1855 and was at first seen as a vigorous and energetic reformer. Statements by many Europeans that Theodore was insane may well have been prejudiced, but understandably, as a man surrounded by religious and diplomatic power struggles, constantly threatened by armed rebellions and untrustworthy subordinates, he became obsessively suspicious. Feeling slighted by the failure of British governments to answer his letters Theodore began to imprison a number of Europeans including missionaries and the British consul, Captain C.D. Cameron, formerly of the Indian Army. Indeed the prisoners were held for several years, but the subject did not become prominent in Britain until the *Pall Mall Gazette* took up the story in 1865-67, partly because it was a wonderful human interest tale, partly because it increased circulation, and partly because as a journal with Conservative sympathies it tended to embarrass the Liberals. In August 1867 the Derby ministry decided on a military campaign to rescue the prisoners and to chastise Theodore, but delayed any public announcement until November. From that moment until confirmation of the successful conclusion of the campaign on April 27, 1868, news of the Abyssian Expedition dominated the papers.[33]

Samuel Martin's first mention of Abyssinia was on December 7, 1867, when he wrote:

THEODORE OF ABYSSINIA,
YOU'RE IN DANGER? OLD FELLOW,
and if you are guilty of even one-half of the crimes attributed to you, the penalty for your *British* doings should be
SHARP! SHORT!! AND DECISIVE!!!
A SMALL WAR, BUT VERY COSTLY.

However, Martin did not believe people would begrudge the cost and went on to praise the army and navy as the instruments that had made Britain great, powerful, prosperous and "made our magnificent constitution and glorious country the admiration of the world." He exhorted the commander of the expedition, gallant Sir Robert Napier, to bring the brutish Theodore to his senses. Then, with words reminiscent of his patriotic and racial sentiments during the Indian Mutiny, Martin wrote:

> Soldiers! now's the time. 'Tis a splendid opportunity to try the SNIDER GUNS upon Theodore's wild legions. Aim fair and fire away, brave boys,

> let no mistaken sympathies withhold your firm arms and bold hearts from keeping up a steady fire. Send it among them like hailstones - astonish the barbarians - scatter them like chaff. Let them really see what British Soldiers can do, and the war will likely soon be over.[34]

Early in 1868 the British expedition, which had actually come from India, began to advance due south from Massawa on the Red Sea toward Theodore's mountain stronghold of Magdala. Martin cheered enthusiastically from the sidelines, claiming that the British troops were anxious for the fun to begin, that this was a fine opportunity to gain experience with breech loading rifles, and that philanthropy before total victory would be a mistake. Martin added in typical patriotic vein:

> That's the way to deal with far off insolent braggadocio absolute monarchs. Trample upon their comparatively pigmy armaments, and thus keep up the pristine position of *Britain, the leading power of the world*, who, while ever anxious for peace with HONOUR, is ever prepared to chastise insolence and crush despotism *whenever* and *wherever* attempted against her Institutions or her Subjects....they'll astonish the Abyssinians, doubtless thrashing them to their hearts' content, which may possibly bring headstrong and bloodthirsty THEODORE to complete humiliation, or perhaps to destruction, *if* not to his senses.[35]

Sir Robert Napier's column encountered no opposition *en route* and by April 9 the British force was within sight of Magdala. In a gesture of reconciliation Theodore released his prisoners, but even so British troops stormed his fortress on April 13 and the emperor committed suicide rather than surrender or be captured. In fact, the campaign was virtually bloodless on both sides and from a military standpoint its importance and interest lay mainly in the logistical problems of moving troops from India to Massawa and then advancing hundreds of miles over wild and rough country. In that the captives were released, Theodore destroyed and British prestige restored the expedition was a success and the news of the capture of Magdala greeted enthusiastically in Britain at the end of April.[36]

Martin's advertisement published on May 2, 1868, was full of exaggeration and bombast. He proclaimed a glorious assault upon and the capture of Magdala, and took evident pleasure in the death of Theodore, "thus ending a *useless* life in a cowardly manner." Martin claimed, in a vast over estimate, that five hundred of the enemy were killed and fifteen hundred wounded without any British fatalities. Martin wrote with approval of troops with modern breech-loading rifles defeating primitive tribesmen, exclaiming, "Oh! what a grand scene to have viewed our gallant fellows peppering and doubling up the Abyssinians." His concept of the nobility and courage of the British soldiers in this action was clearly revealed when he wrote:

> Then Regiment after Regiment march up, all eager for the front, to have the first dash at the enemy - COOL and STEADY, ON, ON THEY GO - every man's heart as steady and firm as his hands, all prepared to die if needs be in maintaining the honour of their Queen and Country, and to let the world see what British Soldiers could do, *notwithstanding the great disparity in numbers, and impregnable looking* position of the enemy.[37]

Not for the first time Martin's patriotic exuberance had overtaken any sense of balance, but, of course, it must be remembered that he was not attempting to compose an accurate journalistic account or a thoughtful editorial. Rather he was indulging his chauvinism and sense of the dramatic, reflecting the mood and pride of his compatriots in the feats of the Victorian army engaged in imperial police actions, and maintaining his own reputation in Aberdeen as someone whose advertisements were highly unusual and worth a few moments to read for diversion if nothing more. Clearly his advertising technique also sold a lot of hats.

In the years 1865-68 Martin continued to have his finger on the pulse of public opinion. His support of the Liberals and parliamentary reform, his reverence for royalty and acceptance of social class, albeit he showed concern for the economic welfare of the lower classes, and his rampant patriotism, suspicion of and frequent contempt for foreigners, and unabashed racism were all marks of a man who epitomized mid-Victorian Britain.

NOTES

1 *The Herald*, July 22, 1865, p4, col 2.
2 *The Herald*, September 9, 1865, p4, col 2.
3 Herbert C.F. Bell, *Lord Palmerston*, Vol II, p420.
4 *The Herald*, October 21, 1865, p4, col 2.

5 *The Herald*, November 4, 1865, p4, col 2.
6 *The Herald*, December 30, 1865, p4, col 2.
7 *The Herald*, March 3, 1866, p4, col 2.
8 *The Herald*, April 28, 1866, p4, col 2.
9 *The Herald*, May 19, 1866, p5, col 4.
10 *The Herald*, July 7, 1866, p4, col 2.
11 *The Herald*, November 3, 1866, p4, col 2. Martin referred to "the most modern weapon of warfare, the famous 'Needle Gun'," and reminded readers he was the son of a British officer, and as such welcomed anything that improved the welfare and well-being of private soldiers.
12 *The Herald*, December 29, 1866, p4, col 2.
13 *The Herald*, January 5, 1867, p4, col 2.
14 *The Herald*, February 23, 1867, p4, col 2.
15 *The Herald*, April 6, 1867, p4, col 2.
16 *The Herald*, August 24, 1867, p4, col 2.
17 *The Herald*, September 28, 1867, p4, col 2.
18 *The Herald*, September 28, 1867, p4, col 2., and November 2, 1867, p4, col 2. Martin's essay into social history was published in italics, and read: "UMBRELLAS *were not brought into general use in* SCOTLAND *until the year* 1781 *or* 1782, *at which time a gentleman in Glasgow brought one with him on his return from* PARIS, *which was the* FIRST *seen in the city, and attracted universal attention. This Umbrella was made of heavy Waxcloth, with cane ribs, and was a* PONDEROUS *article. The early specimen of the English Umbrella, made of oiled silk, were, when wet, exceedingly difficult to open or to close; the Stick and furniture were heavy and inconvenient, and the Article generally very expensive; the substitution of Silk and Gingham, for the Oiled Silk, however, remedied the above objection. The Umbrella was originally formed and carried in a fashion the reverse of what now obtains. It had a ring at the top, by which it was usually carried on the finger when furled (and by which it could be hung up within doors), the wooden handle terminating in a rounded point to rest on the ground."* An umbrella something like the style of 1782 and a modern style could be seen in Martin's window, a large stock of umbrellas, including pretty silk ones, were available at prices ranging from twelve shillings and sixpence to eighteen shillings.
19 *The Herald*, December 28, 1867, p4, col 2.
20 *The Herald*, January 4, 1868, p4, col 2.
21 *The Herald*, March 14, 1868, p4, col 2.
22 *The Herald*, April 11, 1868, p4, col 2. Martin hoped the visit of the Prince of Wales to Ireland would be but the prelude to many others by the royal family to view the beautiful scenery of that country.
23 *The Herald*, October 24, 1868, p4, col 2.

24 *The Herald*, December 19, 1868, p4, col 2. Martin confided, "although years are accumulting upon MARTIN'S, alas! *Grey Hairs, pompatum hardly having its accustomed effect of keeping them dark*, and tho' feeling a few bodily ailments occasionally, some of which he *heroically* manages to shake off while others he finds rather *grippy....*"

25 See Chapter Five for Martin's comments regarding royal visits in 1865 and 1866.

26 *The Herald*, August 25, 1866, p4, col 2.

27 *The Herald*, May 25, 1867, p4, col 2, and August 24, 1867, p4, col 2.

28 *The Herald*, May 23, 1868, p4, col 2. See also August 21, 1869, p4, col 2, and May 21, 1870, p4, col 2, where the same innkeepers and their establishments were awarded public praise. On May 18, 1872, p4, col 2, Martin added even more details in eight verses devoted to the pleasures of Deeside including such useful information as:

Bonnie BRAEMAR has *two* splendid HOTELS,
Large Public rooms for comfort and ease,
Airy *large* Bed-rooms there are in great plenty,
And M'NAB or FISHER most anxious to please.

29 *The Herald*, August 15, 1868, p4, col 2, and September 19, 1868, p4, col 2.

30 *The Herald*, May 4, 1867, p4, col 2.

31 *The Herald*, June 22, 1867, p4, col 2.

32 *The Herald*, November 2, 1867, p4, col 2.

33 See Thomas E. Marston, *Britain's Imperial Role In The Red Sea Area 1800-1878* (1961), especially Chapters IX-X, XIII, and XVI-XX.

34 *The Herald*, December 7, 1867, p4, col 2.

35 *The Herald*, February 8, 1868, p4, col 2.

36 See Thomas E. Marston, *Britain's Imperial Role In The Red Sea Area 1800-1878,* Chapter XX; C.R. Markham, *History of the Abyssinian Expedition* (1869); and H.M. Hozier, *The British Expedition To Abyssinia* (1969).

37 *The Herald*, May 2, 1868, p4, col 2.

CHAPTER SEVEN

MILITARY PRIDE AND THE ABERDEEN WAPINSCHAW. 1868-1876.

Samuel Martin was intensely proud of his family's military connections, and of the courage, endurance and achievements of the British army and navy. Whenever fighting erupted, be it in the Crimea, China, India or Africa, Martin was never slow to feature the conflict in his advertisements and to lavish praise on the armed forces of the crown. In peacetime, too, his martial enthusiasm was quickly aroused, and he was ever an ardent advocate of better pay, improved promotion prospects and reasonable living conditions for soldiers. He wondered, for example, why Scottish regiments scheduled for a tour of duty in India seemed to be sent to Fort George a short time prior to embarkation, or else went abroad directly from Aberdeen, since such postings were more likely to acclimatize them to cold rather than to hot weather.[1]

In Gladstone's first ministry, December 1868 to February 1874, the oft debated, and equally oft postponed, question of army reform was finally taken up. Despite the obvious shortcomings revealed in the Crimean War little had been done to improve military organization and to rectify abuses in the system. In part that was due to innate military conservatism and traditionalism, and in part to the influence of vested interests. The motives of the Gladstone government in addressing the question of army reform were mixed, and the desire to achieve economies was probably as great as the wish to improve efficiency. Fortunately, the Secretary for War, Edward Cardwell, was a man who was able to combine greater efficiency with improved economy, and he was aided in his campaign for reform by the startling Prussian victories against France in 1870-71, victories which were attributed to superior organization and greater professionalism, qualities which pointed up British deficiencies.

Not surprisingly, Martin, despite his Liberal convictions and general support for tax reductions, was hostile to Gladstone's attempts to cut military and naval expenditure. However, the patriotic hatter's opposition to one of Cardwell's major proposals, the abolition of the system whereby commissions in the army and promotions could be purchased, possibly needs some explanation. One might surmise that Martin was himself a conservative and a traditionalist in military matters, often looking backward rather than forward for his inspiration in this field. His attitude was very possibly reinforced by his ideas about social deference.

At all events, in January 1869 Martin was asking whether economy and efficiency were compatible, and giving a guarded positive response to his own question. He even ran a headline:

THEN THUNDER AWAY MR. GLADSTONE,
REDUCE THE TAXATION,
BUT EVER HAVE AT HEART THE
EFFICIENCY OF OUR DEFENCES AND
DEFENDERS.

Martin added, for the benefit of Gladstone and his President of the Board of Trade, John Bright:

> So fire away, Mr. Gladstone, be prepared to strike while the iron's hot, and don't be alarmed or surprised if MARTIN THE HATTER reminds you, if needs be, of your promises and your duty.
>
> - - - - - - - - - - - - - -
>
> So Gladstone do right, stand forward John Bright,
> Retrenchment is no easy matter;
> But reduce the Taxation - *that's* if you can,
> And then you'll please MARTIN THE HATTER.[2]

By 1870, however, Martin evidently believed that the Chancellor, Robert Lowe, had gone too far in cutting military expenditure, commenting that some reductions could well turn out very costly in the long run. Martin advanced the opinion, "with all due deference to Mr. LOWE'S transcendently financial abilities...that any reduction that was thought requisite in ARMY matters might with safety have been left more in the hands of MILITARY MEN," whom Martin believed to be fully as likely as the Chancellor to know what kind of organization was needed for Britain to maintain her position in the eyes of Europe. He added:

> ...There are matters connected with *Military* reductions recently made that are of too sweeping a nature for the safety of the country, and which are beginning to be seen, but MARTIN is glad to think that it is not *yet* too late to remedy the evil, and he would respectfully suggest to legislators the sooner the better....[3]

In May that year Martin, in welcoming Queen Victoria to Deeside, included three pointed verses:

> If MARTIN had chance he'd explain to the Queen
> A matter that's alarmingly plain to be seen;
> He'd show that it was illogical blarney
> In the "Budget" to reduce the strength of the army.
>
> Government, no doubt, new laws can make,
> But reducing "the army" is quite a mistake;
> Tho' anxious for peace, 'tis the best way by far
> To have our defenders efficient for war.
>
> Our Soldiers have fought on many a field,
> To economy that hurts them 'tis dangerous to yield;
> Reducing the army should have been left alone,
> It may yet be required in upholding the throne.[4]

Already, in March 1870, Martin had been able to give a personal demonstration of his affection for the army, and for Scottish regiments in particular, a preference his Aberdeen readers doubtless shared, on the occasion of the arrival in the Granite City of the 93rd Highlanders. The regimental advance party had reached Aberdeen on the evening of March 28, after an absence of fourteen years from the city due to an extended period in India. *The Herald* recorded the scene, noting:

> ...The signs of welcome, other than those manifested by the crowd, were few in number. From one or two houses in Union Street rockets and blue lights were discharged, notably from the premises of Mr. Cattenach, military tailor. Mr. Samuel Martin waved a flourish with his sword and welcomed the Highlanders with a blast from his trumpet, as well as by appropriately emblazoned sentiments....[5]

Martin himself expressed his delight at the reception the troops received on their arrival,[6] and he was soon recording his pleasure that a company of the regiment, commanded by Captain Nightingale, had been stationed at Ballater as the Queen's bodyguard.[7] Nevertheless, before very long he was making a suggestion that he thought would improve the arrangements:

Martin saw these gallant men arrive
Under Nightingale's command;
But was rather disappointed
They did'nt bring their band.

O, 'twould surely very pleasant be
If on Deeside it was seen
Discoursing charming music
At Balmoral to the Queen.

It would doubtless give great pleasure
To hear it playing there,
And, if agreeable to "Her Majesty,"
Play in Ballater Square.

May the *Colonel* or the *Major*
Favourably view the matter;
It might be beneficial to the men;
So thinks MARTIN THE HATTER.[8]

Martin's regard for the 93rd Highlanders was evidently reciprocated, as was shown in June 1871 when the regiment left Aberdeen. Once more *The Herald* recounted the event:

> DEPARTURE OF THE 93D SUTHERLAND HIGHLANDERS. - This distinguished regiment, with the depots of the 92d and 78th regiments, left Aberdeen on Thursday morning per special train for Edinburgh. Rain fell pretty heavily during the morning, in consequence of which the number of spectators on the route to the station was comparatively small to what it would in all likelihood have been had the weather been more favourable....On passing the premises of Mr. Samuel Martin that gentleman appeared at one of the windows, waving a banner in his hand, bearing the friendly expression "Good-bye," "Haste ye back," the officers as they passed bowed an acknowledgement to Mr. Martin's compliments, and a cheer burst forth from the crowd on the street.[9]

The success of the Prussian army against France did not lead Martin to demand that Britain imitate her system of conscription. Indeed, the reverse was true. Under the headline **"MILITARY AFFAIRS AND THE OPENING OF PARLIAMENT"** Martin observed in February 1871, and was somewhat critical of the fact, that it was difficult to pick

SCOTLAND WELCOMES HER HIGHLANDERS.

WELCOME! 93D.

A REMINISCENCE OF BALAKLAVA.

Sir Colin looking calmly on,
  The Russians charge, fifteen hundred strong ;
Steady ! *Highlanders!* reserve your fire,
  These cavaliers must not trouble us long.

I know ere this my northern lads,
  How well you all can fight ;
Aim fair, my lads, at the Russians' heads,
  And make them take to flight.

These noble sons of Scotia's land,
  Whom Britain's foes all fear,
Sent a volley at the Russian ranks
  Accompanied with a cheer.

Well done ! Well done !! Sir Colin cries,
  You've done it to my mind ;
For when the smoke had cleared away
  No Russians could he find.

Now 93d, I knew it well,
  You'd die before you'd yield ;
And thus Sir Colin thanked these men
  On Balaklava's field.

These are the men, Ballaterians,
  That's come Deeside to view ;
Receive them with *three* hearty cheers,
  And thus your duty do.

Hip ! Hip ! Hurrah ! for the 93d,
  On Deeside now they're seen ;
A body-guard, as they deserve,
  To Britain's well-loved Queen.

One cheer more for the 93d,
  Now enjoying Deeside's Vale ;
Welcome, Lads, to your Highland hills ;
  Forward ! gallant Nightingale.

O greet our Highland Soldiers,
  'Tis ever a pleasing matter ;
Health and strength to the 93d,
  So says MARTIN THE HATTER.

Observe!—**SAMUEL MARTIN.**
HATTER TO THE PEOPLE,
34, UNION STREET (WAREHOUSE ABOVE SHOP),
ABERDEEN.
ESTABLISHED THIRTY TWO YEARS.

up a newspaper that was not full of "animadversions and strictures" upon the British military system. While some writers were clearly well informed, that could not be said for all. "With all due deference to the opinion of others," Martin believed it would be a retrograde step for Britain to abandon her well tried scheme of voluntary enlistments, especially as conscription might have detrimental economic consequences. He went further in claiming that any deficiencies in the British system were more due to cheeseparing economies than to any inherent faults.[10] He was also critical of the idea of civilian M.P.s legislating on military matters about which they knew so little.[11]

Despite Martin's reservations Secretary for War Cardwell was able to push through a much needed and fairly comprehensive scheme of military reform during Gladstone's first ministry, (though the absence of a general staff and the lack of a clear command structure would prove to be liabilities in the Boer War at the end of the century). As late as August 1873 Martin was still bemoaning the fact that while he was satisfied with the efficiency of the Royal Navy, he was not so certain about the army, which seemed to him to have been cut to a dangerous level in the interests of false economies. He revealed his attachment to tradition by writing:

> ...MARTIN is, and (if he does not hear a better line of argument than he has yet heard), ever will be, opposed to the doing away of
>
> THE PURCHASE SYSTEM IN THE ARMY.
>
> Facts show that, under the purchase system, our Army has ever been well officered, and non-commissioned officers and private soldiers well cared for and to be depended upon in time of need; thus, why change the system. But, indeed, it appears to MARTIN that we are getting far too much of the Foreign element into our ideas of managing military affairs.[12]

Britain was, perhaps, fortunate not to face a major war before 1899, but there were always imperial adventures to excite the general public and to provide advertising copy for Samuel Martin. By late 1873 Martin was devoting attention, much of it in verse, to the Ashanti War in West Africa and anticipating the triumph of Sir Garnet Wolsey.[13]

Martin's interest in military affairs was not confined to the regular army, and, being opposed to any scheme of conscription on Continental lines, he naturally took a great deal of interest and pride in the activities of the part-time volunteers at both the national and local level. Military pageantry always appealed to his patriotism, and was likely to stimulate the muse in him. Martin had, for example, drawn the attention of his readers to the annual meeting of the National Rifle Association at Wimbledon in July 1867, which combined shooting competitions with parades, reviews and the visits of members of the royal family. He viewed the volunteer rifle movement as one of the most glorious developments of the previous hundred years, a movement that would help to ensure the safety of the nation providing adequate practice and manoeuvres took place.[14]

Martin did not limit his interest to national reviews, but was willing to bestow his plaudits upon the local Aberdeen volunteers. He did so in verse in 1868,[15] and in song in 1869. On the latter occasion his composition, which urged Aberdeen city and county riflemen to attend the shooting competition held on the links, was entitled "Come To The Wapinschaw," and was to be sung to the tune of "Blue Bonnets over the Border." Martin commended the men on their general appearance, but hoped that every opportunity would be seized for drilling in large formations and for volunteers and regulars to exercise together.[16]

Whatever the popular opinion of Martin's ability as a song writer he felt sufficiently encouraged to display his talents in this direction again in June 1870 with his "March To The Wapinschaw," to be sung to the tune of "March to the Battle Field."[17] By this time the annual Aberdeen wapinschaw was sure to generate an equally regular response from Samuel Martin, though happily, perhaps, in 1871 he abandoned a musical tribute and returned to his own line in poetry in honour of the volunteers and their officers. The subject seemed sufficiently important to Martin in 1871 for him to celebrate it with no less than fifteen verses from which the following have been selected:

> Ye gallant sons of Bon-Accord,
>   Loyal subjects of the QUEEN,
> Muster well at the Wapinschaw-
>   Three cheers for Aberdeen!
>
> Officers know their duty well,
>   And all goes on serene;
> Pleasant, as it ought to be-
>   Hurrah! for Aberdeen.

Drill you've studied well, my lads,
Results are plainly seen;
Persevere at Duty's call-
Hurrah! for Aberdeen.

Your marching's known o'er a' the lan',
Aye fam'd it's ever been;
None surpass *Our* Riflemen-
Hurrah! for Aberdeen.

Your shooting's good; all well know
No faults there are to screen;
Fire away as you're wont to do-
Hurrah! for Aberdeen.

The prizes are worth shooting for;
You've a' guid han's, and een
Carry off the *feck* o' them-
Hurrah! for Aberdeen.

If foes should dare attempt our shore,
They'll find out what we mean,
We'll face them as we ought to do -
With a cheer for Aberdeen.[18]

In 1872 Martin again featured the wapinschaw in his advertisements, and he outdid his own performance the previous year by writing seventeen stanzas on the subject. He also stressed once more the need for joint exercises involving the regulars and the volunteers, who might well learn something from each other.[19]

In the late 1860s and early 1870s Martin did not limit himself simply to verbal encouragement of the volunteer movement and the annual wapinschaw. He was a regular contributor to the expenses of the movement and the shooting competition, and in 1869, 1870, 1871, and 1872 Martin's name appeared on the list of subscribers for the sum of two guineas on each occasion.[20] In 1872 he also took up a suggestion made in *The Herald* in 1866, when the paper proposed that local tradesmen offer prizes to be competed for at the Aberdeen wapinschaw,[21] and with a mixture of patriotic and civic duty with commercial self interest he announced:

AT THE NEXT WAPINSHAW
MARTIN
INTENDS
TO GIVE A CUP,
TO BE FIRED FOR IN ACCORDANCE WITH HIS SUGGESTIONS.
God Bless the QUEEN, Hurrah![22]

Martin was as good as his word, and on April 5, 1873, he reported that the cup he was donating to the Aberdeen Volunteer Association could be seen in his east window that day and on the two succeeding Saturdays.[23] His gift was confirmed in the subscription list published in *The Herald* on June 14[24] which further reported in July that "Several additional Cups were also competed for, including one from the redoubtable Mr. Samuel Martin, hatter."[25]

No doubt the 1873 event was special in Martin's eyes, and in anticipation of the occasion he wrote in part:

The WAPINSCHAW of Eighteen Seventy-Three
Will be a glorious meeting all may see.
Donations plenty, lots of prizes-
CUPS and BROOCHES, tasteful sizes.
With powder dry, and steady aim,
Best Shots will *the* Best Prizes gain.
Forward lads, hold well your *Sniders*;
Bull's-eyes make, but no outsiders.
Eyes front, and keep your spirits up-
The *best shot's* to get our GOOD QUEEN'S CUP.
There'll be a tug, the matter's certain,
To him that gets the Cup frae MARTIN.[26]

In 1874 and 1875 Martin's name was again featured on the subscription lists for the Aberdeen wapinschaw. On each occasion he made his usual contribution of two guineas.[27] In its report on the wapinschaw in 1876 *The Herald* carried the results of the shooting competitions which included the details of the regulations regarding Martin's prize:

FIX BAYONETS.

SAFETY NOT AGGRESSION.

STEADY hands and firm hearts,
Success from care oft flows,
Ready to defend ourselves,
Commands respect from foes.

ABERDONIANS!
FORWARD TO THE WAPINSCHAW,
HURRAH!

Riflemen of Aberdeen,
 Defenders of our QUEEN,
Forward to the Wapinschaw,
 And let yourselves be seen.

We're well aware, without a doubt,
 You're perfect at your drill ;
Forward to the Wapinschaw,
 Your duty there fulfil.

Officers *your* duty do,
 Pleasing all beholders ;
Muster well your gallant men,
 Acquit yourselves like soldiers.

The prizes are worth firing for—
 Show your powers are keen ;
Keep them frae bein' taen awa
 Frae the men o' Aberdeen.

The splendid Cup from our LOVED QUEEN,
 T'would surely be a pity
If that gem was carried off
 From the *famous Granite City*.

Then fire away with steady aim,
 Make bull's eyes, one and all—
Forward to the Wapinschaw
 Ready at Bugle Call.

Other prizes try well for,
 Which to you may fall ;
By good shots and centres
 You may get them all.

The Ladies' Cross, a pretty prize—
 Steady your eyes and hands,
Your gallantry for *this* prize
 Will be heard in foreign lands.

Sniders you have lately got,
 'Tis hop'd the Corps they please ;
Fire away, nor powder spare,
 You can rest at *stand at ease*.

Your marching past is very good,
 And you're pretty good at *double*—
What you do you do in style,
 Nor does it cause you trouble.

All are pleased with our Riflemen,
 Near perfect as they are ;
Skirmishing might be improved,
 So *might* forming square.

Now forward, gallant Colonel Jopp,
 Your sel' and others ken
The good *Old Granite* City
 Is proud of her riflemen.

County Corps, we welcome you,
 Be early on the scene ;
Tak' a' the prizes, *if ye can*,
 Frae the Men o' Aberdeen.

No doubt you'll do your best, lads,
 To take VICTORIA's Jug,
But afore you get it ta'en awa',
 Ye'll hae a gey stiff tug.

Unlimber guns, Artillerymen,
 Your distance science display ;
Make some splendid shots, brave boys,
 Tho' with *Balls* you fill the *Bay*.

Then forward to the Wapinschaw—
 Duty you'll never shun—
Let *Old Scotia's* sons exclaim,
 Northern men—Well done.

Hip ! Hip ! Hurrah for our Riflemen,
 The fact is plainly seen,
They please SIR SAMUEL *that's to be*
 And our beloved QUEEN.

XIII. - MR SAMUEL MARTIN'S CUP.

And £25 added by the Association, in 22 Money Prizes. Open to all efficient volunteers. 7 shots at 400 yards. Prizes:- 1st, Challenge Cup, presented by Mr. Samuel Martin, hatter to the people. To be held for one year by the winner and to become the property of any competitor gaining it twice, though not in succession. In the event of not being won within three years, to become the property of the competitor making the highest score for it during that period, and £5. 2nd, £3; 3rd, £2; 6 of £1 each, and 12 of 10s each; also £3 to competitor making the three highest scores. Entry money:- 2s each entry. Competitors may enter as often as they choose, but no competitor can take more than one prize.[28]

From 1868 until the mid-1870s Martin maintained his interest in military affairs, and never hesitated to offer advice to the government of the day on the subject, or to comment for the benefit of the Aberdeen public. As was to be expected he was against military retrenchment, but it was somewhat surprising to find him opposed to some of Secretary for War Cardwell's reforms. He urged his readers never to forget what British troops had achieved in the past, prophesying that a nation that neglected its defenders must be prepared to suffer a loss of respect.[29]

Martin was not only an admirer of the regular troops, especially the 93d Highlanders with whom he appears to have had a particular affinity, but he was also a keen supporter of the volunteer movement. He had expressed his faith in these part-time soldiers since the days of the French war scare, and he retained his faith in the locally based riflemen throughout this period. In particular he supported the annual Aberdeen wapinschaw, a yearly occasion for military practice and show, and, no doubt, an important feature in the Aberdeen social calendar.

NOTES

1 *The Herald*, November 13, 1869, p4, col 2. Martin requested the government:

> Be kind to our brave soldiers,
> May their comforts be complete;
> Be kind to our defenders,
> That stand both cold and heat.

Remember that they fight for all,
And oft have far to roam;
And on their march in foreign lands,
Oft think of friends at home.

2 *The Herald*, January 23, 1869, p4, col 2.

3 *The Herald*, April 30, 1870, p4, col 2.

4 *The Herald*, May 21, 1870, p4, col 2.

5 *The Herald*, April 2, 1870, p3, col 3.

6 *The Herald*, April 2, 1870, p4, col 2.

7 *The Herald*, May 21, 1870, p4, col 3. Martin's advertisement headed **"WELCOME! 93D."** consisted of nine verses in the main praising the regiment's Crimean War record. It ran alongside his regular advertisement of fourteen verses commemorating the Queen's first visit to Deeside in 1870.

8 *The Herald*, August 20, 1870, p4, col 2.

9 *The Herald*, June 17, 1871, p5, col 5. On October 7, 1871, p4, col 2, Martin wrote in nostalgic mood:

Martin mused again on the 93d-
They're gone! O'er true a tale.
Well liked they were in Aberdeen-
Adieu! INNES and NIGHTINGALE.
He thought on many happy hours-
The smoke created thirst;
So with *half* a glass of ---- and water,
He drank good health to the 91st.

10 *The Herald*, February 4, 1871, p4, col 2.

11 *The Herald*, April 22, 1871, p4, col 2.

12 *The Herald*, August 16, 1873, p4, col 2. Martin added: "What may do in *Russia* with her serfs, or even in *Prussia* with her nobles as soldiers, will not do in *Britain*; we are people of a different (if not nature) at anyrate temperament, and knowledge, and besides, Britain has been accustomed to *lead*, never to *follow*, Continental Powers in the idea of managing armies, and when Britain is unable to *lead* she must be prepared to sink from her pristine position as the leading Power of the Earth."

13 *The Herald*, November 8, 1873, p4, col 2.

14 *The Herald*, July 27, 1867, p4, col 2. Accounts of the Wimbledon meeting may be found in *The Herald*, July 20, 1867, p2, cols 5-6, and p3, col 1; also July 27, 1867, p7, cols 1-2.

15 *The Herald*, June 27, 1868, p4, col 2.

16 *The Herald*, June 26, 1869, p4, col 2. A sample verse ran:

MARCH! March! Aberdeen Riflemen-
Come to the Wapinschaw marching in order.
March! March! JOPP and HOGARTH's men-
May your zeal for the cause never grow colder.
Come from the workshop, the office, the wareroom,
Ready to put Britain's foes in disorder.
Let foreign nations see Scotchmen will ever be
Firm in their ranks marching in order.

17 *The Herald*, June 25, 1870, p4, col 2.

18 *The Herald*, July 1, 1871, p4, col 2.

19 *The Herald*, June 29, 1872, p4, col 2.

20 *The Herald*, May 8, 1869, p1, col 4; May 7, 1870, p1, col 4; May 27, 1871, p1, col 4; and June 1, 1872, p2, col 4.

21 *The Herald*, May 26, 1866, p5, col 3.

22 *The Herald*, July 13, 1872, p4, col 2.

23 *The Herald*, April 5, 1873, p4, col 2.

24 *The Herald*, June 14, 1873, p1, col 3.

25 *The Herald*, July 5, 1873, p4, col 6.

26 *The Herald*, June 21, 1873, p4, col 2.

27 *The Herald*, June 6, 1874, p1, col 3, and July 10, 1875, p1, col 2.

28 *The Herald*, July 1, 1876, p8, col 3.

29 *The Herald*, November 2, 1872, p4, col 2.

CHAPTER EIGHT

LIBERAL SUPPORTER AND ROYAL SYMPATHIZER. 1868-1874.

Samuel Martin did not give his attention in the years 1869-1874 exclusively to the military matters discussed in Chapter Seven. The victory of the Liberal Party, led by William E. Gladstone, in the general election of November 1868 brought to office a government whose policies Martin broadly approved, and was more than willing to comment upon.

One of the leading characteristics of Martin's advertisements over the years had been attention to party politics and parliamentary affairs, and this feature continued during the period of Gladstone's first ministry, (November 1868 to February 1874). It should be understood that Martin's preoccupation with national and local politics was not idiosyncratic, even if the introduction of such topics into commercial advertising copy was unusual. In the virtual absence of popular heroes, or heroines, in the fields of sport or entertainment, in an age prior to the electronic or mass media, many people derived what interest and excitement that entered their mundane lives from the proceedings of parliament and the speeches of such political giants as Gladstone and Disraeli. The personal and political confrontations between the two protagonists, their clashes in the House of Commons or on the hustings, were reported widely and at length in the press and read and discussed by a large and often fiercely partisan audience. The Reform Act of 1867 had also served to increase both the size of the electorate and the public interest in politics. Samuel Martin's readers may be presumed to have been both well informed and intensely interested in political matters, and the Aberdeen trader could be relied upon not to disappoint their expectations that he would offer some entertaining and original comments.

In advocating reductions in taxation Martin, without a doubt, struck a popular chord,[1] but his liberal attitude toward the disendowment and disestablishment of the Anglican Church in Ireland, a topic forced to the fore by Gladstone in 1868, was more controversial, though likely to reflect the majority opinion in Scotland. In late February 1869 referring to the rivalry between Gladstone and Disraeli, as well as the Irish Church question about to be placed before parliament, Martin wrote:

Meantime, each thinks his victory sure,
Because professing tactics pure,
If GLADSTONE gains the first affray,
DISRAELI may try a move some other way,
And say, with GLADSTONE I'll yet cope
By stratagem or for-lorn-hope;
And if victory's gained by his disaster
Of his place I'll soon be master.
But, GLADSTONE seeing his place at stake,
May be more than ever wide-awake.
Tho' DIS. may put him in the lurch
About his scheme about the Church,
'Tis dangerous ground, all well know,
Who through this happy country go,
To tamper with institutions old,
That in the "people's" minds have hold,
Many love their church, that's quite right-
And support it with a willing *mite*,
But, to keep it up with *stress*, some say,
No need that *other* churches pay.
In trade 'tis understood full well,
And, facts do show it all can tell,
That, if you buy at a certain price,
You pay but once, 'tis not asked twice,
Then, why should one man expect his brother
To pay for his *own* church and *another;*
Equivalence for what you pay you fairly merit,
Exacting more accords not with a Christian spirit,
Thus! there's surely justice in this clatter
Soliloquizes MARTIN THE HATTER.[2]

The Irish Church bill passed its third reading in the House of Commons on May 31, but its fate in the Lords seemed in doubt. On June 12 Martin reminded the peers that the will of the majority of the country, as shown through their elected representatives, was in favour of the bill, and he called upon them to pass it as a matter of common fairness.[3] Despite some moments of suspense the bill became law on July 26.

According to the Liberal inclined *Aberdeen Herald* in its editorial columns, nowhere had Gladstone's recent career been followed with keener interest than in Aberdeen, and nowhere were the principles that

"The wise and active conquer difficulties
By daring to attempt them."

Prudence and Firmness are Great Requisites in Statesmen.

"Prudence is that Virtue by which we discern what is proper to be done under the various circumstances of time and place."

THE BUDGET.

THE CHANCELLOR OF THE EXCHEQUER SPEAKING PLAIN AND PLEASANT.

MARTIN, THE HATTER, WOULD RESPECTFULLY SAY TO HIM—"PRAY, SIR, WHAT'S YOUR OPINION OF AFFAIRS IN GENERAL?"

THE Chancellor of the Exchequer, a very smart man,
Is going to do immense good if he can,
By trying to lower our enormous taxation,
Which, if he does, will give consolation.
Tho' to the rich it may be little relief,
To the poor it may lessen the price of their beef,
And to the many who use coffee and tea,
Ask their opinion and they'll all agree
That, to get these things cheaper would be their desire,
And coals at a price to *ensure* a good fire.
We hear of great men who do noble actions,
These sort of men have many attractions.
He'd be a great man, there can't be a doubt,
To make *all* people happy the way would find out.
The rich enjoy comforts because they are able
To pay for the nice things that cover their table;
But many there are, with truth we can say,
Whose comforts are scarce by the taxes they pay.
And when we consider the rents of the houses,
'Tis not surprising so few men get spouses.
Tho' earning good wages *one's* comforts we fear
Are alarmingly small, with all things so dear.
But stop! here's the "Budget," and all must confess
The Taxes not more but considerably less,
But, tho' efficiency's good, its been carried too far,
Nine Millions seems dear for the Abyssinian War.
But cutting and pairing is all very fine,
If it don't leave a deficit in the year sixty-nine.
The Chancellor t'was said would be millions behind,
But he's got over that in the BUDGET you'll find.
A reduction on income appears on the card,
Otherwise, it might have been *felt* very hard,
And *felt* very hard all will declare
Isn't so pleasant as *Soft Felt* to wear.
But necessaries of life it really seems queer
How they should continue kept up so dear,
But matters *look* pleasant, then away with all fears,
Taxes may be less, for a series of years,
So Mr. Lowe tho' t'was no easy matter,
You've reduced taxes gently, and pleased MARTIN THE HATTER,
But indeed if you had'nt filled your position with grace,
The QUEEN might have pop'd MARTIN INTO YOUR PLACE.

SAMUEL MARTIN'S Stock of Hats, Caps, Glengarry Bonnets, Umbrellas, &c. &c, is, *from the magnitude of his Trade, ever Large, Fresh, and Fashionable*, and as he purchases his goods at the best markets upon the best cash terms, he is enabled to sell his goods at moderate prices, and thus keep up the celebrity of his *world-wide* famed Establishment.

Beautiful SATIN HATS, exceeding pretty, New Shapes, 8/6, 10/6, 12/6, 13/6, 15/6, 16/6, and 17/ each.

Best Quality (London-made) SATIN HATS, 18/ each.

Observe!

SAMUEL MARTIN,
HATTER TO THE PEOPLE,
34, UNION STREET (WAREHOUSE ABOVE SHOP),
ABERDEEN.
ESTABLISHED THIRTY-ONE YEARS.

April 9, 1869.

guided the Prime Minister more heartily supported. *The Herald* expressed these opinions on the occasion of a decision by the Town Council, after an unusually harmonious meeting, to offer Gladstone the freedom of the city, an honour he politely declined at that moment due to pressure of work in preparing for the next session of parliament.[4] Such an invitation did not go unnoticed or unremarked by Samuel Martin. Indeed, he devoted the whole of his advertisement on October 2, 1869, to a light-hearted treatment of the subject. Martin noted that Mr Gladstone had been recruiting his health at Balmoral in preparation for a strenuous parliamentary session in the offing. Martin was of the opinion that the fact that his name had not appeared in any way in connection with the offer by the Town Council to the Prime Minister might have convinced Gladstone that the invitation was of little importance. The present Lord Provost, and future holders of that office, if anxious to thrust honours on other great men, might bear in mind Martin's influence in high places. Martin was himself a little disappointed that Gladstone had been forced to decline the honour extended as he would have liked to have heard and perhaps met the Liberal leader. However, even this disappointment would not deter him from remaining lively and selling his stock as cheaply as ever.[5]

Among Martin's stock of satin, felt, tweed and velvet hats, and plush, tweed and cloth caps were the "Alpine" hat, worn by the Prince of Wales and by Martin himself, the "Tyrolese" hat and the "Neapolitan" hat. He pointed out that:

> MARTIN'S HATS fit with ease, and are *firm* in the *brim*, which enables the wearer to lift his Hat gracefully to a Lady, a great point, as MARTIN is a thorough believer in politeness; it makes society sweet, and adds very materially to individual pleasantness.[6]

Apparently Martin sold enough hats in 1869 to describe it as, "a year of his business prosperity thoroughly up to his expectations," and a vindication of his system of business. He assured the people of Aberdeen at the beginning of 1870 that he enjoyed his usual good health, though he sometimes felt "what may be called certain grips, as it were, indicating that he is getting older, grey hairs increasing rapidly, &c." He had begun to think he was growing taller, but on examination discovered he was getting a little bald. He would never be backward in giving his opinion on passing events and if he occasionally differed from others he hoped never to offend. However, he claimed his right, as a British subject, "to look at matters through his own eyes, though he occasionally requires to use spectacles to see plain."[7]

Martin's good health did not prevent him from making provision, in his own inimitable style, for the inevitable final event. *The Herald* was obviously impressed with Martin's far-sightedness and perspicacity when, only a month later, in February 1870, it ran the following news item:

MR. MARTIN'S MURAL MONUMENT

\- - - - - -

For that which thou canst do thyself
Rely not on another.

OUR townsman Mr. Samuel Martin, who never seems to trouble himself with any other rule of life than his own independent notions of what is right and fitting, and who in consequence has said and done many brilliantly original things, has this week struck out a new idea by erecting in Nellfield Cemetery his own tombstone - a very handsome granite monument built into the south side of the middle wall of the cemetery and bearing on its tablet the following inscription

THE
LAST RESTING PLACE
OF
SAMUEL MARTIN
HATTER TO THE PEOPLE,
ABERDEEN.

A late citizen of Aberdeen is said to have preferred the earnest dying request - "Don't, don't let the awkward squad fire over my grave!" By filling up his own tablet in a simple but business-like and characteristic fashion, Mr. Martin has protected himself against this risk. Nobody will subject his memory to the maudlin stuff with which well-meaning survivors whose heads are still softer than their hearts sometimes disfigure the tombs of our public burying grounds.

Fame to our ashes comes, alas! too late:
And praise smells rank upon the coffin plate.

The monument is a massive and handsomely finished structure. The design does credit to Mr. Martin's good taste, and the whole idea of the thing speaks eloquently to his native strength of mind and force of character. Everybody can enter into the spirit of the Buchan wit's last prayer "Dinna bury me like a beast!" but there are not many who could have the moral courage to ensure an answer to the prayer so effectually as Mr. Martin has done. It seems as if he were snapping his fingers in the face of the last enemy - and why not? Those who are not fit to die are not fit to live. We

> trust the time is far distant when it will become the mournful duty of Mr. Martin's executors to fill up the blank left for the date on his monument; and it will not come a day sooner because he has made preparation for it. Long may he have as little appearance of being likely soon to want the accommodation he has provided for his mortal part. Long may he personally assure us that "Martin's stock of hats and caps is at present," &c besides entertaining and instructing us, by the racy and versatile emanations of his enviable literary fertility, anent the characters and questions of the day.[8]

No doubt Martin enjoyed the notoriety that his actions on this occasion bestowed upon him. Martin loved to play practical jokes, and had, in fact, already made use of his acquisition of his own future burial site to attempt a jest at the expense of his friend and legal adviser James Collie, co-founder with his brother of the firm of advocates of James and George Collie. Martin bounced into James Collie's room in the firm's offices at 25 Union Street, almost opposite Martin's shop, and said:

"Ah, Mr. Collie, I have just bought an estate, and I hope you will act for me."

James Collie was slightly surprised, but asked how big was it, having first assured Martin he would, indeed, be pleased to carry out the transaction. Martin replied:

"Oh, it is quite small, 10 feet by 6 feet."

This comment revealed that Martin was actually referring to a lair which was, and is, treated in law as a heritable estate. Martin's moment of triumph was spoiled, however, when, without looking up from his desk James Collie asked:

"And pray may I have the date of entry?"

Martin was crestfallen that his joke had backfired and his lawyer friend had had the last word.[9]

If Martin was well prepared for the future, he nevertheless continued to be greatly concerned with the present, including the unhappy state of Ireland, his mother's home country, and the land where he grew up. Having managed to pass an Irish Church Act, Gladstone next intended an Irish Land Act to ameliorate the agrarian poverty and discontent in that country. Martin welcomed this prospect, including a snippet on the subject in his advertisement for November 13, 1869:

HURRAH! JUSTICE TO
IRELAND.
'Tis said the Irish Land question is to be
improved; much need, better late than never.

\- - - - - -

MAY our brethren of the sister isle
Soon tire of agitators,
And be pleased with what is done
By British legislators.[10]

The opening of parliament at the beginning of February 1870 drew forth from Martin his routine plea for low rates of taxation and advice to Gladstone, John Bright at the Board of Trade and Robert Lowe at the Treasury. Martin also continued to support land reform in Ireland, and he combined all these subjects in a new song to the tune of "John Anderson," of which the following are the last two verses:

Now! Mr. Gladstone, go a-head!
Opponents' tactics scan;
No need to tell you, *cannie* Will-
Keep office long's you can;
Ireland's land, and tenant rights
Are subjects for your mettle-
Show firmness in a righteous cause,
And Ireland's troubles settle.

Let justice be your watchword,
Keep colleagues firm together,
And let all see the Session end
In political fine weather.
Dizzi will watch your movements,
And facts may try to scatter,
Don't let him jump into your shoes
And thus vex MARTIN THE HATTER.[11]

Two months later Martin was able to argue that the political horizon was comparatively quiet and the government progressing steadily with its proposed measures including the Irish land bill which would give justice to the land of St. Patrick.[12] The Irish Land Act was actually approved on August 1, 1870, but this achievement failed to elicit any comment from

Martin who had by this time turned his attention to the Franco-Prussian War. In fact the 1870 Irish Land Act never worked effectively, but its shortcomings were not immediately obvious either to the government or to Martin.

Somewhat surprisingly Martin did not comment in any way upon another major legislative achievement of 1870 - W.E. Forster's Education Act, which may be seen as one of the forward steps in educational provision in the nineteenth century. Rather less surprisingly Martin also failed to refer in his advertisements to the 1870 Married Women's Property Act which was equally epochal in its field. Nevertheless, Martin did include an indirect reference to education in the summer of 1870 when he argued that the future welfare of the country, both politically and commercially, depended upon the proper education and moral training of the rising generation. As his contribution to the instruction and uplifting of the next generation, bearing in mind that, *"the Boys of the present age will be the men of the next,"* Martin published a series of proverbs he trusted would be useful to many of the youth of his day as they grew into manhood, (Martin made no mention of education for girls). Martin's pearls of wisdom included such maxims as, "Think much of a trifle, though small it appear, Small sands make the mountain, and moments the year," "What we hope to do with ease we must learn to do with diligence," and "An idler's like a watch that wants both hands, As useless when it goes as when it stands."[13] Martin's attention may also have been distracted from public affairs in the summer of 1870 by the fact that he had recently returned from "a very pleasant few weeks' jaunt in the country," though he was sure his readers would be pleased to know he felt much the better for the break.[14]

In fact, Martin really devoted the second half of 1870 to the Franco-Prussian War which broke out in mid July. A military clash between France and Prussia was possibly inevitable sooner or later, but the immediate cause was the candidature of Prince Leopold of Hohenzollern-Sigmaringen for the throne of Spain. France objected to Leopold becoming King of Spain because of his Prussian connections, while Prussia resented the French attitude.[15] Martin took up the subject for the benefit of his readers and customers on July 23 when he asked the question:

> **What's all the Row About?**
> 'TIS NOT MUCH,
> **SPAIN ASKS FOR HERSELF**
> **A KING!**
>
> But the amiable PRINCE LEOPOLD OF HOHENZOLLERN - a COLONEL IN THE PRUSSIAN GUARDS - tho' offered the Crown, is not (in the meantime) to be King, tho' it seems he has many qualifications to justify him in accepting the proffered honour; but he has the great misfortune, *in the eyes of France*, of being a distant relative (something like half cousin), of the King of Prussia, and Napoleon, evidently finding himself smartly snubbed by the King of Prussia for his arrogant and dictatorial interference in the matter, declared War. This appears, at present, the simple cause of the War....

Martin believed the two countries had been preparing for war with each other for several years, and only waiting for a pretext to start hostilities. He bewailed the fact that it would be the young men of each nation who would be killed to satisfy the grasping ambition of the leaders. His novel solution to the problem was that if he had the power he would introduce a law which provided:

> ...that all Crowned heads, particularly those past the age of sixty, should, on declaring War, be *obliged* to submit to a medical examination by a Board of Physicians appointed for the purpose, to satisfy their subjects and the world of their sanity, and of having a cause justifying them going to War. And if found going to War simply for the sake of grasping at more power and outwitting each other to the annoyance of their more peacefully inclined neighbours, and thus inclined to sacrifice the lives of their subjects unnecessarily, then to be at once made subject to the ordinary laws of Lunacy, which will keep them out of harm's way, and be for the general good and well-being of their respective subjects and mankind generally....[16]

That Martin was following the military and political developments closely is clear from his advertisement published on August 13 which made mention of the series of French defeats at the beginning of the month, the resignation of the French ministry and the threat to Napoleon III's position. Martin admitted he had little, if any, sympathy with either combatant, but on balance found France deserving of the greater share of the blame for starting the war. The best result for Europe might well be the mutual weakening of both Prussia and France.[17]

By the time Martin returned to the subject in late September the situation had become desperate for France. A continuing series of military reverses had culminated in the disaster of the battle and surrender at Sedan and the downfall of Napoleon III. Moreover, the formation of a French Government of National Defence and the proclamation of a republic left matters, both political and military, somewhat confused. However, the war had not yet ended and the seige of Paris began on September 19. Little wonder Martin began his advertisement with the question **"IS IT PEACE?"** and then went on to plead that "LOVELY, MAGNIFICENT PARIS" be spared from destruction. He made an open appeal to the leaders of Prussia:

> Has the cries of thousands, and tens of thousands of *Widows* and *orphans*, starving and dying miserable deaths by this war, and the emanciated and diseased state of your thousands of prisoners, no claim upon your sympathy of Christian feelings! Oh! men think on what you are, what you are doing, and your awful responsibility. Have the horrible groans of the *wounded, maimed, disfigured,* and oh! drearily dying Soldiers (awful to contemplate), no effect upon your humanity! Is there no way of glutting your uncalled for (yes, uncalled for are the words) thirst for Vengeance but in a further display of brute force, by in a manner murdering the *non*-combatants, helpless women and children, amongst the combatants when opening your batteries upon Paris! Oh! men rouse up your apparently dormant feelings of humanity, and try, oh! try mediation before you begin to destroy lovely Paris.[18]

Similar sentiments were repeated in October,[19] but by the end of that month the French position had become even more hopeless with the Prussian occupation of Orleans and Strasbourg and the surrender of a large French army at Metz. Martin's tender feelings were touched by the plight of the French people in general and the Parisians in particular. The swing in Martin's opinion, from blaming France for the war and applauding Prussian success, to expressing compassion and sympathy for France, especially after the departure of Napoleon III, and denouncing Prussian ambitions, was typical of shifting British public reactions to the war.[20]

Taking advantage of the situation Russia on October 29 announced that she would no longer consider herself bound by the Black Sea clauses of the Treaty of Paris of 1856 forced upon her at the end of the Crimean War. The British response was to deny that one party to a treaty could unilaterally denounce all or part of an agreement, changes could be made only if all parties concerned were willing. This placed Britain on the diplomatic moral high ground, while at the same time making later concessions possible. Naturally, the Russian move reawakened Martin's latent Russophobia and he responded in December with a virtual call to arms. He also penned nine verses criticizing the Russian Chancellor, Prince Gortchakov, while applauding the British Foreign Secretary, Lord Granville.[21]

Certainly, there was much for Martin to ruminate over at the end of 1870, especially the sad situation in France and the heavy casualties due to "The horrid War." These thoughts turned his mind to the transitory nature of life, which he wrote would be a first-rate text for a sermon in the hands of an able minister. He was not himself a minister and did not seek to preach, "and whatever merit (ahem!) there may be in his advertisements, he certainly never aimed at making them actual sermons, although he trusts they will ever be found advocating *sound* principles...." Despite the occasional need for serious thoughts, Martin believed he had a lively and happy temperament, which was conducive to both mental and physical wellbeing, *"having a beneficial effect upon the digestive organs,* which more or less ever affect the BRAIN."[22]

Having given repeated attention to the Franco-Prussian War in the second half of 1870, Martin dropped the subject entirely in 1871, except to use it to promote the need for military preparation. Perhaps he felt the Aberdeen public had lost interest, especially after the surrender of Paris to the Prussians on January 28 after a seige lasting 131 days. Perhaps other topics of interest arose that claimed his attention or seemed more likely to catch the eye of potential customers.

Royal visits and events, however, and the subject of Martin's own imminent elevation to the rank of knight or better, remained perennial favourites. Martin's loyalty to the royal family in general, and the Queen in particular, was unquestioning, and as such quite remarkable, since Victoria's popularity reached its nadir by the late 1860s and early 1870s. The reasons for this decline in the status of the Queen in the eyes of many people were her prolonged retirement from the limelight following the death of the Prince Consort in 1861, and the widespread feeling that she had neglected her public duties. This led to resentment and even popular protests about the large parliamentary grants awarded both to the Queen herself and to other members of her family. The fall of the imperial regime in France, and the proclamation there of a republic, precipitated a rise in republican sympathies in Britain where a number of Republican Clubs were founded, including one in Aberdeen.[23]

None of the above reasons weakened Samuel Martin's intense loyalty and ardent attachment to the royal family and to the institution of monarchy. The Queen's visit to Deeside in May 1869 produced the by then customary poem by Martin, the third verse, (of eleven), showing concern for Victoria's continuing grief over the death of Prince Albert:

A lonely heart may oft be found
Where all looks bright and quite serene,
Oh! rank can't sooth the sorrowed heart,
God bless our kind, our widowed Queen.

However, in a shift of mood Martin added three additional verses on the subject of his own possible knighthood.[24] Only a month later he had devised another tongue in cheek scheme for the public recognition of his own contribution to the life of Aberdeen. After applauding the widening of the footpath at the south-west corner of the Union Street Bridge he suggested that this civic improvement might be completed by erecting:

A Statue Opposite "The Prince."

It certainly has not yet been actually proposed, but now is the time (better late than never) for the "People of Aberdeenshire" to get up a statue

TO MARTIN THE HATTER.

'Tis a happy opportunity, a nice granite base and column and chaste cornice, &c., with a full-length Statue of MARTIN. Costume - Knickerbockers, Military Cap, &c. &c., Attitude - with his right hand leaning on the hilt of his drawn sword, his left hand holding the scabbard, from which hangs gracefully a scroll displaying the motto - "DUTY." But why, it may be asked, with a drawn sword? why? because Martin is happy in being a *Soldier's Son*, and thinks he knows a little about how to *Draw, use* and *sheath* a sword; and

Drawn Swords and Fixed Bayonets,

Being ever handled sharply by our brave defenders, has had a great deal to do in making our great and glorious country *what she is*. But about the Statue, t'would be much in keeping with the opposite corner of the Bridge, as

THERE **WAS** only **ONE "PRINCE ALBERT"** And
THERE **IS** only **ONE SAMUEL MARTIN**,
HATTER TO THE PEOPLE.

Thus it would be tasteful to have "the Column" finished in accordance with "THE PRINCE," viz., "MARTIN" printed in bold letters on the front. It may be asked what claims has MARTIN to expect to get a Statue? Why, among many, may be mentioned that he has attended well to his own business, is a very Loyal Subject, is a conspicuous and prosperous man *(few instances of Statues being proposed to poor men, or men that don't mind themselves, or have not made what is called a certain standing or conspicuous position in the world)*, and has never been backward in doing what he thought his duty in advocating principles and matters that he believed would be conducive to the honour, welfare, and *safety* of the country,

and *because he thinks that he is*

RESPECTED BY "THE PEOPLE,"

more rational claims and reasons, he thinks, than perhaps could be given for getting up many Statues met with now-a-days.[25]

In August Martin published two poems alongside each other welcoming both Victoria and the Prince of Wales to Deeside, and wishing the Prince good luck in the hunting season while blatantly soliciting a brace of grouse. He also seized the occasion to praise the local countryside and even the army barracks at Ballater, which, as someone who in his childhood had lived in a number of military posts, he felt qualified to do.[26] He repeated his welcome to the Queen in both May and August 1870, on each occasion heading his patriotic verses "ODE (AS USUAL) BY SAMUEL MARTIN."[27]

The early months of 1871 provided an additional opportunity for Martin to compose a poem to celebrate a royal event with the wedding of the Queen's fourth daughter, the Princess Louise, to the Marquis of Lorne, the eldest son of the Duke of Argyll. While the popular resentment at the Queen's virtual retirement from public life and at the cost of the monarchy led to large public meetings in Birmingham and Nottingham, which passed resolutions condemning the grants voted to the young couple,[28] the city of Aberdeen marked the royal marriage with a banquet, grand ball and supper.

A committee that included several local members of the aristocracy, the Lord Provost of Aberdeen, Members of Parliament, representatives of the academic and business communities, officers from the Aberdeen

Volunteers and the 93rd Highlanders, and many others, organized a banquet in the Music Hall at 2.00 p.m. on Tuesday, March 21, tickets 3s. 6d., and a ball and supper at 10.00, tickets 15s. for gentlemen and 10s. for ladies. The accomplished band of the 93rd Highlanders played at the banquet.[29]

Prior to both events, the impending marriage and the banquet, Martin reported, perhaps not with complete accuracy, that there were great rejoicings in the country, and that Aberdeen was doing her duty in style. He also informed his rapt readers that, "MARTIN THE HATTER WILL APPEAR AT THE BANQUET," before presenting his ode on the marriage.[30]

The Queen's regular visit to Balmoral in May was also given its normal welcome with the usual intertwined remarks regarding the beauties of Deeside and Martin's deserved promotion.[31] In October he combined his regular affirmation of loyalty to the Queen with the extension of good wishes to the royal newly weds. He wrote:

> If the MARQUIS OF LORNE and his Royal bride
> Were to visit Bon-Accord the fact would'nt hide,
> 'Twould be a great honour, and not indiscreet,
> If they'd call on SAM MARTIN, 34, Union Street.
> MARTIN would receive them with pleasure and glee;
> He's a right loyal subject soon they'd see.
> 'Twould be very kind, he'd much like the call,
> If invited *he'd* certainly visit *Birkhall*.[32]

The scant public regard for the royal family began to change in late 1871. The Queen herself received some sympathy due to her indisposition in the autumn, but the real turning point in popular affection was the serious illness of the Prince of Wales in December which brought the heir to the throne close to death with enteric fever. The Prince's recovery led to outbursts to enthusiasm for the monarchy, none more sincere than Martin's when he took a retrospective look at 1871:

> To our Royal House it brought sad grief,
> Let all thank God, that sent relief;
> Man's power is small, 'tis prayer prevails,
> Health's restored to the PRINCE OF WALES.

A nation's prayers, oh! how sincere,
When Death was thought so very near;
God bless the PRINCE'S devoted wife,
The greatest belssing of his life.

Let all bless ALICE, nor rank deride,
A loving *Sister* at his sick bedside;
A faithful *Daughter*, a model wife,
God grant ALICE a long, long life.

If 1871 brought mixed fortunes to the royal family, though laying the foundations for the enormous popularity the Queen enjoyed in the last quarter of the nineteenth century, it was, apparently, a good year for Samuel Martin. In reviewing his personal and business affairs at that time he stated:

MARTIN THE HATTER

THANKS "THE PEOPLE" MOST HEARTILY AND SINCERELY

For their kind support during the past year, a year of His Business prosperity quite up to his expectations. "The People" will no doubt be highly pleased to hear that MARTIN is in good health, tho' he is certainly not free from *all*

"THE ILLS THAT FLESH IS HEIR TO,"

being occasionally troubled with Rheumatism, and it might be thought Gout, but which in no way affects his activity in business, but being fashionable complaints they might be attributed to his living in the *West End*. MARTIN is no doubt getting up in years, but Father Time is laying his hand gently on MARTIN, as he feels no indication of *Round Shoulders, Weak Knees,* nor does the length of his *Whiskers* in any way interfere with his *hearing*. His moustache is certainly grey, but nevertheless comely. His sight is good, and his teeth answer all the purposes of mastication, and his digestive organs are generally in good order, and his appetite good about *Dinner-time*, all indications of soundness. Indeed MARTIN has *reason*, and *is* very very thankful for *all* his mercies.[33]

From a business point of view there was one development in 1871, which if not of immediate or serious concern to Martin, was nevertheless pregnant for the future. On November 18 *The Herald* published, alongside Martin's advertisement in that edition, the following:

OPENING ANNOUNCEMENT.

JOHN C. M'LEOD,

(ABOUT 30 YEARS WITH MR. SAMUEL MARTIN, HATTER),

WOULD respectfully announce to his Friends and the Public, that he has Commenced Business in the Shop

46, UNION STREET,

(Directly Opposite Adelphi Court),

With a New and Fashionable Stock of

GENTLEMEN'S DRESS HATS (New Shapes),
SHELL AND FELT HATS,
CAPS and GLENGARRYS, of every description,
LEATHER HAT CASES,
LEATHER, CANVASS, CARPET, DESPATCH,
AND COURIER BAGS,
UMBRELLAS, &c.

J. C. M'L. hopes, from his long experience and connection with the trade, and by strict personal attention to business, keeping first-class goods, and selling at moderate prices, to merit a share of public patronage.

November, 1871.

If John C. M'Leod had indeed been "ABOUT 30 YEARS WITH MR. SAMUEL MARTIN," it meant he had been at 34 Union Street since the early 1840s and been a close observer of Martin's business practices. There is no clue available as to why M'Leod chose to set up on his own account at this moment, although he and Samuel Martin appear to have parted on amicable terms. Clearly, M'Leod felt it a commercial advantage to stress his previous connection with Martin. The opening of a rival hat shop only a few doors along Union Street was unlikely, however, to have been entirely welcomed by the proprietor of number 34. Whatever inroads M'Leod made into Martin's trade he made no effort in the succeeding years to enter into competition in the advertising field. Whether the appearance of M'Leod upon the scene was instrumental or not Martin reminded his readers in March 1872 that his establishment had been open for thirty-four years and announced the refurbishment of his premises. The shop had been painted and decorated inside and out, new plate-glass windows had been installed which looked magnificent and were tastefully dressed.[35] Another change in Martin's business was his acceptance of the view that shorter working hours were beneficial to the health and happiness of employees:

Working hard and no play
Is not the fashion of the day:
Working men should have some leisure,
And after work enjoy some pleasure.

Martin announced, therefore, a slight reduction in his hours of business by his intention to close his shop at 3.00 p.m. every Wednesday afternoon in May, June, July and August 1872. This change would be good for himself, pleasing to the young men in his employ and ought not to inconvenience the public.[36]

Martin's general support for social and economic reforms was often clear from the text of his advertisements,[37] and early in 1872, on the eve of the opening of parliament, he stated that no county could be great unless the main aim of legislation was the welfare, well-being and general prosperity of the people. While some people might think he should have been elected as an M.P. ere this time, Martin could not really spare the time from his business, and in any case his entry into politics might endanger Mr Gladstone's position. Nevertheless he took this opportunity to chide the politicians for their lack of constructive legislation in the last session and to offer advice for the coming one.[38] Near the end of the year Martin returned to the theme that the welfare of the working classes was the real strength of the country, and that politicians should remember this when fixing tax scales. He warned Gladstone to keep this fact in mind, or to make way for Martin as Prime Minister. The opening verse of his song devoted to these ideas ran:

O! Mr. Lowe, just keep in mind,
And Mr. Gladstone too,
The country well kens what she wants,
So thus your duty do.
Reduce the Taxes soon, Sirs,
As muckle as ye can,
And mak' the burdens lighter, Sirs,
Upon the working man.[39]

Whatever his disappointment with the achievements of Gladstone's government, Martin remained a loyal supporter of the Liberals, as demonstrated in June that year on the occasion of the parliamentary election held in Aberdeen caused by the death of the sitting Liberal

REASON IS EVER IN SEASON.

SHORTENING BUSINESS HOURS

THE ORDER OF THE DAY,

AND CONDUCIVE TO HEALTH.

Health that greatest blessing,
That makes all Nature look so sweet.

Shortening the working hours, and a little recreation,
Should meet with wise men's approbation.

THE SHORT-HOUR MOVEMENT IS GOOD.

'Tis right, 'tis reasonable, 'tis common-sense that the working classes should have *some* spare time for intellectual improvement, rational enjoyment, *and to get better acquainted with their homes and their families*, when after work

"They meet their rosy children at the door
Prattling their welcomes."

And which may be accomplished without inconvenience to Employers, if willingly arranged ; and which will facilitate the way to the working classes to fulfil their duty satisfactorily to themselves as taxpayers and citizens of this great commercial country where labour accomplishes so much.

Working hard and no play
Is not the fashion of the day ;
Working men should have some leisure,
And after work enjoy some pleasure.

Serfs may do for foreign lands,
But are not wanted here.

MARTIN, HATTER TO THE PEOPLE,

believes that a trip to the country now and then, at this genial season, is, in the highest degree, invigorating and conducive to *mental* and *physical* health, and has the pleasing tendency of enlivening the spirits, thus prolonging life.

There's "tongues in trees,
Books in the running brooks ;
Sermons in stones."

and intellectual education in taking a walk in the country.

MARTIN, being in the enjoyment of the best of health and spirits, which he is ever thankful for, and wishing to continue in this happy state as long as possible *(he believes that health greatly depends upon how it is studied by proper attention to nature's laws, pure air being one of the great elements)*, has made up his mind, in accordance with the *progress* of the age, to shorten his business hours slightly, by having

A WEDNESDAY'S HALF-HOLIDAY,

Which he thinks he can do with beneficial effect to himself, and which will no doubt be highly pleasing to the young men in his employment, and *WHICH HE HOPES AND FIRMLY BELIEVES* without in the slightest degree inconveniencing

"THE PEOPLE,"

Who have, by their kind support, enabled MARTIN to live very comfortably for the last THIRTY-FOUR YEARS, a continuance of which kind support it will ever be his study to deserve. HEALTH is naturally a matter of great moment to MARTIN, *BUT LET "THE PEOPLE" THINK ON THE LOSS IF* MARTIN *WAS TAKEN FROM THEIR MIDST.*

ON WEDNESDAY, 1st May,

And every WEDNESDAY during the months of MAY, JUNE, JULY, and AUGUST, 1872, MARTIN intends to Shut his place of Business at

3 O'CLOCK Afternoon,

And hopes that THE PEOPLE will encourage him in this movement by purchasing goods at his Establishment as early as convenient *before* 3 o'clock, on the *Wednesday* Afternoons.

MARTIN thinks this is a move in the right direction, and being in accordance with the feelings of the age, he hopes it will be pleasing to "THE PEOPLE." Shortening the Hours of Labour and business being the order of the day, and which, when done in a proper Christian spirit, will turn out ultimately to be satisfactory to *All*, being in the highest degree conducive to the health and happiness of the

EMPLOYERS AND EMPLOYED,

who, the longer they work together harmoniously in their respective positions, will ever have the best effect in keeping up the dignity and prosperity of

THIS GREAT AND GLORIOUS COUNTRY.

SO THINKS

MARTIN THE HATTER.

MARTIN'S Stock is very Large at present with FRESH GOODS, *New* and *Fashionable Styles*, and, from the Largeness of his Business, he is enabled to continue to Sell his Goods at very Moderate Prices.

Observe!—**SAMUEL MARTIN,**

HATTER TO THE PEOPLE,

34, UNION STREET (WAREHOUSE ABOVE SHOP),

ABERDEEN.

ESTABLISHED THIRTY-FOUR YEARS.

EVER THANKFUL FOR THE SUPPORT OF "THE PEOPLE."

19th April, 1872.

member, Colonel Sykes. Martin remained ardent in the Liberal cause, as a newspaper account of the election indicates:

> The polling commenced yesterday morning at eight o'clock. The voting continued with considerable briskness until four o'clock, when the poll closed. The day was very wet throughout the morning. As it is now illegal for the candidates to hire conveyances one stirring feature of previous contested elections was wanting. Notwithstanding the excited state of public feeling the utmost order was preserved. Slips giving the state of the poll were issued from the committee rooms of the different candidates every half-hour, and were eagerly scanned.
>
> Our friend, Samuel Martin, had a large card in each window of his shop with the inscription, "Vote for Mr. Leith." He also exhibited a photograph of Mr. Leith. A flag graced each window upstairs, where a sweeping brush was also prominent. At the close of the poll he displayed a large board on which was the word "Victory" in large letters. Mr. Martin himself appeared in a fancy dress and blew his trumpet.[40]

Mr Leith's comfortable majority was, no doubt, a source of pleasure to Martin, but even political triumphs were overshadowed in Martin's mind, and certainly in his advertisements at this time, by his homage to the Queen whose vacations on Deeside in 1872 fell either side of the election. Her visit in May prompted Martin to write no less than thirteen verses of welcome, incorporating his usual strong suggestion that the time for him to be honoured was surely overdue, plus seven stanzas on the pleasures of Deeside and two on the royal body guard.[41] In August he presented his readers with fifteen verses, each beginning "Happy Land!" and reciting the pleasures and benefits of living in Britain. He added that when he received his knighthood he might build a mansion on Deeside, not as large as Balmoral, "but possibly with a bold attempt to take the shine out of **INVERCAULD OR GLENMUICK**, and the Mansion might be opened by a *Tea Garden* party, at which HER MAJESTY might graciously deign to appear, and, after a *flourish of trumpets*, name the Mansion **MARTIN HALL**...."[42] Martin claimed to have seen the Queen several times during her second visit, and was delighted to see her looking so well, and speculated that she was pleased to see him in good health.[43]

He confirmed his business and physical health in his advertisement for January 4, 1873, when he welcomed the new year and bade farewell to the old year without too many tears:

1872, is off without regret,
He really was so very wet.

Martin claimed his physical and mental energies were as great as twenty years earlier, that he was "blessed with a good *appetite* and *drinkitite*," both of which he enjoyed in moderation.[44]

Before the meeting of Parliament in February 1873 Martin warned Gladstone and Lowe that "They have a stiff session to face that will require all their philosophy, tact, and ability to surmount."[45] This, as it turned out was an accurate prophesy.

At the beginning of the new session Gladstone, anxious to continue to meet Irish grievances, introduced an Irish University Bill designed to create a university which Roman Catholics would be willing to attend, unlike Trinity College, without offending Protestants. Inevitably, perhaps, the bill fell between the two stools, and was defeated on its second reading in the House of Commons by 287 votes to 284 in the early hours on March 12. Gladstone and his government resigned the next day, but did not ask for Parliament to be dissolved and for a general election, being nervous about the result. Gladstone expected Disraeli to form a minority government, but the Conservative leader saw no advantage in this and declined office, also refusing to recommend a dissolution. Gladstone was forced to resume office on March 18, but he had suffered a loss of power and prestige and the days of his government were clearly numbered.[46]

Martin made clear reference to the complicated political situation in his advertisement for April 5, two weeks after the crisis. However, his view that Gladstone had somehow outmanoeuvred Disraeli, a view coloured no doubt by partisan feelings and maybe wishful thinking, was at odds with reality since most observers believed the reverse was true. Even so Martin's views are worth quoting at length:

"ALL'S WELL THAT ENDS WELL."
MR. GLADSTONE, how do you do,
You have your troubles if a' be true.
It's no easy job I fear
To fill the place of A PREMIER.
Parliament's lately been disjointed,
But the Opposition's disappointed;
You were *out*, but now you're *in*,
And going back is no a sin.

"ALL'S WELL THAT ENDS WELL."

MR. GLADSTONE, how do you do,
You have your troubles if a' be true.
It's no an easy job I fear
To fill the place of A PREMIER.
Parliament's lately been disjointed,
But the Opposition's disappointed;
You were *out*, but now you're *in*,
And going back is no a sin.
Disraeli thought to out-wit you,
And of your office fairly strip you;
But, William, man, tho' you were out,
Weel you ken'd what you were about;
Parliament you had resolved
Not by you should be dissolved.
Thus your chance you did'na slip
To take Disraeli in the hip.
He saw the Commons to him averse,
Thus his doings would reverse.
Thus tho' willing, he saw 'twas vain,
Your office at present to obtain.
So by your few days' transposition,
He gain'd defeat and you *re*gain'd position;
The matter was so neatly done,
'Twas really like a piece of fun,
On *your* part, William, just to see
If the Opposition could agree,
If Dissi and his friends were wide-awake,
You and your supporters' place to take.
And now you've found the matter out,
O' that there canna be a doubt,
Now you're firmer in your seat,
While they're disheartened by defeat.
M. P's. like laddies at the school,
They aft go a-head that keep most cool.
Now, William, the late assault you nobly stood,
No doubt 'twas owing to your *Scottish* blood.
The country's pleased that's plainly seen,
But you must no more annoy "THE QUEEN,"
Or if you do the matter's certain,
You'll hear o't soon frae SAMUEL MARTIN,
And he's no a man to be tamely slighted;
Besides, he'll no doubt soon be KNIGHTED,
And tho' not *at present* in your sphere,
When you're out *again he* may be made PREMIER;—
Man's life is like a well-contested race,
Each strives to get the foremost place.
You return'd to office with becoming grace,
Else MARTIN *might* have got your place;
As matters went this was prevented,
"THE QUEEN," *no doubt*, would have consented;
To many 'twould be an amusing matter—
The New Premier, MARTIN THE HATTER.
Mr. LOWE's reinstated, we dinna grudge it,
So come awa, ROBERT, wi' you're Budget.

Disraeli thought to out-wit you;
And of your office fairly strip you;
But, William, man, tho' you were out,
Weel you ken'd what you were about;
Parliament you had resolved
Not by you should be dissolved.
Thus your chance you did'na slip
To take Disraeli in the hip.
He saw the Commons to him averse,
Thus his doings would reverse.
Thus tho' willing, he saw 'twas vain,
Your office at present to obtain.
So by your few days' transposition,
He gain'd defeat and you *re*gain'd position;
The matter was so neatly done,
'Twas really like a piece of fun,
On *your* part, William, just to see
If the Opposition could agree,
If Dissi and his friends were wide-awake,
You and your supporters' place to take.
And now you've found the matter out,
O' that there canna be a doubt,
Now you're firmer in your seat,
While they're disheartened by defeat.[47]

Political preoccupations would not have blinded Martin to the arrival of yet another rival in trade. On May 10, 1873, there appeared alongside his own advertisement not only a message from John C. M'Leod thanking friends and public for their liberal patronage since he began business with his hat shop at 46 Union Street, but also the opening announcement of the Aberdeen Ready-Money Hat and Cap Warehouse at 31 Broad Street. The proprietor, William C. King, intended by selling for cash on small profit margins and by personal attention to place his establishment second to none in the city.[48]

Neither politics nor business matters deterred Martin from commemorating the Queen's 1873 visits to Deeside,[49] and in June and July he commented on the visit of the Shah of Persia to London. It was Martin's suggestion that he ought to visit Aberdeen and see the sights of the town.[50]

In October 1873 Martin recorded a swing in the political balance in the country and in public opinion in favour of the Conservatives, and predicted a change in the government. Change, he pointed out, was an important word and fact, and social and political changes were often necessary. While no-one could be sure of the identity of the new Prime Minister, it might even be Martin:

> But be the PREMIER whom he may,
> He'll get MARTIN'S approbation,
> Who keeps up *the dignity* of the CROWN,
> And the *Prestige* of THE NATION.

Even such a portentous political possibility as the fall of the Gladstone ministry did not divert Martin's attention entirely away from local matters, and in the same advertisement he argued in favour of the lighting up of the clock in the new Town House. As the citizens of Aberdeen had paid for the building through their rents and taxes they had the right to expect the clock to be illuminated regularly and not just when it suited the convenience of the Town Council.[51]

Only three months later, in January 1874, Martin was again publicly critical of the Town Council, this time over the topical debate regarding the positioning of a horse trough. Martin objected to the so-called Castle Street improvement, which involved the placing of a drinking fountain, or horse trough, depending on one's point of view, in front of the statue of the Duke of Gordon then sited in the Castlegate. A Town Council meeting on January 19 failed to reach any agreement on the subject,[52] and, as so often, Martin made his feeling known in verse:

> Methought I heard the *Stone* DUKE say,
> Oh! pray take this vile trough away,
> Councillors might very well suppose
> 'Twould spoil my view and offend my nose.
> Truly, if I could get away,
> I would no longer near it stay;
> 'Tis most unseemly to the eye -
> Remove it quickly let "The People" cry.
> Oh! 'twould surely be a pity
> To insult my memory in the "Granite City."
> In good "old times" 'twas plainly seen
> I was much respected in Aberdeen.

What! a Knight of "The Thistle and the Garter"
To associate with every passing Carter -
Oh, shame! the matter's out of place -
Remove "this trough" from before my face -
Top of Castle Street there's lots of space.
Behind me would be its *proper* place;
I've often drawn my Sword in Battle -
Could I draw it now, I'd make it rattle
Upon this "trough" and paltry lamps,
Which want of taste *their* position stamps;
I thought at first the whole a myth
Till I heard the working of a *Smith*.
But, take the "trough" from me away,
That is what I mean to say;
To leave it and me in our present place
Would *Bon-Accord* and *me* disgrace.
So hold a Council on the matter *specially*,
And I will loudly shout Long Life to PROVOST LESLIE.[53]

Martin bade farewell to 1873 in his usual style,[54] and greeted 1874 with an almost maudlin outpouring of sentimentality as regards Scottish traditions and culture, especially those associated with the New Year.[55]

Despite some reshuffling of his cabinet, forced on him by the revelation of irregularities in the administration of the Post Office, the Gladstone ministry grew increasingly unpopular in late 1873. In consequence Gladstone finally requested that Parliament be dissolved on January 26, 1874, and a general election was held in February with Gladstone holding out the promise of the abolition of income tax if re-elected. In fact, the Conservatives secured a majority of about fifty seats, to Martin's chagrin. On February 28 he published his thoughts on the matter with such headlines as "TURNING THE TABLES WITH A VENGEANCE," "MR. GLADSTONE OUT OF HIS CALCULATIONS FOR ONCE," "DISRAELI JUBILANT" and **"WOLF-LIFE RUSH FOR OFFICE."**

Martin clearly wrote with feeling when he addressed remarks to Disraeli on the political situation and held up to view the merits of the Gladstone ministry, merits that he had not always perceived himself in the past:

> But how can you make the country believe that you can carry on the coming Parliament upon *Conservative* principles. *A Conservative,* as you well know, *is one who wishes to maintain an institution in its* PRESENT *state*. The late Government's acts are established by Law. Well, Sir, if you carry on upon this principle you will be furthering the Acts of MR. GLADSTONE'S Liberal Government, which has done more for the general prosperity of the Country than any Government during the last fifty years. Yet, strange as it appears, they have been pushed out of office ("facts winna ding") because they have done so much *good*. A Ministry that has done wonders! Yes, that's the proper name, and were upon the eve of gratifying the Country still more by the Abolition of the "Income Tax." Yes, such were the Ministry that have been pushed out of office to make room for you and your incongruous crew, who apparently promise *nothing*, and doubtless will fully act up to their promise. Truly Sound Legislation appears little appreciated now-a-days. That's no hard to see, but some folks like a change, and *hope* for the best.[56]

Clearly the electorate had not shared Martin's view of the record of the Gladstone government, which was seen as failing to resolve the Irish problem, refusing to allow peaceful picketing during strikes, as the author of unpopular education and licensing acts, as unable to pass needed social reforms, and as a ministry that had conducted a colourless and passive imperial and foreign policy. For example, the Geneva arbitration award, arising out of the so-called *Alabama* claims which dated from the American Civil War, rankled with the British public, and certainly infuriated Martin.

During the conflict between the North and the South in America the Confederacy, lacking in conventional naval power, had turned to commerce raiding. A number of cruisers, several built in Britain, had inflicted severe damage on the northern merchant marine. The most famous of these commerce raiders was the *C S S Alabama*, built in Liverpool and manned by a mainly British crew. Between September 1862 and June 1864, when she was finally sunk off Cherbourg by a northern warship, the *USS Kearsarge,* the *Alabama* destroyed over sixty American merchant vessels and one ship of the northern navy. The British government had taken a narrow view of the Foreign Enlistments Act of 1819, and argued that so long as vessels were not actually fitted out as warships in Britain no offence had been committed. Even so the British government was in the process of ordering the seizure of the ship when she sailed on a so-called trial run, but made instead for the Azores where she took on arms and supplies. The claim for damages by the American owners of the merchant ships and the cargoes destroyed amounted to over fifteen million dollars, or more than three million pounds. Since the British government declined to admit responsibility the affair dragged on for years embittering Anglo-American relations. Eventually the May 1871 Treaty of Washington, which resolved a number of differences between the two countries, referred the *Alabama* claims to an international tribunal which met in Geneva in 1872. In September that year, after a certain amount of diplomatic manoeuvring and posturing, the tribunal awarded the United States fifteen and a half million dollars in damages because the British government had been negligent in preventing the building and arming of the *Alabama* and other commerce raiders.

Martin had been anti-American even before the Civil War, and, in 1861-1862 over the *Trent* affair, he had rejoiced at northern discomfort when they were forced to return the southern envoys, Mason and Slidell. In early 1863 he had been equally bombastic when relations were soured by the escape of the *Alabama*.[57] Not surprisingly, therefore, his reactions to the *Alabama* claims and the Geneva award were equally acerbic. Initially, however, in response to the Treaty of Washington, which did not itself resolve the claims but laid down the procedures for doing so, Martin's attitude was one that welcomed reconciliation, albeit in a patronizing manner:

THE ALABAMA CLAIMS.
JONATHAN AND JOHNNY.
THE WASHINGTON TREATY.

- - - - - - - - - -

Jonathan was a naughty boy
　　That cried to get the moon
Or, something just as likely
　　His ALABAMA claims paid soon.

Johnny was a shrewd boy,
　　Useless quarrels he'd shun;
Thus, he smiled at Jonathan's claims,
　　As nonsense, if not fun.

Says *Jonathan* the treaty's plain,
The meaning's so and so;
And if *you* don't agree to this,
The settlement's no go.

No, says *Johnny*, you construe it wrong,
The meaning you distinctly *strain;*
How *you* can view it as you say,
I've tried to see in vain.

Says *Jonathan*, I guess you're cute,
There *may* be some mistake;
I'll *not* push matters further now,
Meantime, your hand I'll shake.

Says *Johnny*, peace is my intent,
So thus your hand I'll take;
But, in future, mind *young friend,*
I am always wide-awake.

Says *Jonathan*, I guess you are,
And friendly in your manner;
But, when you make out Treaties, John,
Try and write *good grammar.*

So *John* and *Jonathan* are friends again,
A very pleasing matter;
Gratifying to *them* both,
And to MARTIN THE HATTER.[58]

The cordial note upon which Martin's verses ended did not outlast the actual Geneva award in September 1872, which he saw as a humiliation. Thus in October he was calling the tribunal and its decision a farce, and complaining that justice was more blind than usual in this case. Martin found it odd that Britain was to pay damages for injuries inflicted by some Americans on other Americans, especially as that country was now reunited. He wished the present British government, headed by Gladstone, had shown more of the spirit of former statesmen like Chatham, Pitt, Fox, Wellington, Aberdeen, Grey, Melbourne, Peel and Palmerston, "who would never have submitted to this stigma, this indignity upon the British flag, by this one-sided absurd Arbitration Court."[59]

From December 1868 until February 1874, the period of Gladstone's first ministry, Martin provided the population of Aberdeen, or at least those who read the *The Herald*, with a running commentary on political events. he clearly favoured Gladstone and the Liberals, as against Disraeli and the Conservatives, and made mention on a number of occasions of the rivalry between the two party leaders that so much engrossed parliament, press and public at this time. Martin's advertisements repeatedly urged tax cuts, but as seen in Chapter Seven he did not support such reductions at the expense of the armed services and national defence. Perhaps because of his family connections and childhood experiences Martin showed a sympathy for Irish grievances and encouraged Gladstone to seek solutions for them. Martin's sympathies were also clearly with Queen Victoria and the royal family throughout this period, and his loyalty was unwavering despite public antipathy to the monarchy for part of this time. Martin showed equal resolve in his continuing campaign to become a knight, or even a baronet, and missed no opportunity to draw the attention of the citizens of Aberdeen or the residents of Balmoral to his claims. His self-promotion found new expression in these years with his suggestion for a statue of himself, and his purchase of his own final resting place. At the local level Martin may have derived some amusement from such matters as the controversy over the drinking fountain in the Castlegate, but he was also touching on a subject of local interest that divided the Town Council.

As regards foreign affairs Martin's attitudes toward the Franco-Prussian War, and his changing sympathies, mirrored British public opinion. His anti-American prejudices showed themselves in his intemperate reactions to the Geneva arbitration award in 1872, but were again in line with public sentiments.

All in all, therefore, Martin seemed to be keeping his finger on the pulse of public opinion, perhaps because to a large degree he genuinely epitomized that opinion. Of course he sometimes differed from the majority, as when he supported the Liberals in the general election of February 1874 which saw a decisive Conservative victory.

Throughout this period we have Martin's word that both his body and his business remained healthy despite the entry into the retail hat trade of at least two new competitors. Certainly his spirit and his sense of humour were undimmed, and his penchant for attracting public notice was as acute as ever.

NOTES

1 *The Herald*, January 23, 1869, p4, col 2, and April 10, 1869, p4, col 2. In the latter announcement Martin referred to "the celebrity of his *world-wide* famed Establishment."

2 *The Herald*, February 27, 1869, p4, col 2.

3 *The Herald*, June 12, 1869, p4, col 2. Martin added:

> My Lords, your House we all respect,
> But keep your feelings coolish,
> And pass "the Bill" at once, my Lords,
> To thwart it would be foolish.

4 *The Herald*, September 25, 1869, p5, col 2. See also p6, col 1, for a report of the Town Council proceedings and the exchange of correspondence.

5 *The Herald*, October 2, 1869, p4, col 2. It is interesting that both Martin and the editorial writer in *The Herald* felt constrained to stress the unusual sight of the Town Council acting in cordial harmony. The freedom of the city was actually presented to Gladstone in 1871, but drew no comment from Martin at that time.

6 *The Herald*, December 4, 1869, p4, col 2.

7 *The Herald*, January 1, 1870, p4, col 2. Martin assured his readers that if he drank a glass of wine that day, which he thought very likely, he would toast the good health and happiness of all the people.

8 *The Herald*, February 5, 1870, p5, col 6.

9 The author is indebted to Mr George F. Collie, grandson of James Collie, for the details of this story. Mr George F. Collie recalls that his father, George Duncan Collie, also an advocate in Aberdeen, often spoke to him about Samuel Martin.

10 *The Herald*, November 13, 1869, p4, col 2.

11 *The Herald*, February 5,1870, p4, col 2. On February 12, 1870, p4, col 2, Martin described the opening of parliament, referring to the Queen's speech as long, ambiguous, prosy and ingenious.

12 *The Herald*, April 2, 1870, p4, col 2.

13 *The Herald*, July 2, 1870, p4, col 2.

14 *The Herald*, June 11, 1870, p4, col 2.

15 For the background to the outbreak of the war see G. Bonnin, ed., *Bismarck and the Hohenzollern Candidature for the Spanish Throne* (1957), and Michael Howard, *The Franco-Prussian War. The German Invasion Of France, 1870-1871* (1961).

16 *The Herald*, July 23, 1870, p4, col 2. Martin might have added that Leopold was also distantly related to Napoleon III. The reference to Napoleon having been snubbed by the King of Prussia presumably refers to

the famous "Ems Telegram" incident. Anticipating how British public opinion might react to the war Martin wrote:

Bravery on either side
May create a hearty cheer,
But British subjects' policy
Is not to interfere.

17 *The Herald*, August 13, 1870, p4, col 2. As a totally unconnected footnote to this particular advertisement, referring to the visit of the Prince and Princess of Wales to Abergeldie, Martin added:

Prince and Princess, hope you are well-
    Long may you visit your jolly old house,
Prince! birds are in plenty, use your gun freely,
    MARTIN will accept a brace of plump grouse.

18 *The Herald*, September 24, 1870, p4, col 2. Martin's compassion for the people of France and of Paris did not extend to the fate of Napoleon III.

19 *The Herald*, October 8, 1870, p4, col 2. Martin composed two verses that were printed at this time:

France and Prussia end this strife,
    Let this horrid carnage cease;
O hear the prayer of neutral friends,
    And let there soon be peace.

God bless our Queen, long may she reign,
    And every good attend her;
King William it would pleasant be,
    If news of peace you'd send her.

20 *The Herald*, November 12, 1870, p4, col 2.

21 *The Herald*, December 24, 1870, p4, col 2. The third and fourth verses of the nine published ran, referring to the actions of the Russian Bear toward Britain:

Advantage he would therefore take
    To put her in a fix,
By saying he'd no longer stand
    To the Treaty of Fifty-six.

So Gortschakoff a missive wrote
    In a very offensive style,
But he and the Czar were thunderstruck
    By the answer from Granville.

In fact a conference was held in London in January 1871 which upheld the principle that Granville was enunciating, but also conceded the Russian demands. Thus face was saved though it was in reality a diplomatic retreat by Britain of which Martin made no mention.

22 *The Herald*, December 31, 1870, p4, col 2. At the end of another year Martin extended his usual thanks to the people of Aberdeen for their patronage: "The support of 'The People' has enabled MARTIN to enjoy many happy years in Aberdeen. 'The People' have been kind and MARTIN is grateful. 'The People' will doubtless be delighted to hear that he is in his usual good health. He is, no doubt, getting up in years, but he is happy in thinking that 'time' (as yet) has made no visible effect upon his *Stature*; his hair he finds thinner and not so *curly* as it used to be, but physicaly he is active as ever. As to his *mental* abilities 'the People' will likely judge for themselves, as he in the meantime proposes continuing his *advertising* propensities, and will never be backward in expressing his opinions upon passing events (and while he may occasionally differ from others, he trusts to do so without any wish to offend), neither seeking favours nor fearing censure from the *great* where he thinks his opinions may be useful in keeping up the *honour and dignity* of the country...."

23 Philip Magnus, *Gladstone. A Biography* (1954), pp207-218, and R.C.K. Ensor, *England 1870-1914* (1936), pp26-27.

24 *The Herald*, May 15, 1869, p4, col 2.

25 *The Herald*, June 12, 1869, p4, col 2. Martin added that he would prefer a Scottish artist to get the commission.

26 *The Herald*, August 21, 1869, p4, cols 2-3. In his welcome to the Queen Martin included a reference to his campaign to secure himself a knighthood:

> He's given the hint very often,
> Nay, spoke on the matter quite plain;
> If the honour don't come very soon
> He'll have laboured a good deal in vain.

27 *The Herald*, May 21, 1870, p4, col 2, and August 20, 1870, p4, col 2. On the earlier occasion Martin included a verse to say:

> Reports, t'would seem, are very soon carried -
> The report was of late "the Queen's to be married,"
> Some thought it a very unlikely matter,
> Some thought it might be to MARTIN THE HATTER.

28 R.C.K. Ensor, *England 1870-1914*, p26.

29 *The Herald*, March 4, 1871, p4, col 3.

30 *The Herald*, March 18, 1871, p4, col 2. Details of the Aberdeen city celebrations to mark the wedding, and an account of the banquet of cake and wine attended by six hundred ladies and gentlemen, appeared on March 25, 1871, p2, cols 2-6, and p3, cols 1-2. The lists of those present confirmed the participation of Samuel Martin.

31 *The Herald*, May 20, 1871, p4, col 2.

32 *The Herald*, October 7, 1871, p4, col 2.

33 *The Herald*, December 30, 1871, p4, col 2. This advertisement included the sentence, "MARTIN is really and truly thankful that the PRINCE OF WALES has, it may be said, recovered from his recent all but fatal illness."

34 *The Herald*, November 18, 1871, p4, col 1.

35 *The Herald*, March 23, 1872, p4, col 2.

36 *The Herald*, April 20, 1872, p4, col 2. Martin expressed the opinion that shorter hours were a move in the right direction, a reflection of the prevailing spirit and opinion of the day and likely to be satisfactory to all. On August 24, 1872, p4, col 2, Martin announced that he intended to make the 3.00 p.m. early closing on Wednesdays a permanent arrangement to operate all year.

Nearly twenty years earlier, in 1854, the shop assistants working for the drapers, clothiers and hatters in Aberdeen had attempted to organize a Wednesday half-holiday and had published a list of those shopkeepers who had agreed to their request. Martin's name did not appear upon that list, though Alexander Steele and W.M. Miller & Co. did so. This is certainly not conclusive evidence that Martin opposed the shorter hours at that time, but equally he does not appear to have been an enthusiastic and vocal supporter. As the 1854 movement did not receive unanimous support it collapsed after a couple of weeks trial. See *The Herald*, April 29, 1854, p4, col 4, May 6, 1854, p8, col 3, and May 27, 1854, p4, col 3.

37 See, for example, *The Herald*, July 8, 1871, p4, col 2, and August 12, 1871, p4, col 2.

38 *The Herald*, February 3, 1872, p4, col 2.

39 *The Herald*, November 16, 1872, p4, col 2.

40 *The Herald*, June 29, 1872, p5, col 4. Colonel William Henry Sykes, 1790-1872, died in June 1872. He had contested, but lost, the Aberdeen seat in 1847, but was the member in the Liberal interest 1857-1872.

41 *The Herald*, May 18, 1872, p4, col 2. Martin added the sentiment that he was happy to hear that the Prince of Wales had quite recovered from his recent illness.

Alongside Martin's announcement in this number of *The Herald* there appeared a sizeable advertisement, across two columns, by Fyffe's Great Hat & Cap Mart, 18, St. Nicholas Street, Corner of Netherkirkgate. Fyffe claimed, "EVER thankful for the past, but resolved that if exertion can gain, or money procure it, the future career of my Establishment shall excel everything I have hitherto attempted. My Wholesale Warehouse and Manufactory being new situated in Manchester (the great seat of Commerce and Manufacture), and being well known as one of the largest buyers in the trade, I am this season prepared to offer by far the largest variety of all classes of HATS, CAPS, SHIRTS, TIES, and COLLARS I have ever had the pleasure of submitting to the public, and at least Twenty per cent. cheaper than any establishment in Aberdeen.

42 *The Herald*, August 24, 1872, p4, col 2. At this time Martin proposed a novel arrangement to suit himself during the shooting season:

> **NOW THAT PARLIAMENT** is prorogued, the *Grouse* shooting going on, and the *Partridge* season about to commence, MARTIN would pleasurably suggest to his M.P. friends *not to inundate* him with presents of too many birds at once during the months of September and October. *One* or *two* brace a-*week* would do nicely, and which might be sent in to MARTIN by rotation - thus the M.P. for Aberdeen might send his present of birds on the *first* week of September, and the *Senior* and *Junior* M.P.'s for the County on the *second* and *third* weeks, the M.P.'s for the neighbouring Counties sending in their presents of birds on the *fourth* and *fifth* weeks, and so on. This arrangement might not inconvenience *them* and would suit MARTIN admirably, as too many Luxuries at once might disarrange MARTIN'S usual style of living. Nevertheless, a Brace or two of Birds would be acceptable at *any* time from "HER MAJESTY" or the "PRINCE OF WALES," and would be duly appreciated. Indeed, they might have a tendency to improve MARTIN'S appetite marvellously; then a glass or two of Claret -ahem!

Possibly Martin's scheme worked, as in *The Herald* on October 5, 1872, p4, col 2, he was able to claim that he had received several brace of grouse from friends in high places, though not yet from the Prince of Wales.

43 *The Herald*, October 5, 1872, p4, col 2.

44 *The Herald*, January 4, 1873, p4, col 2. Martin maintained once more that Father Time had laid his hand but gently on him, though admitting:

> His grey hairs are certainly in the ascendant, and he finds more hair on the *sides* than on the *top* of his head, from which it might be inferred that he has lately been growing *through* his hair. His moustache is fierce as ever, and his beard comely. His teeth of *youthful growth* are not too plentiful, but answer all the purposes of mastication, and sharpen up wonderfully with a glass of good "Old Port." He occasionally wears spectacles, perhaps because they are becoming fashionable; however, they suit him admirably, and his nasal organ holds them up nobly. There is an old saying that old age brings its troubles *it has brought* MARTIN *a great many comforts that he could not get at in his youth,* THANKS TO THE SUPPORT OF "THE PEOPLE."

45 *The Herald*, February 1, 1873, p4, col 2. See also March 8, 1873, p4, col 2.

46 Philip Magnus, *Gladstone. A Biography*, pp224-25, and R.C.K. Ensor, *England 1870-1914*, pp24-25.

47 *The Herald*, April 5, 1873, p4, col 2. In this particular advertisement Martin also made a reference to the difficult personal and political relationship between Gladstone and the Queen. He remarked that if Gladstone continued to annoy her he would have to deal with an irate Martin.

48 *The Herald*, May 10, 1873, p4, col 1.

49 *The Herald*, May 17, 1873, p4, col 2, and August 16, 1873, p4, col 2. In May Martin mentioned Victoria's kindness to the exiled Empress Eugenie of France, whose husband, Napoleon III, had died at Chislehurst, in England, on January 9.

50 *The Herald*, June 21, 1873, p4, col 2, and July 12, 1873, p4, col 2. Martin regretted that due to some oversight he had not received a lock of the Shah's hair, a shake of his hand, a pearl-mounted sword, or a bag of diamonds as a parting gift. In fact Nasar Od-Din Shah, who ruled 1848-1896, visited Deeside in 1889, alas too late for Martin to enjoy or to commemorate the event.

51 *The Herald*, October 4, 1873, p4, col 2. By this time W.C. King's emporium, now called The Broad Street Hat Shop, was claiming to be recognized as the cheapest in town for good and durable hats, bonnets, shirts, ties and braces. See *The Herald*, October 4, 1873, p4, col 1.

52 See *The Aberdeen Journal*, January 21, 1874, p5, col 3, for an account of the Town Council proceedings of January 19.

53 *The Herald*, January 24, 1874, p4, col 2. The statue of George, fifth and last Duke of Gordon (1770-1836), was later removed to its present position in Golden Square. The reference to *Smith* was presumably to the Aberdeen city architect.

54 *The Herald*, December 6, 1873, p4, col 2.

55 *The Herald*, January 3, 1874, p4, col 2.

56 *The Herald*, February 28, 1874, p4, col 2.

57 See herein Chapter Four on Martin and the American Civil War.

58 *The Herald*, March 23, 1872, p4, col 2.

59 *The Herald*, October 5, 1872, p4, col 2. Martin thought that America might well exclaim:

> Brother John, we've done you clean
> By the Geneva Arbitration,
> You must admit, big Brother John,
> You're behind in Legislation.
> You have to pay the piper, John,
> And the payment's pretty smart,

But hand to *us* the *Sovereigns*, John,
And do not break your heart.

Martin also included an oblique reference to the Geneva award in his advertisement of November 8, 1873, p4, col 2, which was otherwise concerned with the Ashanti War.

CHAPTER NINE

THE FINAL YEARS ON UNION STREET. 1874-1885.

The electoral success of the Conservatives led to the creation of a government headed by Benjamin Disraeli that would remain in office for six years, February 1874 until April 1880. Disraeli faced the future with the pleasant prospect of a safe majority in both houses of parliament, a united cabinet and a harmonious relationship with the monarch. On the other hand, the Liberal Party, which Samuel Martin had supported, was in disarray following its defeat, and Gladstone was so downcast by the result that he wished to resign the leadership of the Liberals. The immediate task before the new ministry was the writing of a budget for the next financial year, and the result was a compromise measure that did not propose to abolish income tax, as Gladstone had advocated, but reduced it by one penny, while also ending the duty on sugar, a proposal Martin had oft times recommended himself.[1]

The new parliament opened on March 18, 1874, and Martin was offering comment and advice within days. He made it clear at once that he did not welcome a Conservative government, especially as it was unlikely to continue Gladstone's policies in general and abolish income tax in particular. He referred to the meeting of the do-little parliament, noting the paucity of legislative proposals brought forward, and expressed the view that he could have made a better speech himself at the opening ceremony. Martin recommended a cut in taxes, especially income tax, that should be designed to shift the burden from the working man. If Disraeli, whom Martin acknowledged as a man of great talent, used the existing governmental financial surplus to reduce taxes he could prolong the life of his ministry. Martin then wrote a few lines for Disraeli's benefit, including a reference to the fact that the new Prime Minister was in his seventieth year:

> MARTIN thinks this is good advice to lengthen your tenure in office, Old Gentleman, if you see it in the right way; and you might suggest *Knighthood* to MARTIN for the hint. He's been expecting the honour for some time: which, doubtless, was known to the late Government, but has evidently been overlooked. So, if you want to make a favourable hit to strengthen your power by pleasing "THE PEOPLE" for the late

> Government's apparent neglect of MARTIN, now's the time. But understand, MARTIN seeks no honours under false colours; he's a Liberal Conservative, but not Conservative in the original sense of the word; but, indeed, as to that MARTIN is inclined to think you're no far frae that kind of politics yersel'. Time works wonders, Sir, and the pleasures of office are sweet.[2]

At first sight it is surprising to note that after March 1874 Martin did not take up a political theme again for nearly a year. The explanation of this unusual abstinence from comment on the parliamentary scene may possibly be found in his advertisement on January 2, 1875, when in reviewing the previous year Martin remarked that for a short time in 1874 he had been laid up "with one of the many diseases that flesh is heir to." Although he claimed that with the aid of a strong constitution, a lively temperament and the support and sympathy of the people he had made a complete recovery in body and mind[3] Martin's health was to prove suspect in the future as subsequent events would show.

Whatever the truth regarding his well-being Martin was not deterred in 1874 from paying his usual respects to royalty. In May he expressed somewhat belated good wishes on the occasion of another royal wedding. On January 23 Victoria's second son, Prince Alfred, Duke of Edinburgh, married Grand Duchess Marie Alexandrovna, daughter of Czar Alexander II, in St. Petersburg. The public celebrations in Aberdeen on that day included a procession, fireworks and street illuminations. *The Herald* published full details of these events the following day, including comments on the buildings and businesses that made particular contribution to the show, but, unusually, made no mention of a display by Samuel Martin.[4] Martin did publish a new advertisement that day, but it was the one that referred to the offensive horse trough or drinking fountain at the Castlegate and the statue of the Duke of Gordon. There is no clear reason why Martin chose to ignore the event in his advertisements at the time, unless his Russophobia temporarily overcame his normal feelings of loyalty and respect toward the royal family. At all events, Martin was in apparent good humour a few months later, in May, when he wrote:

> MARTIN'S wish is true happiness
> To the PRINCE and his RUSSIAN BRIDE;
> They might on MARTIN make a call
> On their visit to DEESIDE.

And if the CZAR himself would call,
MARTIN would be delighted;
And, if *agreeable*, step up with *him*
To BALMORAL, to be KNIGHTED.

Then Bon-Accord would ring her bells,
There might be an illumination,
"THE PEOPLE" so well pleased would be
With MARTIN'S elevation.

And jolly cheers would then be heard
From BALLATER to BRAEMAR,
At the meeting of OUR GOOD KIND QUEEN,
With MARTIN and the Czar.

Then let *all* hope the time *has* come,
With *Parliament's* approbation,
That THE QUEEN, THE CZAR, and MARTIN,
MEET IN FRIENDLY SALUTATION.

In fact, as Martin noted, preparations were afoot in London for the visit of Alexander II. Martin observed how time altered circumstances, but hoped that the royal marriage would lead to peace between the two countries. He also noted with apparent regret, that as Prince Alfred had married the Czar's only daughter, Martin could not himself become the Czar's son-in-law.[5]

Martin's advertisement for July 25, 1874, though modest in size and very unremarkable in content by his normal standards, was innovative in one respect at least. For the first time he featured in his weekly announcement in *The Herald* a sketch of his shop-front, which in the absence of photographic evidence is particularly interesting as it gives an artist's impression of the famous establishment at 34 Union Street.[6] Oddly enough Martin had been using a slightly different etching of his shop-front on his bills or invoices since at least 1859.[7]

In fact, Martin ran this same advertisement for thirteen consecutive weeks, July 25 to October 17, 1874, inclusive. This was a very unusual circumstance, and may be an indiction that this was the period in 1874 when Martin was unwell. Not until October 24 did he change his text to remind readers of the approach of winter.[8] Martin, after all, passed his sixtieth birthday in 1874, and his claim in January 1875 that he was quite recovered from his illness has to be viewed with some caution. In Martin's obituary, published in *The Evening Gazette* and *The Daily Free Press* in January 1888, it was recorded that Martin was a man who enjoyed life, "But these blythesome times passed, and days of pain and dowieness came sure and suddenly. Twelve or fourteen years ago Mr Martin was stricken with paralysis, and he was never the same man after. Though, following a brief confinement, he was able to be daily at 34 Union Street, yet the attention was a trying task...."[9] It is impossible, at this distance in time, to know whether Samual Martin suffered a stroke, or something similar, in 1874, or whether the illness he had was but a forerunner of a stroke that occurred in the next year or two.

Martin, however, was sufficiently recovered at the beginning of the 1875 parliamentary session to devote his advertisement of February 27 to that subject. He claimed to observe that Disraeli had a hard time keeping his own supporters in order, and offered little hope for any reduction in taxes under the Conservatives. Martin also wrote three verses about the new Leader of the House of Commons, Lord Hartington, who had replaced Gladstone as leader of the Liberals in the Commons, (while Lord Granville led the party in the Lords).[10] This advertisement ran for six weeks before being replaced by a plea for a larger military garrison in Aberdeen.[11]

In May Martin divided his attention between the Queen's first visit to Deeside that year, and the dangerous diplomatic situation developing in Europe. That month had witnessed a war scare due to the apparent intention of Germany to launch a preemptive war against France, who had recovered remarkably quickly from the defeats of 1870-1871. Britain had associated herself with the diplomatic protest and pressure exerted on Germany by Russia, and this had led to a difference between the British government and the German Ambassador in London, Count Munster. Martin made a critical mention of the Ambassador's "recent...uncalled for Speech," and believed it no part of a diplomat's function to interfere in, or to comment upon, the political affairs of the country to which he was accredited.[12]

By July Martin was devoting his announcement to the forthcoming visit of the Prince of Wales to India:

GREAT
PREPARATIONS FOR THE
PRINCE OF WALES' TRIP TO INDIA.
"HAPPY PRINCE,"
A trip to India and all expenses paid.
That's the way to do it. HURRAH!

O! that MARTIN THE HATTER had been born a PRINCE, but it is perhaps better as it is as the "PEOPLE" enables MARTIN to enjoy many trips that cost much less than

£142,000.

The preparations for the trip are nearly ready, and MARTIN hopes that the results will be highly beneficial. Many might suppose that it would have been more complete, and

A GRACEFUL ACT ON THE PART OF
"HER MAJESTY" TO HAVE
KNIGHTED MARTIN,

and appointed him to accompany the PRINCE OF WALES to India. His advice and presence might have been of much service to the PRINCE, as in many parts of India MARTIN'S name might be as well known to some of the NATIVE CHIEFS as the PRINCE'S. But this is a matter that has evidently been neglected on the part of the "QUEEN," so that

MARTIN'S KNIGHTHOOD AND OTHER
HONOURS

Are yet to come, and the sooner the better. MARTIN cannot say that he is wearying, but, nevertheless, he is anxious; but hope keeps him up wonderfully, which might be well supposed from his philosophic mind.[13]

At the end of the 1875 parliamentary session Martin published an advertisement that expressed both criticism of the government and disappointment at "ONE of the most unsatisfactory Sessions that has happened in the annals of British history." Martin complained that for six months M.P.s had trifled away their own and the public's time achieving almost nothing unless one counted the blocking of bills that would have benefited the public. He wondered if this was due to old age impairing the faculties of legislators, if so he recommended an infusion of younger blood into the cabinet.[14]

On this occasion either partisan preference blinded Martin to the achievements of Disraeli's government, or his political perspicacity deserted him, since most observers would view the 1875 session as a particularly successful one, even "an *annus mirabilis* for useful domestic legislation."[15] The major measures of social reform passed in this session included two acts favourable to trade unions - the Employers and Workmen Act and the Conspiracy and Protection of Property Act - the Artisans Dwellings Act, an Agricultural Holdings Act, a Sale of Food and Drugs Act, a Factory Act, a Friendly Societies Act and a Public Health Act.[16]

On New Year's Day 1876 Martin thanked his customers, as usual, for the last twelve months in which his business had lived up to his best expectations, thus endorsing his system of business, namely selling quality goods at moderate prices. He also claimed to be in wonderful good health for his time of life, and also in good spirits since he habitually looked on the bright side and avoided a great deal of anxiety. He summed up his philosophy with the verse:

> Then strive to be happy is the best plan,
> And shun life's troubles long as you can;
> All in this world have some part to play,
> But a happy mind may keep troubles away.[17]

This apparently happy mood was reiterated two weeks later when Martin wrote that he was beginning 1876, "with a very happy flow of spirits, being very grateful for prosperity and having a Large and Well-assorted Stock of Seasonable Goods, *Easy-fitting, Light,* and *Durable, and at Moderate Prices.*"[18] Another indication that Martin's health was not as good as he claimed, and wished his readers to believe, is that he ran this seasonable advertisement for eleven weeks. He did not replace it until April 1, 1876, and then mainly to write about the spring weather.[19]

In early May Martin was able to comment on a change of some significance in his business and advertising career. *The Herald* was taken over by the proprietors of the rival *Aberdeen Free Press*, and though in the short run *The Herald* continued to enjoy a separate existence, in November the two titles merged as *The Herald and Weekly Free Press.* Martin marked the change of ownership in May with an advertisement which scotched one rumour about the costs of his announcements in *The Herald* under the old regime:

OLD FRIENDS DEPART
BY DEATH OR OTHERWISE.

- - - - - - - - - -

This being MARTIN'S *first Advertisement in the "ABERDEEN HERALD" under the New Proprietorship, he thinks it a duty on his part to say that he was always well pleased with the polite attention and charges under the old management, although some people seemed to think that* MARTIN *got his Advertisements inserted for nothing (which was a mistake); yet, if the New Management comes to the conclusion of doing so,* MARTIN *has no objection. They might be inclined to do so upon the hypothesis that the friendly feelings of new friends might make up, to a great extent, for the absence of old familiar faces.*[20]

Neither infirmity nor the novelty of the new proprietorship of *The Herald* deterred Martin when it came to a royal event of note, and in the same advertisement of May 6, 1876, he used the debate over the Royal Titles Bill, which made Victoria Empress of India with effect from January 1, 1877, to suggest that this opened up fresh opportunities for the Queen to honour him with a title of some sort.[21]

Martin did not discover a new cause to lay before the people of Aberdeen until the end of September, but he then chose to join the popular outrage which had swept the country in the summer of 1876 over the Turkish atrocities against the Bulgarians. The Balkans had been a seething mass of political and military turbulence for twelve months, and though the situation had been a source of concern to the British government it had not troubled the consciences of the British people until the London *Daily News* published grisly accounts of the actions of irregular Turkish troops. The whole country was outraged by these reports, and in early September William Gladstone leapt back into the public limelight with the publication of *The Bulgarian Horrors and the Question of the East.* This sensational best-seller was one of the most famous political pamphlets ever produced, and it contained the well known demand that the Turks should leave the area, "one and all, bag and baggage."[22]

Martin was as disturbed and affronted as anyone by the revelations of these "HELLISH ATROCITIES," and he called the Turks a disgrace to the nineteenth century and to the civilized nations of the earth. He was aggrieved that Britain wasted time with expressions of indignation and remonstrances against the Turks, when these had no effect in preventing fresh outrages, and he called for firm leadership and action to end these "fiendish atrocities."[23] Whether Martin's indignation cooled suddenly cannot be known, but his anti-Turkish outburst was only included in his advertisement for one week.

The amalgamation of *The Herald* with *The Free Press* in late 1876 did not lead to any change in Martin's practice of reviewing the previous twelve months at the beginning of a new year. Nor did it prevent him thanking the people "sincerely and heartily for their support during the past year," or detract from his determination to "keep up the world-wide *fame* of his well-known, well-conducted, and attractive Establishment." He did, however, make some concession on the subject of his health and age:

> "THE PEOPLE" will no doubt be pleased to learn that MARTIN is in comparatively good health.
>
> No doubt he is getting older, having been nearly *Forty* Years in business in Aberdeen, but getting *old* was quite in accordance with MARTIN'S calculation, as he thought it would *happen* if he *lived long enough*. But age sits lightly on MARTIN as his business abilities are lively as ever, and his juvenile activity of mind, youthful appearance, and polite manners are as conspicuous as ever.
>
> 'Tis a treat to see age
> With a pleasant youthful manner.
>
> In short, MARTIN is wonderfully well, if it was not for a touch of rheumatism or *gout* (which MARTIN is happy in supposing *only* troubles people in *easy* circumstances) which enables him to practise the *Alexandra* Limp, which some people think adds a sort of *dignity* to his general appearance. In fact, he finds it a benefit, as it obliges him to mind his *steps*, which is a great advantage to many people in *treading* their way through this Weary World, which is frequently severely commented upon, but from which comparatively few people seem anxious to part.[24]

One consequence of advertising in the combined *Herald and Weekly Free Press* was that Martin's announcements now appeared alongside those of W. Fyffe, Fashionable Hatter, 3 & 5 St Nicholas Street. However, on February 3, 1877, there appeared the following announcement:

> SALE OF BANKRUPT STOCK - On Thursday afternoon tenders were received for the whole stock-in-trade, shop furniture, &c, belonging to the

trust estate of Mr William Fyffe, hatter, St Nicholas Street, Aberdeen, which were opened in presence of the offerers within the premises. The offer of Mr William King, hatter, Broad Street, amounting to about £900, was accepted.[25]

There is no way of knowing whether Martin had himself entered a bid for Fyffe's stock, but this did not, in fact, mark the end of a competitor, because in November 1877 Fyfe & Co., Hatters & Clothiers, late St Nicholas Street, announced they were now at 7 Market Street. Their exact relationship to William Fyffe is obscure, especially as the spelling of the name had changed.[26] Meantime, the Crown Clothing Company, 17 Broad Street, which claimed to offer rare value in satin and felt hats as well as caps, had followed Martin into verse,[27] and only twelve months later James Hall opened a new hat shop at 55 Union Street.[28]

In April 1877 Martin himself went in for an unusual two column spread for his latest announcement, but it was one of the most poignant of his advertisements. His text was full of nostalgia after nearly four decades trading from the same premises, and in itself virtually a social history of mid-nineteenth century Aberdeen:

ESTABLISHED NEARLY FORTY YEARS

\- - - - - - - -

Forty years; 'tis a long time. Yes! NO Railways at Aberdeen at that time. NO beautiful Market. NO magnificent Municipal Buildings. NO Bank Buildings like Noblemen's Mansions. NO splendid Post-Office. NO attractive Houses and Villas as are now to be seen in the West-End. NO Tramway Cars. NO Cabs and Few Carriages. NO Lorries. NO Wet Dock. FEW, if any, Plate Glass Shop Windows. NO School Boards or Schools like Palaces (yet good solid education at a cheap rate). NOT so many Churches, but better *filled.* NOT nearly so many BOBBIES, but more soldiers. THE same Barracks (for which those that are inclined may thank all the Governments that have been in power up to the present time). AND Last though not Least, NOT so many Grey Hairs in Martin's Head (he had no Moustache at that time). Oh! the changes of time. Forty years ago Martin was a dark-haired comely youth, with lots of philosophy and the world before him, and though now a trifle older his temperament is lively as ever, with a fine eye to business....[29]

Although in the same advertisement Martin noted that the Queen had not consulted him on the Eastern Question, nor invited him to meet the

Russian diplomat General Ignatiev on his visit to London, he fancied the cause might well be that Victoria already knew that he favoured peace with honour in the Balkans. Unfortunately, peace did not survive beyond the end of the month, with hostilities between Russia and Turkey lasting from April 1877 to January 1878, the most notable action being the siege of Plevna. In May 1877 Martin greeted the Queen's visit to Deeside with assurances that she might sleep securely at Balmoral as neither Russians nor Turks were at hand. He added:

> BEACONSFIELD and DERBY have done their best
> To avert the War this Session;
> Now let RUSSIANS and TURKS fight it out,
> It will give them a useful lesson.[30]

In August Martin managed an oblique reference to the war in the Balkans when he ran a headline to the effect that the shooting season had began, particularly in Turkey. However, this was more a lead into his usual seasonal solicitation of a present of a brace or two of grouse rather than a serious comment on foreign affairs. In fact between May and August he had concentrated largely on local affairs including references to the weather and the agricultural prospects for that year.[31] Martin continued to focus on matters of local interest in September when he gave his attention to the meeting of the Social Science Congress in Aberdeen. No doubt it was a matter of regret, he mused, that the Queen would not grace the proceedings and that he would not be reading a paper. On the other hand Martin's absence would allow others to shine.[32]

The last advertisement by Martin in *The Herald and Weekly Free Press* in 1877 was on November 10. Then, without explanation, his insertions in this newspaper abruptly ceased, even though in the following months there were regular advertisements by M'Leod, and occasional notices by Fyfe, Steele, and Hall, but no announcement at all by any hatter from December 21, 1878, until August 30, 1879, when Martin published an advertisement after a gap of twenty-two months.[33]

Martin had not, however, reconsidered the value of advertising and decided to abstain from the columns of the local press. Instead, he had removed his announcements, after nearly forty years, from *The Herald* and its successor *The Herald and Weekly Free Press*, and begun to patronise both *The Daily Free Press* and the *Aberdeen Journal*. No

SUMMER RAPIDLY APPROACHING
THE DAYS LENGTHENING FAST,
BUT DRY WEATHER WANTED FOR SEED-TIME.

THE TIME WHEN SHABBY HATS SHOULD BE OUT OF SIGHT
AND FASHIONABLE NEW HATS APPEAR.

For however well Dressed
From the Necktie to the Feet,
Without a good Hat
You can ne'er be complete.

RIGHT AGAIN, MARTIN.

SATIN HATS.

THE NEW SHAPES.

BEAUTIFUL GOODS.

EASY FITTING, LIGHT, AND DURABLE,
AND AT MODERATE PRICES.

ALSO,
THE NEW
ROUND CROWN SHELL AND TWEED HATS,
IN GREAT VARIETY.

BEST QUALITY
SATIN HATS,
MANUFACTURED BY
LINCOLN, BENNET, & CO., | EDWARD WALMSLEY,
AND OTHER EMINENT HOUSES.

SEE MARTIN'S
ATTRACTIVE ESTABLISHMENT
AND
HANDSOME WINDOWS.

SAMUEL MARTIN,
HATTER TO THE PEOPLE,

34 UNION STREET, ABERDEEN.

ESTABLISHED NEARLY FORTY YEARS.

Forty years; 'tis a long time. Yes! NO Railways at Aberdeen at that time. NO beautiful Market. NO magnificent Municipal Buildings. NO Bank Buildings like Noblemen's Mansions. NO splendid Post-Office. NO attractive Houses and Villas as are now to be seen in the West-End. NO Tramway Cars. NO Cabs and Few Carriages. NO Lorries. NO Wet Dock. FEW, if any, Plate Glass Shop Windows. NO School Boards or Schools like Palaces (yet good solid education at a cheap rate). NOT so many Churches, but better *filled*. NOT nearly so many BOBBIES, but more Soldiers. THE same Barracks (for which those that are inclined may thank all the Governments that have been in power up to the present time). AND Last though not Least. NOT so many Grey Hairs in Martin's Head (he had no Moustache at that time). Oh! the changes of time. Forty years ago Martin was a dark-haired comely youth, with lots of philosophy and the world before him, and though now a trifle older his temperament is lively as ever, with a fine eye to business, and

EVER THANKFUL FOR THE SUPPORT OF "THE PEOPLE."

GOD BLESS THE QUEEN.

THE SUPPORT OF THE PEOPLE
Has enabled HER MAJESTY AND MARTIN to enjoy many of the blessings of this life.

AND ALTHOUGH HER MAJESTY DID NOT CONSULT MARTIN UPON THE EASTERN QUESTION, NOR SEND FOR MARTIN TO MEET GENERAL IGNATIEFF WHEN HE WAS IN LONDON, the cause might be that HER MAJESTY IS WELL AWARE THAT MARTIN'S IDEAS ARE EVER IN FAVOUR OF PEACE WITH HONOUR.

explanation was volunteered other than the bald statement, "A CHANGE. MARTIN'S Advertisements will in the meantime appear in the Friday's *Free Press* instead of the *Herald and Weekly Free Press."*[34] This arrangement was quickly changed with the announcement that Martin's advertisements would be published in *The Daily Free Press* on Wednesdays.[35] Martin had a choice of days of the week with both the *Free Press* and the *Journal* because the former had moved from a twice weekly publication to a daily newspaper in 1872, while the latter had changed from a weekly to a daily in 1876. At the same time Martin announced his shorter opening hours for the winter months, December 1, 1877, until March 1, 1878. In future he would close at seven o'clock in the evenings, (instead of eight o'clock as formally), except for Saturdays when he would conclude business at "Sharp Ten," and for early closing on Wednesdays at three in the afternoon.[36] Even this unpromising subject produced two verses from Martin's pen in December:

One hour more for rational enjoyment
Is really quite a treat,
And may make the hours of business
More agreeable, healthy, and sweet.

To keep us vigorous, healthy, and strong,
The hours of business have been too long;
We should keep in view the *mind* needs *ease*,
To keep the *body* from disease.[37]

One can only speculate on the motives behind Martin's sudden and unexplained switch away from *The Herald and Weekly Free Press.* As he now employed the columns of the *Daily Free Press* it does not seem likely that there had been a falling out with the editors or proprietors of the weekly over either Martin's copy or the editorial views of the paper. Perhaps Martin obtained better rates from the daily papers, or possibly he had been disappointed with the impact of his announcements in the weekly and hoped to reach more potential customers via one of both of the dailies. In fact Martin did pay for a weekly insertion in the *Aberdeen Journal* from November 1877 until May 1878. Thereafter, however, his announcement in that paper became occasional and irregular and only repeated his advertisements in *The Daily Free Press* which did appear regularly every Saturday from November 1877 until September 1879. The great majority of these advertisements, which ran unchanged for several weeks, were brief announcements devoted to strictly mundane business promotion. Only occasionally did Martin revert to his once familiar style of lengthy diversions upon whatsoever political, military or diplomatic matters took his fancy, or else indulge in unusual explanations of the benefits of a new hat bought from his stock. In December 1877, for example, he explained why such a purchase was sound philosophy:

> Reader, if at present you've a Shabby Hat,
> Out of Shape and greasy,
> Try a Soft-fitting Hat from MARTIN;
> If the head is right the mind is easy.
>
> And if you have an easy mind,
> Life's blessings it almost doubles;
> Whereas if your mind is *not* at ease,
> Life's pleasures may seem but troubles.[38]

At New Year 1878 both *The Daily Free Press* and the *Aberdeen Journal* carried Martin's appraisal of the past twelve months, his fortieth year in the city, which he adjudged to be one of the most prosperous in his career. He recalled that he had launched his business on what, forty years later, would seem but scant capital. However, it had enabled him to buy his stock cheaply through prompt payment, and to sell good quality hats at moderate prices, a system that had worked well for four decades. As he explained:

> Forty years is a gie long time
> To keep a Business firmly going;
> But MARTIN thinks his reaping well
> Is by his early Sowing.[39]

Although he continued to publish his advertisements in the early months of 1878,[40] he did not produce one that touched upon matters of moment until May, when he focused on the Eastern Question.

The Balkan War between Russia and Turkey in 1877-1878 ended with the Treaty of San Stefano in March 1878, but the terms were so favourable to Russia and the Slavs in general and so disadvantageous to Turkey that Austria and Britain objected and the treaty was totally revised at a European conference, the Congress of Berlin, 13 June-13 July 1878. In early 1878 an Anglo-Russian war seemed not unlikely, and Russophobia and jingoism flourish side by side in Britain. When Disraeli, now Lord Beaconsfield, returned from Berlin with a treaty that seemed to have thwarted Russian ambitions, in a fateful phrase Disraeli claimed he had achieved "peace with honour," he was fêted in London.[41]

Martin was not the man to resist anti-Russian feelings or to object to any outburst of chauvinism or appeal to national honour. At the beginning of 1878 he was expressing the hope that Lord Beaconsfield would make sure that British honour was not tarnished in any Balkan settlement.[42] By late May, before the Congress of Berlin convened, he was applauding the fact that the Russian eagle's wings had been clipped, but warned they might grow again. He added:

> MARTIN was transcendently delighted at the firm attitude of Britain on the Eastern Question. MARTIN is, and ever was, a Liberal-Conservative in politics, being a firm supporter of the Constitution and Institution of our glorious country, and will ever be induced honestly to give honour to whom honour is due. No matter what shade of politics men in office may be, the men that keep up the dignity of the Country are the men that MARTIN admires, and
>
> LORD BEACONSFIELD
>
> and the present Government have done so to MARTIN'S entire satisfaction. Then go ahead, old gentlemen, and prosper. You've nobly revived the *prestige* of our Country to HER former standard and shown to the eyes of the world that
>
> THE BRITISH FLAG MUST EVER BE
> RESPECTED.[43]

Several weeks after the Congress of Berlin was over Martin returned to the subject of the Eastern Question. He used the literary device of recounting a dream, one which related to two imaginary events - a visit by Lord Salisbury, who had replaced Lord Derby as Foreign Secretary in April 1878, to the Czar to settle differences, and a visit by the Prime Minister, Beaconsfield, to Martin's shop before both statesmen went as British representatives to Berlin.[44]

Martin did not repeat this particular advertisement in the following weeks, but merely published short announcements in *The Daily Free Press* each Saturday until the end of the year. The final few months of

1878 appear to have heralded the beginning of an economic depression and a downturn in trade. At the beginning of 1878 Martin had claimed that 1877 had been one of his most prosperous in forty years of business, but twelve months later his mood was more circumspect:

> MARTIN thanks "THE PEOPLE" most heartily for their kind support for the past year. No doubt trade has not been so lively as usual for the last month or two, and, looking at the trade of the country generally, he is a fortunate tradesman who can say otherwise; but MARTIN having had some very good months at the beginning of the year they make up wonderfully for the dull trade, thus *keeping in view the trade feeling in the country, the unhinged state of politics,* the present weather, *the frozen state of the money market, the sagacious looks of bankers, &c.,* MARTIN, looking at the year on the whole, is satisfied and grateful.[45]

Although he was now over sixty, (in fact sixty-four), Martin still claimed to enjoy good health and to have no intention of retiring. Age had not dimmed his martial enthusiasm, and he praised the record of British soldiers in the Afghan War of 1878-79, a conflict which arose out of an Anglo-Russian struggle for influence in that remote but strategically important country.[46] Surprisingly, perhaps, with an imperial military campaign in progress, Martin did not publish another significant and substantial advertisement until August 30, 1879, when an announcement by him appeared in the pages of both *The Daily Free Press* and, after nearly two years, in *The Herald and Weekly Free Press.*

Whereas no adequate account exists to explain why Martin had shifted his advertising away from *The Herald and Weekly Free Press* in November 1877, even omitting his annual reviews at the end of 1877 and 1878, equally no reason was given to explain this return to the fold. The disinclination of other hatters in the city to advertise in *The Herald and Weekly Free Press* in 1879 is another unexplained mystery. After November 1877 Martin's main publicity effort was in the columns of *The Daily Free Press*. His announcements in the *Aberdeen Journal* appeared regularly until May 1878, but were few and far between from then until his New Year's greeting in 1879, after which they disappeared entirely for two years.

Whatever the explanation for Martin's sudden reappearance in the advertising columns of *The Herald and Weekly Free Press*, indeed on the front page, in August 1879, the content of his announcement can scarcely have caused surprise. Perhaps it was not a coincidence that Queen Victoria had arrived in Aberdeen *en route* to Balmoral earlier the same week. At all events Martin chose to concern himself with yet another imperial war, the Queen's visit to Deeside and his own ambition to be knighted. The new military adventure was the Zulu War of January to July 1879, which began with the disaster of Isandhlwana, but ended with the victory of Ulundi and the capture of the Zulu leader Cetewayo. This was just the sort of distant campaign in some far flung corner of the Empire that appealed to Martin's sense of the heroic and the dramatic, ending, as it did, in triumph. His advertisement was in the main a poem, in no less than nineteen verses, relating to a fancied visit by himself to South Africa. Martin's reverie was interrupted, he explained, by the arrival of the Queen in Aberdeen:

> MARTIN was startled by the report of guns,
> Which echoed through the house,
> Caused, he thought by *County* friends,
> Determined to send him *Grouse*.
>
> Then he heard a trumpet's sound
> As if in a barrack yard;
> 'Twas the approach of the Royal Scots,
> Her Majesty's body-guard.
>
> Now the sun came out in Splendid style,
> And beautiful the scene;
> Then ""THE PEOPLE" gave a loud Huzza
> For our good and gracious QUEEN.[47]

Martin ran a modest advertisement, about hats, in *The Herald and Weekly Free Press* from September 13 to December 27, 1879, inclusive, but at the beginning of 1880, he published his regular retrospective view of the past year. He began by reminding his readers that he had opened his premises in February 1838 and claimed, therefore, to have been established for forty-two years, which made his the oldest hat shop in Aberdeen. He included a brief aside about, and New Year greeting to, the Highland troops then serving in the renewed Afghan War,[48] before commenting on both his own, and the nation's commercial situation:

MARTIN thanks THE "PEOPLE" most sincerely for their kind support for the *past* year - *a year (notwithstanding the dull trade in the country generally)* quite up to his expectations, and although the trade of the last few months of the past year was not so good as the corresponding months of the previous year, yet, after being Forty-Two years in business he would think his philosophy terribly at fault, and that his business education had been sadly neglected if *that* had any depressing effect on his naturally good spirits. No! No!! No low spirits for MARTIN. According to MARTIN'S ideas, *a hatter* that has been in business *for a few* years less than *half* a century, and has never *felt* dull trade or the anxieties therefrom, should be considered a *Commercial Hero*; and when taken away from what some people call this *weary* world (yet seem in no way anxious to *leave*) should be buried with

MILITARY HONOURS,

And get a nook in

WESTMINSTER ABBEY,

beside other Heroes. MARTIN finds his hair getting unco white, but it is of *feminine* fineness; as to *whiskers*, they were so *backward* in coming *forward* that he compromised the matter getting a *fierce* moustache and a *becoming* beard. MARTIN'S health is good, and his business energies as lively as ever, but he would *not* attempt to

Dance a hornpipe,
But could *whistle* a reel.

The remainder of Martin's advertisement, which ran for a full column, was a new song entitled "Keep Your Spirits Up," to the tune of Auld Langsyne, which dealt with the dull state of trade but expressed optimism for the near future.[49]

Martin reverted to a more prosaic and modest advertisement in *The Herald and Weekly Free Press* from January 10 to August 7, 1880, a period of thirty-one weeks, before publishing a few verses on harvest time and bountiful crops, but which also showed concern for the health of Mr Gladstone who had returned as Prime Minister in April.[50]

Meantime, apart from his January 1, 1880, announcement, Martin disappeared from the pages of *The Daily Free Press* after September 1879 when he began once more to patronize *The Herald and Weekly Free Press*. It was something of a surprise, therefore, when he published an advertisement in *The Daily Free Press* on April 3, 1880. Despite the fact that Lord Beaconsfield had dissolved parliament in March 1880 and a general election campaign had then taken place, with the majority of the results being declared in the first week of April, no mention of these stirring political events had been made by Martin. Instead, his advertisement of April 3, published in the midst of the declarations of election results, devoted three verses to the depressing effects on the mind of wearing a shabby hat, and four verses to the evergreen subject of a knighthood for himself. He was able to add a new twist to the situation since his namesake, Theodore Martin, a well known literary figure in the second half of the nineteenth century, who was also close to the Queen, had been made a Knight Commander of the Order of the Bath in 1880 on the completion of his five volume biography of Prince Albert.[51]

The remainder of this advertisement was directed to advising potential purchasers of the becoming styles available at his establishment and the exceptional value of Martin's snug fitting hats at that time. Martin declared he was ready to use all legitimate means to keep up his trade, and continued to be attentive to customers, especially as he never felt more happy than when behind his counter attending to his clientele.[52]

Why Martin did not take the opportunity to make political, indeed partisan, comment, as he had often done before at election times, is obscure. Possibly his health prevented him having the time or inclination to compose apt comments. Perhaps difficult commercial conditions made him reluctant to risk offending potential customers. Despite his earlier Liberal sympathies maybe his own political preference was unclear in 1880, for as a self confessed Liberal Conservative the choice between Gladstone and Disraeli may have been difficult.

Having returned to the columns of *The Herald and Weekly Free Press*, Martin reemployed, in September, the device or recounting a dream to his readers, the subject being the visit of the Queen to Milton of Crathes, where he was staying. In his verses Martin managed to include laudatory remarks about Crathes, and praise for the train service from Aberdeen and the local stationmaster. There was also a reference to "*Squire* Brown" acting as an intermediary between himself and the Queen, which was very possibly an allusion to John Brown. Not surprisingly, Martin's dream ended with him being knighted, whereupon:

Then the news was wired to Aberdeen;
    The PROVOST called a Council meeting,
And 'twas resolved by one and all
    To give MARTIN a special greeting.

Then the Council Chamber was lighted up;
 There were flags on the Town-house steeple.
And loud huzzas for the new-made Knight -
 The Hatter to the PEOPLE.[53]

From September 25, 1880, until the beginning of 1881, Martin followed what had emerged as the new pattern of his advertising, namely publishing the same short announcement relating to his stock for several weeks - fifteen weeks in this instance. The practice of publishing lengthy advertisements in either late December or early January, was, however, continued in 1881. At that time he rehearsed the familiar themes - thanks to the people of Aberdeen for their support, satisfaction with his own business achievements and prospects despite the depression in trade, assurances that he was himself hale and hearty, and good wishes for the royal family. He was also full of praise for General Roberts famous march from Kabul to Kandahar, 320 miles in twenty-three days, during the recent Afghan War.[54]

Throughout the whole of 1881 Martin ran the same brief announcement in the weekly editions of *The Herald and Weekly Free Press*, but on January 7, 1882, he published his regular annual review. Once more he thanked the people of Aberdeen, claimed his own business was prosperous and that he had no cause to grumble despite the continuing depression in many manufacturing districts. His advice was to make the best of things since grumbling would do no good anyway. He added:

Commercial prospects are decidedly better,
 In fact, trade begins to look bright;
And when FARMERS get quit of their grievance,
 Matters will become rapidly right.[55]

He concluded with an eleven verse poem speculating on a contemporary controversy as to whether human heads were getting smaller, a subject that allowed him to be amusing without offending anyone. For the remainder of 1882 Martin's insertions in *The Herald and Weekly Free Press* were all short and conventional. The fact that by this time his advertisements were not being rewritten on a regular, or even an irregular, basis might have been an intimation that he was finding it increasingly difficult to keep up with his business affairs, and was no longer taking the detailed interest in the text of his advertisements that had once been his trademark.

He did, however, maintain the tradition of a New Year's greeting to the people of Aberdeen in 1883, coupled with the equally traditional expression of thanks for their support:

> In thanking the *People* for their *continued support,*
> MARTIN does so with feelings sincere;
> He wishes *them* health and the same to *himself,*
> And lots of enjoyment during *the* year.

He was able to continue in a fresh vein, with the frequent use of plays on words, and some humour at the expense of the town council by praising the scheme to introduce electric lighting in the streets. For a four month period from December 23, 1882, Guild Street, Bridge Street, Market Street, Union Street and Castle Street were equipped with electric lights as an experiment.[56] Martin believed this would enlighten the town, and he thought "the appliances for testing the matter are very well POSTED, and will be looked up to." He added:

> Many may think we have plenty of Gas,
> And to give us more light is mere stuff;
> But the *Council* have given us a more luminous light,
> With the *aid* of kind Councillor DUFF.
>
> And this *Luminous* light is in the *Town-Hall,*
> And is very conspicuous *there,*
> An 'tis *surroundings* that give the *effect*
> *Where luminous lights are but rare.*[57]

Martin went on to praise the Lord Provost, Peter Esslemont, "the City improver," and to suggest that both he and the Provost be knighted the same day. They might both later that year attend the opening of Duthie Park by the Queen, if she could be persuaded, as this would give the seal of royal approval to the city improvements.[58] Martin was right to be proud of the considerable civic energy being displayed at this time, but he would have been partially disappointed since when Duthie Park, the gift to the city of Miss Elizabeth Crombie Duthie of Ruthrieston, was opened formally on September 27, 1883, the ceremony was not performed by

Queen Victoria but by Princess Beatrice.

The Princess interrupted her sojourn at Balmoral to travel by special train from Ballater to Aberdeen to perform the dual tasks of opening the bazaar in aid of the Hospital for Sick Children, of which she was patroness, as well as to attend the opening of Duthie Park to the public. Despite the cheerless and generally wet weather it was reported that, "Never, probably, in the whole course of its chequered history has the city of Aberdeen given itself so much up to the display of holiday trappings and to outward manifestations of ardent welcome to a scion of Royalty as it has done to-day." The "enthusiastic loyalty" shown by the city was described as "unbounded." Castle Street, Union Street and Market Street were replete with patriotic decorations, especially the offices of the major banks and insurance companies. Martin's indisposition was not sufficient to prevent him participating in the spirit of the occasion, and it was noted that, "Among other attractive displays in Union Street, mention may be made of the exhibition on the shop of Mr Samuel Martin, who, with a rich profusion of banners, presents the characteristic devices, "A loyal people," and "A Queen beloved."[59]

Three months later, on January 1, 1884, Martin greeted the New Year with enthusiasm and with his usual sentiments. As ever he was anxious to encourage people to pay attention to their appearance:

Attention to Dress has claims on us all,
There's lots of authorities on that;
But, Dress as you like, you can never look well
With a *Bad-fitting, shabby, Dress Hat.*

Your Coat may be fine and made to perfection,
And your *Boots* may be stylist and easy;
But there's *one* part of Dress 'tis better to shun,
That's a hat when it begins to get *greasy.*[60]

Unbeknown to the Aberdeen public at the time Martin's last advertisement appeared on September 12, 1885,[61] by which time one might suppose negotiations were already in hand for the sale of the business. The Aberdeen public was apprised of the change that was taking place on October 21, 1885, when John C. M'Leod, the longtime former employee of Samuel Martin, announced in the conventional and formal language of the day which was deemed appropriate for such an occasion,

JOHN C. M'LEOD,

HATTER. 34 & 46 UNION STREET,

IN returning his grateful thanks to his Friends and the Public for their very liberal patronage since he commenced Business, would intimate he has taken the Shop, Stock, and Good-will of Business, at 34 UNION STREET, belonging to Mr SAMUEL MARTIN, so long known in the trade, and would solicit a continuance of the patronage of his former and Mr Martin's Customers.

A CLEARING SALE of Old and Surplus Stock will be held at 34 for a short time, after which the Shop will be Re-opened with a Fresh and Fashionable Stock.

J. C. M'L. would also intimate the arrival at 46 of a large and varied Stock of New Goods for the Season.

Dress Hats—Lower, Medium, and finest quality.

Felt Hats—all the leading Shapes and Colours—Soft, Flexible, and Stiffened.

Ladies' Soft Felt Hats, Tweed Hats, Caps, and Tam o' Shanters.

Boys' Felt Hats, Sailor Caps, in Serge, Cloth, and Velveteen; Glengarrys, Polo, and Jockey Caps. Great variety of Gentlemen's Tweed Hats and Caps, Winter Caps—in Plush, Witney, Fur, Sealskin, &c. House Caps, in Tweed, Velvet, Cloth, Turkish Fez, Pullman Car, &c., &c.

Ladies' and Gentlemen's Umbrellas, superior quality, in Silk, Zanella, Russell Cloth, Separate Covers, Bands, Tassels, and Rings.

Winter Gloves, in Cape, Calf, Cloth, &c. Fur Tops, Spring Clasp, &c. Skating and Sleighing Gloves—New Patterns. Knitted Gloves, Gauntlets, Mitts, and Cuffs.

Albert Tan Driving Gloves, Lined and Plain.

Superior Class of Braces—Elastic, Girth, Web, Buck, and Calfskin.

The New British Argosy Brace, superior to any previously made.

Body or Riding Belts, with and without Elastic.

Football Jerseys, Hose, Belts, Cowls, and Shin Guards. Velvet, Trophy, and Club Caps made to order.

Hat Cases, Knapsacks, Travelling Bags, Mauds, Cardigan Jackets. Mufflers, in Silk, Cashmere, and Woollen. Leather and Elastic Garters. Livery Hats, Bands, and Cockades. Mourning Bands and Weepers.

SPECIAL AND ODD HATS MADE TO ORDER.

34 AND 46 UNION STREET Oct., 188[illegible].

that he had bought out his onetime master. The statement, which marked the passing of a veritable Aberdeen institution, read:

> **JOHN C. M'LEOD,**
> **HATTER, 34 & 46 UNION STREET,**
> IN returning his grateful thanks to his Friends and the Public for their very liberal patronage since he commenced Business, would intimate he has taken the Shop, Stock, and Good-will of Business, at 34 UNION STREET, belonging to Mr SAMUEL MARTIN, so long known in the trade, and would solicit a continuance of the patronage of his former and Mr Martin's Customers.
>
> A CLEARING SALE of Old and Surplus Stock will be held at 34 for a short time, after which the Shop will be Reopened with a Fresh and Fashionable Stock.[62]

Thus, fourteen years after he had branched out in his own right in November 1871, John C. M'Leod had, in a manner of speaking, returned to 34 Union Street where he had spent so much of his working life. And, of course, Samuel Martin vacated the premises he had occupied for over forty-seven years and disappeared from the advertising columns he had graced and enlivened for so long.

Martin's last ten years as the proprietor of 34 Union Street were not easy. According to reports his health was suffering, and there was a depression in trade in the early 1880s. Yet, despite such personal and economic difficulties, Martin maintained a brave front. He claimed every year to be enjoying remarkably good health, for his age, and regularly thanked the people for their support, which kept his business prosperous. The demise of *The Herald* and its replacement by *The Herald and Weekly Free Press* inaugurated a period of unusual flux in Martin's allegiance to the Aberdeen newspapers, which coincided with a decline in the number, size, regularity and originality of his advertisements. His political commitment to the Liberal cause also seemed to falter as he expressed support for Lord Beaconsfield's foreign policies at least, but nothing interfered with his allegiance to the crown, or with his less than serious campaign to be knighted. As he noted in 1878, "MARTIN is a *firm friend* to HER MAJESTY and the THRONE."[63] Foreign affairs still attracted his attention from time to time, and he was ever ready to criticize uncivilized behaviour, and, of course, imperial conflicts still aroused his patriotic spirit. However, the vitality which so characterized Martin's business career and spilled over into the advertising columns of the Aberdeen newspapers was clearly lacking by the mid-1880s.

NOTES

1 For background on the Disraeli ministry of 1874 to 1880 see Richard Shannon, *The Age of Disraeli, 1868-1881: the Rise of Tory Democracy* (1992), especially Parts III and IV, also Robert Blake, *Disraeli* (1966), Part Three.

2 *The Herald*, March 28, 1874, p4, col 2. His disappointment at the political situation did not prevent him keeping one eye on business by adding: "MARTIN'S *busy season generally commences about the beginning of April, and, in anticipation of fine weather, which has apparently already set in, he has lately got to hand Lots of Fresh Goods."*

Apart from the budget the new government intended only to bring forward changes in trade union and factory legislation and a change in the licensing laws. As the Home Secretary, Richard Cross, introduced the necessary legislation he attained instant popoularity in some quarters, and hence the contemporary jingle cited in Robert Blake, *Disraeli* p550:

"For he's a jolly good fellow,
Whatever the Rads may think;
For he has shortened the hours of work
And lengthened the hours of drink."

3 *The Herald*, January 2, 1875, p4, col 2.

4 *The Herald*, January 24, 1874, p4, col 6, and p5, cols 1-4, reported the wedding in St Petersburg and the local celebrations in Aberdeen,.

5 *The Herald*, May 9, 1874, p4, col 2. On June 13, 1874, p4, col 2, Martin published fourteen verses on the Queen's latest visit to Deeside with numerous asides about the Czar and Martin's own wish for a knighthood.

6 *The Herald*, July 25, 1874, p4, col 2. The sketch of Martin's shopfront is reproduced on the back cover of this study. Apart from the novelty of incorporating a drawing, this particular advertisement said little beyond commenting on the fine weather and indications of a good harvest.

7 Two bills or invoices from Martin to Lord James Hay, dated July 5, 1859 and May 6, 1861, both with impressions of 34 Union Street, are to be found in *Accounts and Other Papers Relating to James Forbes of Seaton, Aberdeen, and his Family, 1782-1861,* MS 2414/130 and MS 2414/140 deposited in the Special Collections of Aberdeen University Library. Lord James Hay evidently believed in sharing his custom around as the

collection also contains a bill from Alexander Steele & Co., dated December 12, 1859. I am indebted to Dr Iain Beavan of Aberdeen University Library who drew these documents to my attention.

8 *The Herald*, October 24, 1874, p4, col 2.

9 *The Evening Gazette,* January 7, 1888, p3, cols 3-4, and *The Daily Free Press*, January 9, 1888, p4, col 6.

10 *The Herald,* February 27, 1875, p4, col 2.

11 *The Herald*, April 10, 1875, p4, col 2. Martin reminded his readers that nothing looked worse in the summer sun than an ill shaped shabby hat, and tempted them with his new shapes in satin and shell hats, new styles and colours in easy fitting felt and tweed hats, to say nothing of his stock of leather hat cases, umbrellas, glengarry bonnets, livery hats, gold and silver bands, cockades, etc.

12 *The Herald*, May 29, 1875, p4, col 2.

13 *The Herald*, July 17, 1875, p4, col 2, also October 16, 1875, p4, col 2. See also Robert Blake, *Disraeli*, pp559-561.

14 *The Herald*, August 21, 1875, p4, col 2. Martin also wrote about the shooting season and his willingness to accept any game birds sent to him. He welcomed the Queen on her second visit to Deeside that year, and attributed both her good health and his own to the Deeside air:

> WINDSOR and the ISLE OF WIGHT
> Have attractions no doubt rare;
> But at neither of those places
> Is there DEESIDE'S bracing air.

15 R.C.K. Ensor, *England 1870-1914*, pp35-36.

16 Robert Blake, *Disraeli,* pp552-553.

17 *The Herald*, January 1, 1876, p4, col 2. Martin ventured the opinion that his name had not appeared on the New Year's honours list because, while he and Mr Disraeli admired each other, they were not well acquainted. He also observed that there were no signs that he was about to be presented with a gold tea service by Her Majesty in appreciation of his conspicuous loyalty.

18 *The Herald*, January 15, 1876, p4, col 2.

19 *The Herald*, April 1, 1876, p4, col 2.

20 *The Herald*, May 6, 1876, p4, col 2.

21 *The Herald*, May 6, 1876, p4, col 2. At this time Martin was also modestly referring to the celebrity of his establishment, his immense trade and his own world wide fame.

22 For the background to this affair see Richard Shannon, *Gladstone and the Bulgarian Agitation 1876* (1963).

23 *The Herald*, September 30, 1876, p4, col 2. Martin was never averse to mixing topics in his advertisements, and this time he combined the

Bulgarian atrocities with the presentation of regimental colours to the 1st Royal Scots by Queen Victoria at Ballater and three stanzas on the perennial subject of his impending knighthood.

24 *The Herald and Weekly Free Press*, January 6, 1877, p4, col 2. On the subject of the fame of Martin's business he worked into this advertisement a reference to Captain Sir George Nares and his recent Arctic expedition, writing that it was quite possible that if Nares had got to the North Pole he might well have overheard a conversation about Martin the hatter. Despite this particular piece of levity, it is interesting to compare the tone of this advertisement with that of January 1, 1876, which had a more positive ring about it.

25 *The Herald and Weekly Free Press*, February 3, 1877, p5, col 2. On February 17, 1877, p1, cols 5-6, W.C. King announced the sale to the public of the stock he had bought from the estate of Wm Fyffe.

26 *The Herald and Weekly Free Press*, November 24, 1877, p4, col 2.

27 *The Herald and Weekly Free Press*, March 17, 1877, p1, col 7. The Crown Clothing Company was, in fact, a gentlemen's and boys' outfitters and not just a hat shop, a fact reflected in the six verses in the advertisement. The following is the opening stanza:

The style of the dress has a prominent place
In the thoughts of the grave and the gay,
And the Crown Clothing Shop is one of the best
For the Fashionable Dress of the day.

28 *The Herald and Weekly Free Press*, March 30, 1878, p4, col 4.

29 *The Herald and Weekly Free Press*, April 7, 1877, p4, cols 2-3.

30 *The Herald and Weekly Free Press*, May 26, 1877, p4, col 2. The Queen's return to London, and Martin's knighthood, were the subjects of his advertisement on June 16, 1877, p4, col 2.

31 *The Herald and Weekly Free Press*, May 12, 1877, p4, col 2: July 7, 1877, p4, col 2; and August 18, 1877, p4, col 2. On the last occasion he advertised shooting hats and caps, which, with the aid of a gun, helped to kill game.

32 *The Herald and Weekly Free Press*, September 22, 1877, p4, col 2. Details of the twenty-first annual Congress of the National Association for the Promotion of Social Science held in Aberdeen appeared in *The Herald and Weekly Free Press*, September 22, 1877, p5, cols 2-3, p6, cols 6-7, p7, cols 1-5, and September 29, 1877, p6, cols 3-6, and p7, cols 1-2.

33 *The Herald and Free Press*, November 10, 1877, p4, col 2. The advertisement by Fyfe & Company on January 5, 1878, p4, col 4, which also appeared in *The Daily Free Press* on January 12, 1878, p1, col 9, is worth reproducing in part. After reviewing the hopes and prospects for 1878 the copy writer went on to consider recent advances in the city:

The city rulers found at last
That public voice was quite steadfast,
All wrangling done, agreed to cast
A Granite Bridge to Torry.
The next proposal long foreseen
Is tramway cars to Cults and Skene,
We'll hope no flaw will intervene
To keep them back.
There's one at least we've not yet named,
Whose goods are by the people famed,
Both far and near he's well maintained,
It's FYFE THE HATTER.

34 *The Daily Free Press*, November 12, 1877, p1, col 9. Also the *Aberdeen Journal*, November 13, 1877, p1, col 8, and November 15, 1877, p1, col 8.

35 *The Daily Free Press*, December 8, 1877, p1, col 9, and the *Aberdeen Journal*, December 26, 1877, p1, col 6.

36 *The Daily Free press*, November 12, 1877, p1, col 9, and the *Aberdeen Journal*, November 13, 1877, p1, col 8. Inventive as ever Martin used this occasion to promote new hats which might have been worn by war correspondents.

37 *The Daily Free Press*, December 8, 1877, p1, col 9 and the *Aberdeen ournal*, December 26, 1877, p1, col 6.

38 *The Daily Free Press*, December 8, 1877, p1, col 8, and the *Aberdeen Journal*, December 26, 1877, p1, col 6. Only two of five verses are reproduced here. The advertisement contains a comparatively rare reference to Ladies' Hats.

39 *The Daily Free Press*, January 1, 1878, p1, col 9, and the *Aberdeen Journal*, January 1, 1878, p1, col 7. Due to a typographical error the *Aberdeen Journal* carried the date January 1, 1877. Martin made the claim that he was in wonderful good health and lively as ever in business. He had a well trimmed grey beard and a moustache that might be envied by Osman Pasha, a reference to the Turkish commander at Plevna.

40 See, for example, *The Daily Free Press*, January 26, 1878, p8, col 1 repeated in the *Aberdeen Journal*, January 30, 1878, p1, col 7; and *The Daily Free Press*, March 9, 1878, p8, col 1, repeated in the *Aberdeen Journal*, March 20, 1878, p1, col 7.

41 For the political and diplomatic background to the Congress of Berlin see Robert Blake, *Disraeli* Chapter XXVII, pp629-654.

42 *The Daily Free Press*, January 1, 1878, p1, col 9, and the *Aberdeen Journal*, January 1, 1878, p1, col 7. Martin added the lines:

We don't want war if our honour's safe;
But it can do no harm to keep our powder dry.

43 *The Daily Free Press*, May 25, 1878, p8, col 1, and the *Aberdeen Journal*, May 29, 1878, p1, col 6.

44 *The Daily Free Press*, September 2, 1878, p8, col 1, which was unusually an insertion on a Monday. Also the *Aberdeen Journal*, August 28, 1878, p1, col 6.

45 *The Daily Free Press*, January 1, 1879, p1, col 6, and the *Aberdeen Journal*, January 1, 1879, p1, col 5.

46 *The Daily Free press*, January 1, 1879, p1, col 6, and the *Aberdeen Journal*, January 1, 1879, p1, col 5. Background on the Afghan Wars may be found in Robert Blake, *Disraeli*, Chapter XXVIII, pp655-679.

47 *The Herald and Weekly Free Press*, August 30, 1879, p1, col 7. An account of the Queen's passage through Aberdeen on August 26 was printed on p6, col 6. The same advertisement appeared in *The Daily Free Press*, August 30, 1879, p8, col 1, and September 6, 1879, p8, col 1, but thereafter *The Daily Free Press* did not carry another Martin announcement that year.

48 For details of the new Afghan War see Robert Blake, *Disraeli*, Chapter XXVIII, pp675-679. For once Martin was upstaged by a rival when A.G. Jessiman, 25 & 27 George Street, cashed in on the hostilities in South Africa and Afghanistan by offering for sale Lion and Afghan Felt Hats. See *The Daily Free Press*, May 10, 1879, p8, col 1.

49 *The Herald and Weekly Free Press*, January 3, 1880, p1, col 7. The same advertisement had also appeared in *The Daily Free Press* on January 1, 1880, p8, col 1. The song contained such verses as:

> But we here from southern news
> That trade's reviving fast;
> We find it so in Aberdeen,
> And hope that it may last.

50 *The Herald and Weekly Free Press*, August 14, 1880, p1, col 6. The last of six verses ran:

> We love to hear that friends are well,
> Though we may get no letter.
> Thus we love to hear, from late accounts,
> That Mr Gladstone's getting better.

51 *The Daily Free Press*, April 3, 1880, p8, col 1. Details of Sir Theodore Martin's life may be found in the obituary columns of *The Aberdeen Daily Journal*, August 19, 1909, p4, cols 7-8. As Theodore Martin's sympathetic biography of Prince Albert contributed to his receiving a knighthood, Samuel Martin's praise of the royal family may not have been such a bad idea after all.

52 *The Daily Free Press*, April 3, 1880, p8, col 1, repeated April 10, 1880, p8, col 1.

53 *The Herald and Weekly Free Press*, September 4, 1880, p1, col 7. The same advertisement appeared in the columns of *The Daily Free Press*, September 1, 1880, p8, col 6, and the *Aberdeen Journal*, September 2, 1880, p8, col 6.

54 *The Herald and Weekly Free Press*, January 8, 1881, p1, col 7. See also *The Daily Free Press*, January 1, 1881, p8, col 2, and the *Aberdeen Journal*, January 1, 1881, p1, col 6. In nostalgic mood he wrote, "MARTIN remembers the time when the *First English Railway* was opened, long before *Railways* were introduced into *Scotland.* Contrast this with the *present* time, when you can almost get a *Railway train* to hand you into your Bedroom and a polite *Guard* to put on your *nightcap."*

55 *The Herald and Weekly Free Press*, January 7, 1882, p1, col 7. See also *The Daily Free Press*, January 2, 1882, p1, col 6, and the *Aberdeen Journal*, January 2, 1882, p8, col 6.

56 James A. Ross, *Record of Municipal Affairs In Aberdeen Since The Passing Of The Burgh Reform Act In 1833* (1889), p111. (Copy in Aberdeen City Archives).

57 *Aberdeen Journal*, January 1, 1883, p1, col 8. Also *The Daily Free Press*, January 1, 1883, p8, col 1. As the files for *The Herald and Weekly Free Press* are incomplete for January 1883 it is impossible to know if this advertisement also appeared therein, though it is likely.

58 Lord Provost Esslemont, who with William Macintosh founded the partnership of Esslemont and Macintosh whose store now occupies the site once graced in part by Samuel Martin's shop, was energetic and progressive. According to Alexander M. Munro, *Memorials of the Alderman, Provosts, and Lord Provosts Of Aberdeen, 1272-1895* (1895), pp291-294, "His tenure of office was marked by the completion of many works of great public utility, while a scheme of improvements was inaugurated...."

59 Full details of the royal visit and the various ceremonies appeared in *The Daily Free Press* on September 27, 1883, p5, cols 1-5, and September 28, 1883, pp4-7, The reference to Martin's shop may be found on the latter date, p6, col 3.

60 *Aberdeen Journal*, January 1, 1884, p1, col 8. Also *The Daily Free Press*, January 1, 1884, p8, col 1. Again the files of *The Herald and Weekly Free Press* are incomplete for January 1884.

61 *The Herald and Weekly Free Press*, September 12, 1885, p4, col 7. On September 19, 1885, p4, col 3, the first advertisement appeared by Adam Pratt, "The Premier Hatter," an announcement no longer of any interest to Martin.

62 M'Leod's announcement appeared in the *Aberdeen Journal*, October 21, 1885, p6, col 2-3, and was repeated for the next four weeks. It also

appeared in the *Aberdeen Journal*, October 21, 1885, p8, cols 2-3, and October 23, 1885, p6, cols 2-3.

63 *The Daily Free Press*, May 25, 1878, p8, col 1, and the *Aberdeen Journal*, May 29, 1878, p1, col 6.

CHAPTER TEN

EPILOGUE AND RETROSPECT

If Samuel Martin had reflected in October 1885 on his career as an Aberdeen trader, he would have been able to look back on more than forty-seven years of business in the same field and at the same address. As his advertisement of April 7, 1877,[1] made clear, these had been years of momentous change in the city and in society. When Martin arrived in Aberdeen the population, (within the parliamentary boundary) was perhaps 65,000, but when he retired in 1885 it had grown to over 113,000, with many accompanying developments.

Martin had been a young man, only twenty-three years old, when he opened his doors at 34 Union Street, but he was an elderly gentleman of seventy or seventy-one when he finally retired from business. As his own advertisements attest his physical appearance changed as he grew older, and his dark locks gave way to white hair and partial baldness. In his later years he sometimes wore spectacles, but he kept enough of his own teeth to be able to enjoy his food. He suffered from rheumatism and gout, and probably had a stroke in the middle 1870s that left him with a limp. The annual reviews he published each January in which he claimed to enjoy good health have to be taken with a degree of reservation by the late 1870s and early 1880s.

Martin was a *bon vivant* in the sense that he indulged himself with a good cigar, drank porter, port or wine, and enjoyed a good dinner of grouse or other game birds. Every year he took a vacation or two on Deeside, a district whose beauty, serenity and unspoiled aspect he loved. Apparently Ballater was his favourite resort, partly for health reasons, but also because it was close to Balmoral. He was obviously a welcome guest at the local hotels and taverns along Deeside, whose accommodating proprietors and proprietresses he admired and whose facilities and hospitality he praised.

Whatever the degree of Martin's musical virtuosity when it came to the trumpet, and there is some difference of opinion on the subject,[2] he allegedly had a good voice. According to the nostalgic and sympathetic obituary notice in *The Evening Gazette* and *The Daily Free Press*, Martin enjoyed his holidays at Ballater, and:

> Business forgotten, there at the foot of Craigen-darroch, he would sit with a few chosen friends in the early August evenings, and as the moon came slowly sailing over Craig-Coil, and the hills about Pannanich and Dalmuchy, lighting up the whole glorious valley of the Dee and the Lochnagar range of mountains - there Mr Martin would, with his clear tenor voice, and as appropriate to the silent gloaming feeling, strike into the love ditty with which Mrs Waylett warblingly won the hearts of our fathers and mothers - "Meet me by moonlight alone"....[3]

Why Martin chose to remain a bachelor is unknown. He was certainly prosperous enough to marry and presentable. William Skene in his *East Neuk Chronicles* recalls that people wondered why "Sammy" Martin remained single, after all "He was a very handsome man, and in his brown velveteen coat and white vest, with a 'nobby' hat, he looked the perfect gentleman."[4] Though he "put an antic disposition on," Martin has been described as a genial and kindly man of sterling honesty.[5] A.S. Cook, author of *Old-Time Traders and Their Ways*, who almost certainly knew Martin well, provides the best description of him. According to Cook, Samuel Martin was of medium height and dark complexion, and:

> In figure he was alert and active. He wore a neatly-shaped and well-dressed hat a little to one side, a stand-up collar not very deep, and a long coloured satin scarf with large knot, in which he displayed a cameo gold pin, black velvet jacket, light vest and trousers, boots faultlessly shiny, yellow thread gloves, and in his hand an ivory-handled silk umbrella, closely rolled up, with a couple of large silk tassels appended to the stick. In walking briskly along the street he was a natty, sprightly man, with a pleasant smile and recognition to all whom he knew, and these were many. His get-up was showy, but it was his style.[6]

As he had no family in Aberdeen, Martin's domestic arrangements were those of a financially sound and secure tradesman of the day. His residences in Aberdeen can be traced via the pages of the annual *Bon-Accord Directory* and *Post-Office Directory*, both of which described him as a hat manufacturer. From 1838 until 1850 Martin lived in Cruden's Court, 22 Broad Street, described as Mrs Innes' lodgings. The arrangements must have been satisfactory as he remained at this same address for thirteen years. From 1851 to 1852 he lived at 2 Affleck Street, in all probability still in lodgings conducted by Mrs Innes. From 1853 until 1854 his home was given as 125 Crown Street, an address still shared by Mrs Innes, but in 1855 he was listed as living at 31 Victoria Street West, where he remained until 1862. It is unclear whether, throughout this period, Mrs Innes was his landlady or became his housekeeper. From 1863 until 1867 Martin lived at 66 Dee Street, Mrs Clark's lodgings, and his final home was 23 Albert Terrace, from 1868 until his death twenty years later, still attended by Mrs Clark. Thus over a period of half a century in Aberdeen Martin had only six addresses and only two landladies or housekeepers, and during the majority of his time in the city he had been prosperous enough to live in the fashionable West End.

If Martin had followed the normal pattern of advertising his merchandise in a conventional and conservative manner, then his career would not have differed materially from the pattern of many another Aberdeen shopkeeper. However, from an early date, he chose to give rein to his propensity to advertise in a flamboyant and eyecatching style. Once he had attracted the attention of his readers he never ended without a reminder as to where a good hat could be purchased at a moderate price, and Aberdeen was never short of rival hatters. Martin, no doubt, agreed with an anonymous contemporary book reviewer in *The Edinburgh Review* in 1843, who wrote, "In short, there is no disguising it, the grand principle of modern existence is notoriety; we live and move and have our being in print," and who recommended the ambitious "never to omit an opportunity of placing your name in printed characters before the world."[7]

The question arises as to why Martin chose for forty years to concentrate his advertisements in *The Aberdeen Herald*. Perhaps this was because Martin sympathized with its politics and stand on religious matters, or maybe on account of some personal relationships between himself and *The Herald's* long serving and distinguished editor, James Adam, or the journalist and some time sub-editor William Carnie. Perhaps it was on account of some deal over advertising rates. Maybe Martin was influenced by the fact that *The Herald* was published on a Saturday, or appeared to reach that segment of the Aberdeen public deemed likely to purchase from Martin. Whatever the combination of reasons it was a long running and mutually beneficial relationship, and William Skene was not far from the truth when he wrote, "It used to be said of a certain local weekly paper that it would not be a paper at all without his advertisement, he never having missed a week in it for over 40 years."[8]

It is surely not a coincidence that Martin advertised in *The Herald* and in return that newspaper carried reports of Martin's antics at election times, or described his decorations in celebration of royal events or when there were military parades. On the other hand Martin did not normally patronize the *Aberdeen Journal* and that paper appeared studiously to ignore Martin's manifestations of patriotism.[9]

In his prime Martin was composing a fresh, lengthy, amusing, informative, argumentative, opiniated and often frankly idiosyncratic advertisement every three or four weeks. No one would argue that his announcements were literary masterpieces, though they were often clever. His rhymes were frequently little more than doggerel, often laced with Victorian sentimentality, albeit the sentiments expressed were usually sincere. (Even he never claimed that he was about to be appointed Poet Laureate). Yet the effort that went into their composition must have been considerable, especially as Martin was constantly striving for effect via his use of deceptive headlines, puns, capitals, italics, bold print, various typefaces and other devices. William Carnie, recalled the practice of the staff of *The Herald*, "Every man Jack, and every boy Jim, of us, from portly Editor to puniest devilick," to take part in "Our Annual Trip." This consisted of an outing, described in detail in the next issue of the paper, of some forty persons, including half a dozen prominent citizens present as guests, to a different destination every year including Aboyne, Turriff, Ellon, Alford, Banchory, Perth and Huntly. Carnie remembered:

> The castles, mansions, grounds, the entire domains, indeed, of surrounding proprietors wherever our journey led were generously thrown open for us to wander in and inspect at will. Politically, it cannot be written that we were universally beloved, the editorial pens were too outspoken for that, but apparently everybody liked us; and I only do justice to men now silent in saying that in these days the *Herald* was a power in this northern land. The outcome was that at whatever village or railway station the annual trippers arrived there would be salutation and welcome awaiting us from not a few kindly inclined onlookers. Keen curiosity stood on tip-toe, and who's who, in a humble way, prevailed. Here is an amusing - some of us thought it a doubtful - instance of this complimentary feeling. After partaking of a hearty breakfast on arrival at Huntly, a goodly number of us foregathered in the Square....Well, we are in Huntly Square, and there around the shop door of Rob Smith, the popular parish barber, are assembled a boorichie of critics and other shavers anxiously taking stock of the *Herald* leading

> lights. Having known Rob in his Aberdeen apprentice years I advanced to greet him for auld lang syne. After a few casual remarks - "Man," quoth Rob, "we were jist trying to pick you fellows oot, and guessin' which wiz the real clever chaps. Aye, wiz we, and we wid like fine to ken fitch o' ye writes the advertisements o' Sammy Martin, the People's Hatter!" Oh! the pity of it - but wasn't Sam proud when he was told regarding the Huntly appreciation of his literary gifts and graces![10]

Only one source, William Skene in *East Neuk Chronicles*, has ever suggested that Samuel Martin did not compose his own advertisements. Skene wrote, "A little man of the name of Kelman - a character in his way - was generally credited as the drawer-up of Sammy's advertisements. Whoever wrote them, they did the writer credit."[11] This doubt, which comes close to blasphemy, runs counter to a great deal of evidence that indicates that Martin was, indeed, the author - the proud author - of his own advertising copy. *The Evening Gazette* and *The Daily Free Press* obituary writer in 1888 had no doubts on this subject when he wrote, "As very kindly relations existed between Mr Martin and the Pressmen of the period referred to, there was a feeling that some of these erratic individuals had a hand in the poetic advertisement pie. But such was never the case. The 'practical hatter' was his own author, none, in this respect, being his parallel...."[12]

A.S. Cook recalled that, "'Sammy,' as he was familiarly called, was a genial, hearty soul with an effervescing flow of humour and anecdote. He had a frank and kindly manner, and set off his wares in an attractive and popular style." Cook noted that customers of all classes were served with promptness and satisfaction and that Martin built up a steady and prosperous business. Moreover, "By his original and eccentric advertising he was known far and near, and many strangers called when in town to see the 'funny man' whose advertisements in prose and rhyme afforded them considerable amusement."[13] Martin certainly appeared to have customers from all levels of society, though he often noted, with mock regret, that particular members of the royal family, and even the Czar of Russia, had *not* visited him when they passed through Aberdeen. However, on September 22, 1877, he claimed, without giving details or clues to aid identification, that "MARTIN, ere now, has had a visit from a PRINCE."[14]

That Martin was, indeed, eccentric is scarcely to be denied, but in part, at least, his reputation for eccentricity was the consequence of his pioneering and imaginative advertising practices. In a traditional and conservative business environment like Aberdeen Martin's behaviour and his advertisements first provoked comment and then, sometimes, imitation.[15]

The overwhelming temptation is to call Samuel Martin "The Mad Hatter of Aberdeen," because of his flamboyant behaviour and unique advertising style. The phrase "Mad as a hatter" was popularized in 1865 by the publication of Lewis Carroll's *Alice in Wonderland*, though it is recorded in America as early as 1836 and may be found in William Makepeace Thackerary's novel *Pendennis*, published in 1850. The origin of the phrase is likely to be connected with the fact that mercurous nitrate, used in the making of felt hats, could produce St Vitus's dance or lesser tremblings.[16] Whether Martin's health or mind were affected by what might be termed this occupational hazard is only speculation, but possibly the man himself might have rejoiced in the title, and in this study the phrase is used as a term of affection rather than in any pejorative sense.

The Evening Gazette and *The Daily Free Press* in 1888 wrote that anyone who believed that Martin was either mad or a fool laboured under a mighty mistake. He was a delightful companion and a liberal and genial host. "There were few subjects started in general conversation on which he could not hold his own with the best; while his courage was soldierly, and his instincts in society ever those of a true gentleman."[17] For a man of limited educational opportunities, he had left school aged about twelve, he was extremely well informed about current affairs, perhaps because he read widely, especially British history.[18]

Martin's advertisements showed him to have been a Liberal in his politics for most of his life, even though he was describing himself as a Liberal-Conservative by the late 1870s. Inevitably, he was selective as regards the subjects he chose to highlight in his announcements, whether they related to local, national or international affairs. Even so they contained a wealth of information for his readers and provided extremely valuable insights into contemporary interests and opinions for the historian. Although he has been described as "well qualified for public life," he never aspired to office himself, preferring to make comments from the sidelines.[19]

Martin was usually to be found on the side of civic improvements in Aberdeen, and in favour of social, economic and political reforms nationally. As regards imperial or international affairs he was unashamedly chauvinistic, his statements revealing both conscious and unconscious racism and a dislike of, or suspicion concerning, foreigners that at times bordered on xenophobia. At different times he voiced dislike, fear and suspicion regarding France, Russia and the United States. On the other hand he was intensely proud of being British, and of his own English, Scottish and Irish heritage. His admiration of the British constitution was frequently expressed, and, of course, his praise of the royal family became legendary. Despite his commitment to social and economic reforms to ease the burdens of the working classes, Martin took a stratified and a deferential society for granted. His own pursuit of a knighthood was a standing joke in Aberdeen for many years, neatly combining professions of loyalty and claims of merit with a talent for publicity and self-promotion. Since Martin's comments on the subject, and his solicitations for some reward for his own devotion to the crown, were all of a public nature, there is even reason to believe they were read at Balmoral, but it is impossible to know if he took himself seriously in private. William Skene maintained that there was a division of opinion in Aberdeen on the subject. He wrote that Martin was "an original in every way," but a man who "never realised the dream of his life - that much coveted knighthood, of which he talked so much." According to Skene, "Some people were of opinion that Sammy really wished the honour, and expected to get it; others as strongly maintained that it was all a joke - for advertising purposes."[20]

Martin's amiability and generosity were frequently commented upon, and he was a regular contributor to charitable funds. For example, in January 1860 he contributed ten shillings to the Public Soup Kitchen, in February 1868 he donated two guineas to the fund for Unemployed Operatives in Aberdeen, and in March 1874 he gave half a guinea, (ten shillings and sixpence) to the Stonehaven Lifeboat Disaster Fund.[21]

It is a matter of regret that so little is known about Martin's private life, but he seems to have had a wide circle of friends and acquaintances. After his retirement from business in October 1885 he appears to have lived quietly, and the *Aberdeen Journal* in January 1888 reported that, "He was able to move about among his friends till last summer, since when he has been confined to the house."[22] *The Evening Gazette* recorded that gradually his strength failed in his last years, but he was carefully and kindly tended by those close to him, and he kept up his spirits wonderfully to the last.[23]

News of Martin's death at his home, 23 Albert Terrace, just after noon on Saturday, January 7, 1888, was carried in *The Evening Gazette* the same day, and in *The Daily Free Press* and the *Aberdeen Journal* on the Monday following. The death was officially registered by James Ferrier, a nephew by marriage from Glasgow, and the cause of death was given as softening of the brain over a period of one year. This is a somewhat vague medical diagnosis, which might refer to progressive senile decay, or possibly could have some connection with illness resulting from his life-long profession.

The public of Aberdeen was advised via the press on Wednesday, January 11, 1888, that the funeral would take place that day at two o'clock from Albert Terrace to Nellfield Cemetery.[24] The following day the *Aberdeen Journal* and *The Daily Free Press* both published accounts of the burial. Religious services were conducted at Martin's home and at the graveside by the Reverend Angus M. Mackay, St James's Episcopal Church, where Martin had been a member. The coffin, covered by a number of beautiful wreaths, was borne to the churchyard by six shore porters. The obsequies were well attended, and the chief mourners were Mr James Ferrier and Mr John Gow, both from Glasgow, and Mr George Clark from Aberdeen. Others present included Mr Robert Westlands from Glasgow; Mr John C. M'Leod the Union Street hatter who had taken over Martin's business; the Reverend James Smith of St George's-in-the-West; Mr William Cooper of Philip & Cooper; Mr James Collie, advocate, and Mr George Duncan Collie, advocate; Mr James Watson, advocate; Professor Smith-Shand of Aberdeen University; Mr A.S. Cook, clothier, of Market Street; Mr F.B. Kelly, clothier; Mr James Hall, clothier; Mr Alexander Nicolson, baker, Waverley Place; Mr George Hutcheson, grain merchant; Mr David Allan of James Allan & Sons, upholsterers; Mr A.R. Gray; Mr William Carnie, Secretary, Royal Infirmary; Mr K. Greig, C.A.; Mr William Cadenhead, wine merchant; Mr Dickson, hatter; Mr Thomas Ogilvie, hatter; Mr William Lindsay, publisher; Mr James Saint, draper; Mr Archibald Campbell, solicitor; Mr Alexander Marr; Mr William Mollyson, manager of the North of Scotland Loan Company; Mr Robert Henderson, draper; Mr John Christie, auctioneer; and Mr Roger, late of Messrs Pratt & Keith. In other words the funeral was attended by numerous friends and acquaintances who represented the trading, commercial and professional classes of the city. Martin had lived and died a respected member of that society.[25]

Thus, eighteen years after he had chosen it and raised the eyebrows of Aberdonians, the "Hatter to the People" was buried in his chosen spot. William Skene, in his *East Neuk Chronicles*, believed that Martin was, without a doubt, eccentric to a certain extent, but he admired his moral courage in erecting his own tombstone during his lifetime. Skene recalled:

> Sammy had his tombstone ready for him for many years in Nellfield Cemetery, with the inscription - "The last resting place of Samuel Martin, Hatter to the People." It used to be a favourite discussion with us boys, when we read it in the cemetery - "What would be the use of the stone if Sammy went out to the bay to fish and got drowned?" However, that catastrophe never occurred; and Sammy lies peacefully and quietly in Nellfield.[26]

Martin's retirement and later death left a gap in Aberdeen life. William Carnie, erstwhile journalist with *The Herald*, lamented in general "the disappearance or dying out of individuals of striking personality, 'characters' in fact," and in particular the passing of Samuel Martin. In Carnie's opinion this was "a distinct loss to the town, his characteristics being all healthy and even amusing." He added:

> "Sammy" (I use the familiar title with all respect), "Sammy" stood out a distinct bit of colour in the picture of our every-day doings - so much so that the mere mention of his name brings vividly before the mind's eye the smart, dapper, jaunty figure, morning after morning for a long series of years, briskly holding on his way to the well-frequented "No. 34 Union Street". And then on occasions of State or Civic ceremony who does not remember our late friend as he bravely stood in smiling Napoleonic attitude in his first-floor winder - the glass and frame removed - clad in impressive Garibaldian or other attractive attire? On such occasions Mr Martin was the observed of all observers, old and young - always a welcome pleasant variety in the ongoings. I have heard the term "mountebank" applied regarding him. If such reference meant anything in the nature of false pretence, or underhand dealing, then the speaker didn't know his subject. Samuel Martin was in word and deed a gentleman, an eccentric gentleman, if you like, with a clear head and a kind heart....and there is fair room for regret that as yet he has no successor in the peculiar *role* he so conspicuously filled.[27]

Samuel Martin's memory was preserved by those who knew him, but, inevitably, the passing of that generation meant that his name, his reputation and his contribution to half a century of Aberdeen life were largely forgotten. Martin was in the tradition of the British Victorian amiable gentlemanly eccentric, who brought colour, excitement, humour and pleasure into the lives of others. His sheer *joie de vivre*, unquenchable spirit, irrepressible good humour and optimism deserve to be remembered. In addition it should not be forgotten that he conducted a successful business for well over forty years, though his estate of £620 0s 1d., was modest.[28] Last, but not least, Martin's name is worthy of mention in any history of nineteenth century advertising. It is hoped that this brief study will do something to revive his memory and re-establish his reputation.

NOTES

1 *The Herald and Weekly Free Press*, April 7, 1877, p4, col 2. See herein Chapter Nine p197.

2 Whereas various reports in *The Herald* suggested that Martin played his trumpet with more enthisiasm than skill, William Skene, *East Neuk Chronicles* (1905), p50, wrote of him "wearing a red Garibaldi shirt and a fancy head-dress, and displaying the everlasting cornet, on which he was quite an expert player."

3 *The Evening Express*, January 7, 1888, p3, cols 3-4; and *The Daily Free Press*, January 9, 1888, p4, col 6.

4 William Skene, *East Neuk Chronicles*, p50.

5 The *Aberdeen Journal*, January 9, 1888, p4, col 6.

6 A.S. Cook, *Old-Time Traders and Their Ways* (1902), p20. There is every probability that this A.S. Cook was also a gentlemens' clothier with a shop in Market Street, and one of the many local people who attended Martin's funeral in 1888.

7 Anonymous, *The Edinburgh Review*, Vol LXXVII, 1843, p2.

8 William Skene, *East Neuk Chronicles*, p50. The claim that Martin had not missed a week in placing an advertisement in *The Herald* was substantially true, though not completely accurate.

9 As an example, when the 93d Highlanders arrived in Aberdeen in March 1870 and left in June 1871 *The Herald* carried reports that made mention of Martin's enthusiasm, (see Chapter Seven), but while the *Aberdeen Journal* also covered both events it did not include any reference to Martin. See the *Aberdeen Journal* for March 30, 1870, p8, col 3, and June 21,

1871, p4, col 6.

10 William Carnie, *Additional Aberdeen Reminiscences. Social, Civic and Personal Pencillings of the Granite City,* Vol III, (1906), pp276-277. It is more than possible that this particular annual outing took place in August 1855 as an account of a trip to Huntly by the staff of *The Herald* was published on August 11, 1855, p5, cols 5-6. Moreover, as this was during the Crimean War it was at a time when Martin was establishing his reputation as local character.

11 William Skene, *East Neuk Chronicles,* p50.

12 *The Evening Gazette*, January 7, 1888, p3, cols 3-4, and *The Daily Free Press*, January 9, 1888, p4, col 6.

13 A.S. Cook, *Old-Time Traders and Their Ways,* pp19-20.

14 *The Herald*, September 22, 1877, p4, col 2.

15 A.S. Cook, *Old-Time Traders and Their Ways,* pp1-3, recalled his apprenticeship as a draper's assistant at about the same time Samuel Martin began his business. "There was no advertising and little or no display," and a great deal of haggling between a salesman and a customer over prices in a process known as 'priggin'."

16 Ivor H. Evans (ed.), *Brewer's Dictionary of Phrase And Fable,* Revised Edition (1981), p696.

17 *The Evening Gazette*, January 7, 1888, p3, cols 3-4, and *The Daily Free Press*, January 9, 1888, p4, col 6.

18 *The Herald*, February 14, 1857, p4, col 2.

19 The *Aberdeen Journal*, January 9, 1888, p4, col 6.

20 William Skene, *East Neuk Chronicles*, p50.

21 *The Herald*, January 14, 1860, p4, col 2; February 22, 1868, p1, col 5; and March 14, 1874, p1, col 5.

22 *Aberdeen Journal*, January 9, 1888, p4, col 6.

23 *The Evening Gazette*, January 7, 1888, p3, cols 3-4, also *The Daily Free press*, p4, col 6.

24 *Aberdeen Journal,* January 11, 1888, p1, col 1, and *The Daily Free Press,* January 11, 1888, p1, col 1.

25 *Aberdeen Journal*, January 12, 1888, p4, col 6; *The Daily Free Press*, January 12, 1888, p4, col 4; also *The Herald and Weekly Free Press*, January 14, 1888, p2, col 8. Details regarding the history of St James's Episcopal Church and a sketch of the career of the Reverend Angus M. Mackay may be found in Alexander Gammie, *The Churches of Aberdeen. Historical and Descriptive* (1909), pp290-293.

26 William Skene, *East Neuk Chronicles*, p50.

27 William Carnie, *Additional Aberdeen Reminiscences*, Vol III, pp272-274.

28 *Calendar of Confirmations and Inventories Granted And Given Up In The Several Commissariots Of Scotland In The Year 1888* (1889), p443.